⌇ CATO ⌇
SUPREME COURT
REVIEW
2 0 0 1 — 2 0 0 2

CATO SUPREME COURT REVIEW

2001 — 2002

ROGER PILON
Publisher

JAMES L. SWANSON
Editor in Chief

ROBERT A. LEVY
Associate Editor

TIMOTHY LYNCH
Associate Editor

CENTER FOR CONSTITUTIONAL STUDIES

INSTITUTE
Washington, D.C.

ISBN 1-930865-35-X

Cover design by Elise B. Rivera.
Printed in the United States of America.

CATO INSTITUTE
1000 Massachusetts Ave., N.W.
Washington, D.C. 20001
www.cato.org

Contents

Foreword
Restoring Constitutional Government
Roger Pilon

The Cato Institute's Center for Constitutional Studies is pleased to publish this inaugural volume of the *Cato Supreme Court Review*— an annual critique of the Court's most important decisions from the term just ended, plus a brief look at the cases ahead. What distinguishes Cato's from other such reviews is its perspective: We will examine those decisions and cases in the light cast by the nation's first principles—liberty and limited government—as articulated in the Declaration of Independence and secured by the Constitution, as amended. We take those principles seriously. Our concern is that the Court do the same.

That is no small concern. James Madison, the principal author of the Constitution, drew upon those principles when he promised, in *Federalist* No. 45, that the powers of the new government would be "few and defined." We've come a long way from that, and the Court has played a major role in the transformation. In this inaugural volume, inspired as it is by our founding principles, it would be useful to set the tone for the essays that follow by recounting here a summary of that transformation and offering a glimpse of what needs to be done to restore limited constitutional government and the freedom it ensures.

First Principles

We are fortunate in America to live under a Constitution dedicated to individual liberty and limited government. For over two centuries the document has served us well, especially in contrast to the experiences of other nations. It has helped us to stay together as a people and to flourish under a fairly stable rule of law. Nevertheless, Jefferson surely was right when he observed that "the natural progress of things is for liberty to yield and government to gain ground."

The Constitution was meant to be a check on that progress. It has done so only to a degree. No one today believes that government in Washington, or in the state capitals for that matter, is seriously limited.

Under our system, it falls ultimately to the Supreme Court to say what the law is. Congress and the states may legislate, and federal and state officials may regulate under that legislation and enforce that law. But if the law is challenged, it is up to the judicial branch to determine whether it is legitimate under our basic law, the Constitution. That is why the Court's work is so important. The Court's decisions either secure or undermine our basic law—and the rule of law itself. And the rule of law is all that stands between us and tyranny.

The Founders understood those fundamentals. When they drafted the Declaration they justified our independence by setting forth their philosophy of government. They began with an appeal to natural law and natural rights, to the idea that there is a higher law of right and wrong from which to derive the positive law and against which to judge that law. That was an appeal to reason, yet to nothing more complicated than the idea that we are all equal as defined by our rights to life, liberty, and the pursuit of happiness.

What that means in practice is that we are all free to pursue happiness as we wish, by our own lights, provided we respect the equal rights of others to do the same. There, in a nutshell, is the basic moral order. It was captured in large measure by the classic common law, grounded in property and contract—"property" referring broadly, as John Locke put it, to "Lives, Liberties, and Estates." Edward Corwin, the eminent legal historian, stated the matter well in his seminal volume, *The "Higher Law" Background of American Constitutional Law*: "The notion that the common law embodied right reason furnished from the fourteenth century its chief claim to be regarded as higher law."

It was with that moral vision in mind that the Founders went on in the Declaration to say that we create government to secure those rights. But not any government will do. To be legitimate, government's powers must be grounded in the consent of the governed. Thus, legitimate government is twice limited—by its ends, which any of us would have a right to pursue were there no government, and by its means, which must be consented to.

The Constitution

Those principles were given practical force 11 years later when the Framers drafted a new Constitution. Madison's task in that undertaking was to craft a plan that afforded enough power to secure our rights and to provide for a few other ends, yet not so much as to undermine those rights, defeating the very purpose of government. Toward that end he began with a realistic conception of human nature, then struck upon the idea of pitting power against power, institutionalizing the idea through the devices we all know— the division and separation of powers, a bicameral legislature with differently constituted chambers, a unitary executive with veto power, provision for judicial review by an independent judiciary, periodic elections, and the like.

But the centerpiece of his design was the doctrine of enumerated powers. That doctrine holds that power rests originally and rightly with the people, who exercise it by right. When they constitute themselves as a political entity, however, they give some of their powers to the government they create, to be exercised on their behalf, enumerating those powers in the constitution that emerges. The doctrine thus serves three fundamental functions: it justifies power by showing how it arises from those who originally and rightly have it; it shows what powers the government has; and, by implication, it limits power, for if a power is not enumerated in the founding document, the government does not have it. At bottom, then, the Founders' theory of political legitimacy is grounded in their theory of individual rights.

The Preamble of the Constitution reveals the foundation of the doctrine: "We the People," for the purposes listed, "do ordain and establish this Constitution." All power, in short, comes from the people. Then in the very first sentence of Article I the doctrine is made explicit: "All legislative Powers *herein granted* shall be vested in a Congress. . . ." By implication, not all such powers were "herein granted." We find most of Congress's powers enumerated in Article I, section 8, of course. Finally, the Tenth Amendment, the last documentary evidence from the founding period, sets out the most explicit statement of the doctrine: "The powers not delegated to the United States by the Constitution, nor prohibited by it to the States, are reserved to the States respectively, or to the people." In a word, the Constitution establishes a government of delegated, enumerated, and thus limited powers.

The Bill of Rights

Indeed, so central was the doctrine of enumerated powers to the Framers' design that it was thought to render a bill of rights unnecessary. When such a bill was proposed at the convention, Hamilton, Wilson, and others responded, "Why declare that things shall not be done which there is no power to do?" Thus, it was the enumeration of powers, not the enumeration of rights, that was meant to be our *principal* protection against overweening government. The Bill of Rights was an afterthought, made necessary to ensure ratification by the states.

In drafting the Bill of Rights, however, a second objection had to be met—that such a bill would be dangerous. Given that we cannot enumerate all of our rights, there being too many, the failure to do so would be construed, by ordinary principles of legal reasoning, as implying that those not enumerated were not meant to be protected. To address that concern the Ninth Amendment was written: "The enumeration in the Constitution of certain rights shall not be construed to deny or disparage others retained by the people." The rights the Framers enumerated were those that in their experience would most likely be at risk. The others would be protected, they assumed, in the normal course of litigation. And in the early days of the Republic, as recent research has shown, judges were not at all reluctant to afford protection to unenumerated rights.

Taken together, then, the Ninth and Tenth Amendments recapitulate the vision first set forth in the Declaration. The Ninth Amendment makes it clear that we have rights, *enumerated and unenumerated alike*, and that the failure to find a right "in" the Constitution is not to be taken as our not having it. For judges, of course, that puts a premium on understanding the theory of rights that stands behind the Constitution, and that has been one of the great problems for the Court, about which more below. The Tenth Amendment, by contrast, makes it clear that the federal government has *only* those powers that are enumerated in the Constitution or are entailed, as means, under the document's Necessary and Proper Clause. That issue is now back before the Court, of course, having been ignored for some 60 years.

The legal regime that emerged from the founding period, then, was essentially libertarian. The federal government's powers were "few and defined," directed primarily to national concerns like foreign affairs, defense, and interstate commerce. Individuals were left free to plan and live their own lives, their rights to do so recognized by the Constitution but protected primarily by state governments, where the general police power was left.

Completing the Picture

That picture was still incomplete, however, for the Bill of Rights, which amended the federal Constitution, protected individuals only against federal violations, not against violations by the states. And the great problem at the center of it all was slavery, which the Constitution recognized obliquely—many Framers hoping the institution would die of its own over time. It did not. It took a civil war to end slavery. And it took the Civil War Amendments to apply the Bill of Rights and the promise of the Declaration against the states. In particular, under the Fourteenth Amendment, individuals finally had federal remedies against state violations of their rights, marking a fundamental change in our federalism.

That advance would soon be compromised, however, for in 1873, in the notorious *Slaughterhouse Cases*, a bitterly divided Court eviscerated the Fourteenth Amendment's Privileges or Immunities Clause, which was meant to be the principal font of substantive rights under the amendment. Thereafter the Court would try to do under the Due Process and, later, the Equal Protection Clauses what should have been done under the better understood Privileges or Immunities Clause. The efforts were largely successful, but uneven, primarily because the Court never clearly articulated the theory of rights that informed the clause, a problem that continues to this day.

Nevertheless, individual liberty and limited government continued for the most part. The reasons were several. For one, the ethos in Congress and state legislatures was such that bills expanding government were usually blocked there. When such bills did get through, however, the executive would often veto them. Thus, in 1887, 100 years after the Constitution was written, President Cleveland vetoed a bill appropriating $10,000 to buy seeds for Texas farmers suffering from a drought, saying, "I can find no warrant for such an appropriation in the Constitution." And of course the courts also did their part, to a large extent, securing the rule of law established by the Constitution.

The Rise of Political Activism

As the 20th century was dawning, however, the climate of ideas in America was changing—and ideas eventually have consequences.

The influences were many: British utilitarianism, with its attacks on American conceptions of natural rights; German schools of "good government" and the social engineering that followed; domestic ideas about democracy—all culminating in the Progressive Era. Elite opinion, especially, was coming to see government not as a necessary evil, as the Founders had conceived of it, but as an engine of good, an instrument for solving all manner of "social problems," the kinds of problems that had accompanied industrialization and urbanization after the Civil War. Far from fearing government, this vanguard was attracted to it. Better living through bigger government captured the spirit of the age—for every problem, a government solution.

The Constitution did not authorize that much government, of course. And the Court, for the most part, was upholding the law. Thus, in 1905, in the famous case of *Lochner v. New York*, the Court found that a state statute limiting the hours bakers might work violated their freedom of contract. But the decisions in that era were uneven. Thus, in 1926, in the case of *Village of Euclid v. Ambler Reality Co.*, the Court upheld a comprehensive municipal zoning scheme against the claims of private owners that their rights to use their property consistent with the rights of others were violated by the scheme.

With the election of Franklin Roosevelt, however, political activists shifted their focus from the state to the federal level. Still, the Court stood its ground, rejecting one New Deal program after another as unconstitutional. Things came to a head just after Roosevelt was reelected. Facing what he took to be an intransigent Court, Roosevelt unveiled his infamous Court-packing scheme, threatening to pack the bench with six additional members. Not even Congress would go along with the scheme. Nevertheless, a cowed Court got the message. There followed the famous "switch in time that saved nine," and the Court began rewriting the Constitution.

Democratizing the Constitution

In essence, the Court democratized the Constitution, doing it in two main steps. In a pair of decisions in 1937 it eviscerated the centerpiece of the document, the doctrine of enumerated powers. Then in 1938 it bifurcated the Bill of Rights, giving us a bifurcated theory of judicial review in the process.

The evisceration of enumerated powers involved the Constitution's General Welfare and Commerce Clauses. Both were meant to be shields against power. The Court turned them into swords of power. The General Welfare Clause was meant to be a restraint on the spending power. Congress could spend for enumerated ends, but that spending had to serve the *general* welfare as distinct from any particular or sectional welfare. In particular, Madison, Jefferson, and others insisted, against Hamilton, that Congress had no *independent* power to spend for the general welfare, for that would have rendered pointless the restraint afforded by enumeration. As South Carolina's William Drayton observed in 1828, "If Congress can determine what constitutes the General Welfare and can appropriate money for its advancement, where is the limitation to carrying into execution whatever can be effected by money?" Yet in 1936, in *United States v. Butler*, the Court sided with Hamilton, even if its opinion on the question was not central to the case. The next year, however, in *Helvering v. Davis*, the Court elevated that dicta to "law." Congress was now free to spend on any end it thought served the "general welfare." The modern redistributive state was thus unleashed.

The Commerce Clause was also meant primarily to be a restraint—but on state power. Under the Articles of Confederation, states were erecting tariffs and other protectionist measures that had begun to interfere with the free flow of commerce among them. In fact, one of the principal reasons the Framers met to draft a new constitution was to address that problem. They did so through the Commerce Clause, which gave Congress the power to regulate—or make regular—commerce among the states. In fact, that is how the clause was read in 1824 in the first great Commerce Clause case, *Gibbons v. Ogden*. It was not read as giving Congress a power to regulate, for any reason, anything that "affected" interstate commerce, which in principle is everything. Yet that is how the 1937 Court read the clause in *NLRB v. Jones & Laughlin Steel Corp.*—and with that the modern regulatory state was unleashed.

After those two decisions, Congress's redistributive and regulatory powers were plenary, in effect, as courts no longer asked that most basic of constitutional questions: Does Congress have the authority to do what it is doing? Yet individuals might still raise *rights* against the exercise of those powers. In 1938, therefore, the Court attended to that impediment to active government. In the famous footnote four of *United States v. Carolene Products Co.*, the notorious filled-milk case, the Court distinguished two kinds of rights and two levels of judicial review. If a measure implicated "fundamental rights" like speech or voting—rights associated with the democratic political process—the Court would exercise "strict scrutiny" and the measure would likely be found unconstitutional. By contrast, if a measure implicated "nonfundamental rights" like property or contract—rights associated with "ordinary commercial transactions"—the Court would exercise "minimal scrutiny" and the measure would likely be found constitutional. Those distinctions are nowhere to be found in the Constitution, of course. They were created from whole cloth to make the world safe for the expansive programs of the New Deal. Limited government would soon be a thing of the past as one program after another poured through the openings the Court had created.

The constitutional revolution the New Deal Court wrought was a textbook example of politics trumping law—not on a small scale, as when a judge ignores the law in a narrow case to reach a popular result, but on a massive, structural scale. The very theory and purpose of the Constitution were upended. The American people had delegated limited powers to the national government. The Court rendered those powers effectively unlimited. The people restrained the exercise of that power and, later, the power of the states through a Bill of Rights, intended to protect both enumerated and unenumerated rights. The Court rendered that design unintelligible. In a word, heeding the politics of the day, the Court turned a document authorizing limited government into one authorizing effectively unlimited government, making a mockery of the rule of law.

An Aftermath of Confusions

We have lived under that regime for over 60 years now and the confusions are everywhere. Take just one aspect, the bifurcated judicial scrutiny theory that emerged from *Carolene Products*. It turns out that gender discrimination required a richer theory, so the Court invented mid-level scrutiny. But when the "must-carry" provisions of the Cable Television Consumer Protection and Competition Act of 1992 were before the Court in 1994, a fourth level of scrutiny had to be invented. Now we have "minimal" scrutiny for ordinary commercial transactions, "relaxed" scrutiny for broadcast television, "heightened" scrutiny for cable television, and "strict" scrutiny for newspapers. Does anyone know what any of that means? One is reminded of nothing so much as medieval geocentric Ptolemaics drawing epicycle upon epicycle to explain the motions of the planets and ward off the onslaught of the heliocentric Copernicans.

But scrutiny theory is only one of the confusions of the body of thought today called "constitutional law." A brief overview of the past 60 years brings out others, related mostly to the role judges now play in our system of government. Start with the surfeit of federal and state legislation the New Deal revolution unleashed, most of it aimed at solving all manner of "social problems"—there being, in principle, no end to such problems. Reflecting the hubris that has always attended central planning, those schemes—regulating commerce, agriculture, labor, retirement, land use, education, medicine, campaign finance, and on and on—have grown ever more complex, often because they generate unintended consequences that require still more regulation, the planners claim. The result is the modern administrative state—massive and effectively unaccountable—and a body of "law" that in fact is policy, reflecting the will of the political forces that have triumphed on a given issue on a given day. It is politics as law in its purest form, with almost no subject beyond its reach.

Much of that legislation and regulation has ended up in the courts, of course, with judges asked to make sense of often inconsistent and incoherent policy—fairly inviting them to be parties to the legislation and hence policymakers themselves. Thus, by parsing often obscure statutory or regulatory language, judges end up setting national policy, something they have traditionally been loath to do. But judges have come to set policy more directly as well. For when government activists fail to achieve their goals in the political branches, they often go to the courts, hoping to find there a sympathetic judge. Regrettably, the Warren and Burger Courts, already deferring to the legislative pursuit of "social justice," were often only too willing to step into the fray, thinking themselves a legislature of nine. A fair amount of what those Courts did was long overdue, of course—nowhere more so than in ending the scourge of Jim Crow. But enough else amounted to nothing less than judicial lawmaking.

Judicial "Activism" and "Restraint"

What such "judicial activism" led to, however, was an equally mistaken reaction that paraded under the label "judicial restraint."

As a result, in recent years we have had two main theories about the proper role of the Court, liberal and conservative, neither of which reflects the original understanding. Modern liberals, having championed the political activism that led to the New Deal, have continued of course to urge the Court to ignore the doctrine of enumerated powers. And they have continued to call on the Court to be "restrained" in finding rights that might limit their redistributive and regulatory schemes, especially "nonfundamental rights" like property and contract. But at the same time they have asked the Court to be "active" in finding other rights, including spurious "rights" never meant to be included among our unenumerated rights.

Reacting to the Court's discovery of such "rights," many modern conservatives have urged judicial restraint across the board. Thus, if liberal programs run roughshod over property or contract rights, rather than ask the Court to protect them—that would encourage judicial activism—much less resurrect the doctrine of enumerated powers—that battle was lost during the New Deal—those conservatives call simply for turning to the democratic process to overturn the programs. Oblivious to the fact that judicial restraint in finding rights is tantamount to activism in finding powers, and ignoring the fact that it was the democratic process that gave us those programs in the first place, too many conservatives have simply bought into the New Deal's democratization of the Constitution. Theirs is a counsel of despair amounting to a denial of constitutional protection.

No one doubts that in recent decades the Court has discovered "rights" in the Constitution that were never meant to be there, even among our unenumerated rights. But it is no answer to that problem to ask the Court to defer wholesale to the political branches, thereby encouraging it, by implication, to sanction unenumerated *powers* that are no part of the document either. Indeed, if the Tenth Amendment means anything it means that there are no such powers. If the Framers had wanted to establish a simple democracy, they could have. Instead, they established a limited, constitutional republic, a republic with islands of democratic power in a sea of liberty, not a sea of democratic power surrounding islands of liberty.

In a word, then, just as it is improper for the Court to find rights nowhere to be found in the Constitution, thereby frustrating authorized democratic decisions, so too is it improper for the Court to refrain from asking whether those decisions are authorized and, if so, whether their implementation violates rights guaranteed by the Constitution, enumerated and unenumerated alike. In the end, therefore, the issue is substantive: the Court must apply the law "actively," but accurately too, and that is a substantive matter. Today, after more than 60 years of constitutional hermeneutics and the cases that have followed, the Court too often loses sight of the Constitution itself, finding comfort instead in the accumulated cases that are called "constitutional law." In addressing that problem, the words "activism" and "restraint" are more misleading than helpful. What is needed, rather, is a return to the first principles of the matter, to the substance of the Constitution.

Toward Restoration

Enumerated Powers

Fortunately, the Rehnquist Court has begun that process, but only begun it. Over the past decade the Court has asked in several cases whether Congress had the authority to do what it did. Constitutional questions do not get more basic than that. Indeed, Chief Justice Rehnquist himself set the tone in 1995 in *United States v. Lopez*: "We start with first principles. The Constitution creates a Federal Government of enumerated powers." That ringing a statement hadn't been heard from the Court since the New Deal. It was a breath of fresh air for those who long to see limited constitutional government and the rule of law restored.

But it was only a breath. Constrained by erroneous precedents, Rehnquist went on to articulate a tripartite theory of the commerce power that enabled Congress to regulate even activities that "substantially affect" interstate commerce. That puts the Court in a business it should not be in—calibrating degrees of affect; it still leaves Congress's regulatory power virtually plenary; and it is not what the Commerce Clause is about. It fell to Justice Thomas in concurrence to note that the Court was still a long way from the original understanding of the commerce power. Indeed, "The Framers could have drafted a Constitution that contained a 'substantially affects interstate commerce' clause had that been their objective," he wrote. They did not.

The importance of the Court's having begun this restoration with federalism and, more precisely, with the doctrine of enumerated powers cannot be overstated. Indeed, the cases have so rattled those who simply assumed that post-New Deal doctrine would be with us forever that they have taken to calling the Rehnquist Court's jurisprudence in this area "activism"—seeming to forget that it was the New Deal Court's activism that gave us that errant doctrine. In its selection of cases, however, as well as its treatment of them, the Court is still at the beginning. One can understand its cautious approach: Leviathan was not created overnight; it will not be dismantled overnight—not by the Court alone, certainly. At the same time, it is crucial that the Court articulate clearly not simply the practical limits it labors under but the fundamental principles before it. And of course its enumerated powers docket should reach well beyond Commerce Clause cases.

Enumerated Rights

Moving from powers to rights, here the Court comes upon what is at once a more promising prospect, as a practical matter, yet a greater intellectual challenge. As noted earlier, the Court has never developed systematically the theory of rights that stands behind the Constitution. What is worse, once democratic theory took hold uncritically, seeming to justify by mere numbers whatever a legislative majority decided, the moral force of an appeal to individual rights diminished. Yet it is precisely the role of the Court to check majorities when their actions are unauthorized by the Constitution or violate rights protected by the Constitution. In that fundamental sense, rights are countermajoritarian notions, which judges are appointed to protect against majoritarian tyranny. And in an individualistic culture such as ours has been from the start—the Declaration, after all, starts with the rights of the individual—it has not been difficult, ultimately, for rights to trump majoritarianism in many areas of life. Not always, to be sure, and not in all areas. But by and large our individualist heritage has remained alive and well. Thus, as a practical matter, restoring constitutional rights may be somewhat easier for the Court to do than restoring the original bounds of the doctrine of enumerated powers.

The difficulties are more likely to be intellectual. For we understand rights and the role of the Court in securing them, for the most part, when rights are easily discerned. When discernment is more difficult, however, problems begin—and judges lose their nerve.

That happens even with enumerated rights. Take property: The Court has had little difficulty upholding the rights of owners to compensation when government takes their property outright. But when *uses* are taken by government regulation, and the owner retains the title, the Court has had difficulty. We all know, from every other area of law, that "property" is a bundle of rights that can be packaged and exchanged in various ways. Yet when the public takes such a package we forget that a private party that did the same thing, assuming the owner agreed to the exchange, would have to compensate the owner. Here too the Court in recent years has revived those basic principles, to some extent, with Chief Justice Rehnquist himself setting the tone in 1994 in the case of *Dolan v. City of Tigard*: "We see no reason why the Takings Clause . . . should be relegated to the status of a poor relation. . . ." But the Court has yet to correctly articulate the theory of the matter, much less apply it consistently, as witness its recent decision in the *Lake Tahoe* case, discussed in this volume.

Unenumerated Rights

Given the difficulty the Court has had, then, even with enumerated rights, it is no surprise that unenumerated rights have fared far worse. Yet in principle, unenumerated rights are no more difficult to secure than enumerated rights. In fact, there is no bright line between enumerated and unenumerated rights. Even enumerated rights, that is, are not self-enforcing: they need to be interpreted and applied in the factual circumstances of the case at hand, as just illustrated with property rights. At that basic, analytical level, then, the distinction between enumerated and unenumerated rights is deceptive and, ultimately, unhelpful—especially if it leads a judge toward legal positivism, one right at a time, and away from the systematic natural rights theory that informs the Constitution.

Moreover, the distinction is especially pernicious if it leads judges to believe that they can recognize and enforce enumerated rights, but it is up to legislative majorities to declare what our unenumerated rights are. There are at least two major errors in that view. First, as noted above, rights are countermajoritarian notions we assert defensively, in opposition to threats from legislative majorities. Imagine if Congress, to clarify religious freedom, specified which were and were not legitimate religions. Second, unenumerated rights are no less a part of the Constitution than enumerated rights. Given that, it would be anomalous at least to say that an individual had an unenumerated constitutional right but that Congress or a state legislature could override it by mere legislation. We would never say that about enumerated rights. Why do we think it is any different with unenumerated rights? After all, we went for two years without a bill of (enumerated) rights. *All* rights at that time were unenumerated, except those few that were included in the body of the original Constitution. Yet no one imagined that judges were powerless to ensure that enumerated powers be exercised consistent with our natural rights. Certainly no one thought that the absence of enumerated rights meant that we had no rights at all against federal power. Yet that is how most jurists today approach the issue of unenumerated rights.

It is at this point that the idea of a systematic theory of rights comes to the fore. In its entirety, this is a complex subject, to be sure, yet at its core it is relatively simple and straightforward—even commonsensical. In fact, the old common law judges did a fairly good job of tracing it out—before the rise of the modern statutory state and its "law" of public policy. Among other things, the theory of rights is not about securing values, at bottom, for rights and values are very different moral notions. Thus, talk of "interests rising to the level of rights" is ordinarily in error. Nor does one pick values randomly—speech, religious expression, privacy, property—and call them rights—the implication being that if enough people ceased to value them they would cease to be rights.

Rather, rights theory looks to entitlements—in the most basic sense of that idea: one determines one's rights by determining what it is one holds title to, free and clear. And one starts at the most fundamental level—logically fundamental, not evaluatively fundamental as the *Carolene Products* Court thought, thereby conflating rights and values. That brings us back to Locke's "Lives, Liberties, and Estates." Once those are secured in the basic justificatory structure, one then derives more specifically described rights like speech, religious expression, and the like. Thus, as an initial matter, each of us has a right to speak freely because no one else has a right that we not do so, and no one else holds that title. Our title to speak, practice our religion, and so forth is something *we* hold, not something held by someone else, unless of course we've done something to alienate it and vest it in another—moved under another's sovereignty, made a promise, committed a tort or a crime, and so on. Explicating the theory of rights is thus a deductive exercise, rooted in reason, concerning property—again, broadly understood. (It is no accident that the classic common law was so intimately connected to property.) The theory can tell us, for example, that our neighbor's addition to his house, which blocks our view, did not violate our rights, for absent an easement indicating otherwise we never had title to that view. In that way it can distinguish legitimate from spurious claims about rights.

What objective reason cannot do, however, is complete the picture. It cannot draw nuisance or endangerment lines, for example, or define "reasonableness" or "probable cause" or tell us what punishments are appropriate. For those kinds of issues we have to introduce subjective values into an otherwise objective, deductive structure, at which point reasonable people can have reasonable differences. In comprehending and developing the theory of rights, then, it is crucial to understand its boundaries and limits. Yet that, again, was never a great mystery for those who understood the difference between law grounded in reason, as natural rights theory was and is, and law grounded in will, as modern democratic theory is.

Those are some of the issues that need to be understood and ordered in working out the theory of rights that informs the Constitution. At bottom, the idea is to ground as much of our law as is possible in reason rather than in values or will or passion. Indeed, it was to avoid the "law" of will that the Framers did *not* give us a democracy—or anything close to it. They roped power in at every turn, hoping that people would thereby be left free, in the private sector, to plan and live their own lives by their own values, not consigned to the tender mercies of the state in everything from day care to education, industry, employment, medical care, and retirement—to say nothing of political speech.

Conclusion

The essays in this and in future volumes of the *Cato Supreme Court Review* will carefully examine the Court's work—criticizing it where necessary, praising it where deserved—all with an eye toward advancing the principles of a free society as captured by our founding documents. We ourselves may not always get it right. We may not always agree among ourselves. But we do agree about the basic task before the Court today. It is to decide cases that come before it in a way that upholds the rule of law the Constitution set in motion over two centuries ago. Given the state of constitutional law today, to say nothing of current conceptions of law, that is often difficult to do. And that is why, in carrying out that task, there is no substitute for returning to first principles.

Introduction

This volume of the *Cato Supreme Court Review* is the first in an annual series that will analyze the most significant opinions of the Supreme Court of the United States. Each year the *Review* will publish essays covering ten to fifteen cases from the Court's most recent term. The volume that you hold in your hands includes cases from the term beginning in October, 2001, and ending in late June, 2002.

In three ways the *Cato Supreme Court Review* is unlike any other publication that follows the Court. First, we are timely. Indeed, our current issue is the first in-depth review of the 2001 October Term—published less than three months after the Court handed down its final decisions on June 28, 2002. Each year's *Review* will appear soon after the term ends, and shortly before the next term begins on the first Monday of October.

Second, because the Constitution is not the exclusive domain of lawyers and judges, we asked our contributors to write articles that will appeal to a diverse and large audience. Although the *Review* is of course a "law" book, in the sense that it is about the Court and the Constitution, we intend it not only for lawyers but also for journalists, editors, broadcasters, publishers, legislators, government officials, professors, students, and all citizens interested in their Constitution and the Court's interpretation of it.

Third, and most important, the *Cato Supreme Court Review* has a singular point of view, which we will not attempt to conceal behind a mask of impartiality. I confess our ideology at the outset: This *Review* will look at the Court and its decisions from the classical Madisonian perspective, emphasizing our first principles of individual liberty, secure property rights, federalism, and a government of enumerated, delegated and thus limited powers. In his Foreword, the *Review*'s publisher, Roger Pilon, has articulated those principles, showing in the process how modern courts have too often ignored them. It is time for a *Review* such as this.

We inaugurate that examination with nine articles about twelve cases decided during the 2001 October Term. Although the term may not have been a vintage one for the Court—that is, we do not have an abundant crop of major decisions involving first principles—nonetheless, the term did produce significant opinions in six subject areas: property rights, federalism, the First Amendment, education, criminal law, and the drug war. The *Review* includes contributions on each of those topics from distinguished commentators including Richard A. Epstein writing on property rights and regulatory takings in *Tahoe-Sierra Preservation Council Inc. v. Tahoe Regional Planning Agency*; Robert A. Levy on federalism and state sovereign immunity in *Federal Maritime Commission v. South Carolina State Ports Authority*; Jonathan Turley on the right to anonymous speech in *Watchtower Bible and Tract Society v. Village of Stratton*; Robert Corn-Revere on child pornography in *Ashcroft v. Free Speech Coalition*, and on obscenity in *Ashcroft v. ACLU*; Clint Bolick on school choice and the establishment clause in *Zelman v. Simmons-Harris*; Timothy Lynch on criminal law and plea bargaining in *U.S. v. Ruiz*; Stephen P. Halbrook on criminal law and sentencing factors in *Harris v. United States*, and on the death penalty in *Ring v. Arizona*; and Roger Pilon on the drug war in *Department of Housing and Urban Development v. Rucker* and *Board of Education v. Earls*. My own contribution discusses judicial elections, political speech, and the First Amendment in *Republican Party of Minnesota v. White*. In a look ahead to the forthcoming October Term 2002, Erik S. Jaffe identifies the cases of greatest interest and the principles at stake.

I thank our contributors for their generous participation: There would be no *Cato Supreme Court Review* without them. I thank my colleagues at the Cato Institute's Center for Constitutional Studies, Roger Pilon, Timothy Lynch, and Robert A. Levy for valuable editorial contributions; David Lampo for producing and Elise Rivera for designing the *Review*; and Elizabeth Kreul-Starr for assistance in preparing the manuscripts for publication.

We hope that this volume, and those to come, chart a journey of the Court toward a jurisprudence grounded on first principles. But we aspire to do more than document the Court's progress. We want the *Cato Supreme Court Review* to be more than a weathervane, merely reflecting the direction of the wind. Instead, we hope that these essays, and those in future volumes, influence, at least in some small way, how the wind blows. Our goal is to reanimate the principles laid down more than two centuries ago in the Declaration of Independence and the Constitution and to apply those principles today to the cases and controversies that come before the Supreme Court of the United States. In so doing we aim to resurrect the spirit of another age when, long before they were eclipsed by the rise of the modern regulatory and redistributive state, the natural rights of liberty and property superseded the will of government and of men. With optimism for the task ahead, we present the inaugural volume of this *Review*.

James L. Swanson
Editor in Chief

The Ebbs and Flows in Takings Law: Reflections on the *Lake Tahoe* Case

Richard A. Epstein

Introduction: A Change in the Winds of Fortune

For the Framers of our Constitution, the principles of good government started with the protection of private property—that guardian of all other rights. The instinct behind their judgment is easy to grasp just by imagining how the world would look if governments could consistently disregard property rights. State bureaucrats could confiscate land at will, not just for public works, but to line their own pockets. Government officials could harvest with impunity crops planted by ordinary citizens, and systematically disrupt all private efforts at long-term planning. It takes little ingenuity to see the moral bankruptcy and economic ruination inherent in any regime devoid of property rights. Nor, ironically, would any of today's preferred freedoms be worth the paper they were written on. How could people pray if they could not keep government officials from snatching away their houses of worship? How could they criticize the government if not allowed to own printing presses and broadcast studios?

Fortunately, none of that has come to pass. One reason for our political stability is found in the Takings Clause of the Fifth Amendment: "nor shall private property be taken for public use without just compensation."[1] By and large, that clause has been sensibly (not ideally, but sensibly) interpreted to block government from seizing and occupying property—the greatest peril to individual freedom—without compensating the owner. Regrettably, the public use

The author thanks Timothy Doweling for his comments on an earlier draft, and Richard H. Helmholz, Geoffrey R. Stone, David Strauss, and David Weisbach, for their perceptive questions at a work-in-progress session at the University of Chicago.

[1]U.S. Const. amend V. For my detailed analysis of the clause, see Richard A. Epstein, Takings: Private Property and the Power of Eminent Domain (1985).

requirement has been watered down, in the name of urban renewal or land reform, to allow takings for private benefit.[2] But in all cases of occupation, the courts have adhered to a well-nigh per se rule that requires compensation whenever government occupies land, including some tiny fraction of a larger holding.[3]

Cases of seizure and occupation are only half the story, however. Government officials (like private individuals) are often tempted to seek the indirect path when the direct route is blocked. If outright occupation of the land requires payment of compensation, why not leave the owner in possession of the land but strip him of his rights to use and dispose of it? Then some particular end, such as urban growth control or the elimination of potential competition, can be advanced without triggering the compensation requirement. To keep matters in perspective, such restrictions on land-use do not pose dangers equal to those arising from unlimited direct occupation. But they are not small potatoes either. In *Euclid v. Ambler Realty Co.*,[4] the seminal zoning case, the Supreme Court sustained an ordinance that reduced the value of the land almost 75 percent. (The ordinance required that a 68-acre plot slated for an automotive plant be devoted exclusively to single-family housing.) The power of regulation becomes still more dangerous when, as is the case with landmark preservation and wetland programs, administrative officials are given broad discretion to designate which lands will or will not be subject to an ordinance.

Given their pervasive use and powerful consequences, such regulations have become the focal point of intense judicial controversy. Over the past 15 years, the Supreme Court has grappled with multiple forms of land-use regulation.[5] But its treatment of the issues has

---

[2] *See* Haw. Hous. Auth. v. Midkiff, 467 U.S. 226 (1984) (allowing forced state transfers to tenants of leased property in order to counter the land oligopoly of the Trustees of the Kamehameha Schools/Bishop Estate); Berman v. Parker, 348 U.S. 26 (1954) (allowing forced state takeovers of viable businesses for local blight removal).

[3] *See, e.g.*, Loretto v. TelePrompterManhattan CATIV Corp., 458 U.S. 419 (1982). Too often, however, the compensation tendered is usually lower than that needed to leave the owner indifferent as to his position before and after the taking. For discussion, see EPSTEIN, TAKINGS, at 182–215.

[4] 272 U.S. 365 (1926).

[5] *See, e.g.*, Dolan v. City of Tigard, 512 U.S. 687 (1994); Lucas v. S.C. Coastal Council, 505 U.S. 1003 (1992); Nollan v. Cal. Coastal Comm'n, 483 U.S. 825 (1987).

at best been halting and incomplete, even if owners have come out on top for the most part. It is no surprise that these decisions often reflect the now familiar right-left split on the Court, with the five conservative justices (Rehnquist, O'Connor, Scalia, Kennedy, and Thomas) arrayed against the four liberals (Stevens, Souter, Ginsburg, and Breyer). But as is equally apparent, that coalition of five contains a subcoalition, with Justices Kennedy and O'Connor precariously positioned midway between the three conservatives and the four liberals.

In the 2000 term, the five-justice coalition held as Justice Kennedy wrote *Palazzolo v. Rhode Island*,[6] one of the Court's stronger and more coherent decisions dealing with property rights. *Palazzolo*'s central holding was that the state could not immunize itself from takings challenges simply by passing a statute and then claiming that individuals who acquire property thereafter are barred from challenging it because they took title "with notice" that the statute was on the books. The Court's "per se" rule—the phrase quickly becomes a term of art—held that the subsequent owner is entitled to raise the same challenges the previous owner could raise. In *Palazzolo*, the subsequent owner was the sole shareholder of a corporation that had been involuntarily liquidated. If he were automatically bound by the new regulation, then it would have been just a matter of time before all owners were so bound: over time, after all, corporations are liquidated; partnerships dissolved; land transferred, by sale, lease or foreclosure, divorce or death. For the time being, *Palazzolo* put an end to the incipient uncertainty in land titles.

Yet the mood of the Court proved most unstable as the pendulum swung sharply in the opposite direction this past term in *Tahoe-Sierra Preservation Council, Inc. v. Tahoe Regional Planning Agency*.[7] The case involved a series of temporary land-use ordinances that prohibited new construction on land near Lake Tahoe. Succeeding moratoria were imposed by the Tahoe Regional Planning Agency (TRPA)—a specialized agency created by California and Nevada— to buy time to develop a comprehensive plan to regulate new construction in the Tahoe basin to preserve the water quality of Lake Tahoe. All of the plaintiffs in *Tahoe* were landowners of undeveloped

[6] 533 U.S. 606 (2001).
[7] 122 S. Ct. 1465 (2002).

7

plots of land located on the edge of the Lake Tahoe basin. Starting in the early 1980s, they have fought a protracted but largely unsuccessful battle with TRPA to build homes on their lands. Of the 700 or so ordinary people who started on this journey, 55 have since died and many others have dropped out of the struggle—their land still unused—from sheer emotional and financial exhaustion. No litigation against government is ever easy. In this case, ordinary citizens, often of limited means, tried in vain to run the gauntlet of TPRA's multiple moratoria and procedural hurdles, which were introduced in the 1970s and have been refined and elaborated over the years.[8]

The legal struggle that reached the Supreme Court centered on two key ordinances that in the early '80s imposed a combined 32-month delay on new construction on key sites, mainly those with the steepest slopes. When TRPA finally produced a plan in 1984, California sought and obtained an injunction against its implementation on the ground that it was insufficiently protective of Lake Tahoe. If the injunction period were taken into account, the moratoria in question lasted some six years.[9] Yet even after that, construction still had to run a formidable gauntlet of permitting requirements.

These post-1980 moratoria were spurred on by consequences of the previous boom period of new construction in the Tahoe basin. As mentioned previously, TRPA's prime justification for refusing to permit development related to the preservation of the once pristine Lake Tahoe. Owing to its high altitude and location, the lake was "oligotropic" in its natural state—it lacked nutrients to support the growth of plant life. In consequence, it enjoyed a matchless, cobalt blue clarity, long celebrated by Mark Twain and by citizens who lived and worked in the region. With development, however, Lake Tahoe had undergone a process of "eutrophication"—plant life was flourishing in the lake, undermining its clarity.

That eutrophication stemmed from a substantial increase in the level of nutrients in the lake as a result of the construction in the

---

[8] Their exact duration is in dispute because not all parcels were treated in the same fashion. In the post-1987 period, some new building has taken place, albeit under restrictive conditions. For a history of the enactments, see *Tahoe-Sierra Pres. Council, Inc. v. Tahoe Reg'l Planning Agency*, 34 F. Supp. 2d 1226 (D. Nev. 1999).

[9] See the dissent of Rehnquist, C.J., point I, for the argument that all three components should be counted in the temporary period. 122 S. Ct. at 1490.

surrounding basin. As natural soil gives way to asphalt and concrete, land in the basin becomes progressively less able to absorb water. The increased runoff sweeps along soil and the nutrients found in soil. These nutrients in turn allow plant life to flourish within the lake, reducing its overall clarity. In response, TRPA divided the land surrounding the lake into seven stream environment zones. The amount of impervious surface allowed in each zone related to the amount of anticipated runoff, such that the least new construction was allowed in those areas designated as most fragile. The restrictions on new construction were intended to prevent an acceleration of the earlier cycle of eutrophication, which everyone rightly regarded as a legitimate social purpose.

The new provisions applied both to owners who had already built up their sites and to those whose land was undeveloped. The impact in the two cases was quite different, however. Owners of existing structures were often barred from building additions, docks, driveways, and the like. Owners of undeveloped lands typically could not build anything at all. The record contains no evidence of measures introduced by TRPA to require modifying existing structures, which appeared to have been grandfathered, in line with common practice. As implemented, the building moratoria and the permit system that followed it have at most prevented an increase in the rate of runoff; they have done nothing to reduce any runoff attributable to prior construction. The onus of preventing further eutrophication of Lake Tahoe has thus been cast on those landowners who did not have the need, foresight, or luck to build on their properties before TRPA's adoption of its restrictive rules.

Clearly, *Tahoe* involves some form of regulatory taking, given that those owners were allowed to retain possession of land that they could not develop. As so often happens in such cases, however, the exact takings question raised is itself the source of some disagreement. In accepting the case for review, the Supreme Court phrased the question as follows: "Whether the Court of Appeals properly determined that a temporary moratorium on land development does not constitute a taking of property requiring compensation under the Takings Clause of the United States Constitution."[10]

---

[10]Tahoe-Sierra Pres. Council, Inc. v. Tahoe Reg'l Planning Agency, 533 U.S. 948 (granting cert.).

Justice Stevens evaluated that question with reference solely to the two ordinances, not the subsequent injunction of the 1984 plan. So limited, the Court did not consider the cumulative effect of the various delays. Nor, as it construed the question, was it permissible to ask whether some circumstances might excuse the payment of compensation. Instead, it opted to decide only whether a per se rule made all total but temporary restrictions on land-use development compensable. So framed, the six-member majority answered that question in the negative, backing off earlier Supreme Court decisions, such *Palazzolo* and *Suitum v. Lake Tahoe*,[11] which involved earlier disputes over building near Lake Tahoe.

In so deciding, the Court unleashed the factional political forces that strong property rights are meant to curtail. With Justice Stevens's blessing, an endless set of legal and planning maneuvers allowed the lucky earlier builders on the edge of Lake Tahoe to exclude or delay the latecomers the like use of their properties. The incumbent residents, as political insiders, used the rolling moratoria to gain the benefit of lower land densities. They parlayed their political power to cast the bulk of the costs of environmental protection not on themselves, who were responsible for the lake's deterioration, but on the latecomers, who bore no responsibility for the deterioration. *Tahoe* represents a dubious morality tale in which the insiders win and the outsiders lose. This is not really a case about property rights. Rather, one group of owners with political power has taken advantage of a second group of owners with less power. Clout counts.

An outcome that misguided does not arise by chance. Here, the causes are both motivational and intellectual. The Court simply does not see why protecting private property against regulation serves an important social function. Because it sees little if any real downside to regulation, it consciously refuses to articulate any consistent approach to takings problems, ranging from the simple occupation of an isolated plot to the complex regulation of many plots. To show the dire consequences of that attitude, and the confusions in current takings law, this essay first explores the relationship between cases of occupation and cases of regulation, comparing two key Supreme Court precedents, *Armstrong v. United States* and *Penn Central v. New*

[11] 520 U.S. 725 (1997).

York. Against that conceptual framework, the essay then critiques Justice Stevens's opinion in *Tahoe.* Finally, we address in preliminary form the larger question of the implications of Justice Stevens's ad hoc approach for the rule of law.

The Conceptual Framework

Armstrong *and Clear Principles*

Some sense of how the Takings Clause should work can be gained by working backward from Justice Black's oft-quoted statement of purpose in *Armstrong v. United States*: "The Fifth Amendment's guarantee that private property shall not be taken for a public use without just compensation was designed to bar Government from forcing some people alone to bear public burdens which, in all fairness and justice, should be borne by the public as a whole."[12]

The statement rings true in the context of that case. Armstrong was a Maine subcontractor who had a right to attach a lien for work and materials on boats manufactured by the Rice Shipbuilding Company for the United States Navy. Before all of the boats were completed, Rice defaulted on its government contract. In response, the Navy removed the boats from Maine, which made Armstrong's lien worthless. He had a huge loss, and the taxpayers of the United States gained a windfall of equal magnitude. Overall, however, the gains and losses do *not* cancel each other out. If the Navy's ploy had worked, then in the long run everyone would suffer from the resulting instability in contracting practices.

That tale of (large) public gain and (larger) private loss links up with the language of the Takings Clause in rigorous fashion.[13] Here is how. The first two questions in any takings case are (1) Was private property taken?, and (2) Was any compensation provided in return? In *Armstrong*, the lien was taken, but nothing was provided in exchange. In the simplest condemnation case, an isolated parcel of land is taken outright from one party and used by the government. Again, something has been taken, but in the absence of cash payment, nothing has been provided in return. Matters can become somewhat more complex, of course. The government need not take all of one's property. It can take only part, which it does when it takes a life

[12] Armstrong v. United States, 364 U.S. 40, 49 (1960), *cited in Tahoe,* at 61.
[13] *See* EPSTEIN, TAKINGS, chapters 8 & 14.

estate, uses business property for a term of years, takes an easement to walk over someone's land, or, most critically, takes a covenant that restricts an owner's right to use or develop his property.

In some cases, the government targets not a single parcel but tracts of land with several different ownerships. The increase in the scope of the government's efforts, however, does not turn a taking into something else. The government's actions are strictly additive. If restrictive covenants are imposed on 100 landowners, then the government has taken property from 100 landowners, each of whom is entitled to compensation. But with comprehensive regulation, the inquiry becomes more complex, for it is necessary to ask whether the restrictions imposed on one landowner count as the compensation to all others—just as when a private developer imposes voluntary and reciprocal restrictions on all plots within a subdivision. If so, then loss and gain may well come back into balance if all of the owners are left better off by the government's scheme than they were before. But there is no guarantee that that will happen. Equality in the *form* of regulation does not guarantee equality in its *impact*. Even if the restrictions in question have a formal equality across users, they could, in practice or by design, benefit people on one side of the railroad tracks at the expense of those on the other.

Just that happened in *Tahoe*: a uniform set of restrictions caused far greater hardship to people who had not built than to people who had. Takings on net do not have to be $100 taken and zero returned, of course. They can be $90 taken and $10 returned, leaving an uncompensated balance of $80. In some cases, moreover, the regulations may be diffuse in their impact so that it is hard to measure who has gained and who has lost. Such is true, for example, with a technical change in the recordation statutes, when it is better to let the matter slide than to try to figure out which millions of people should pay or receive some trivial amounts of money. But at Lake Tahoe the stakes were very high, and the disproportionate impact was the unmistakable sign of a large-scale taking with tiny compensation in exchange.

Penn Central *and* Ad Hoc *Principles*

The *Armstrong* principles speak strongly, then, toward compensation in *Tahoe*. Unfortunately, however, the case does not stand alone. In retrospect, the most important takings case of the past 50 years

is *Penn Central v. City of New York.*[14] In that case the question before
the Supreme Court was whether the landmark preservation statute
of New York, which was invoked to prevent the Penn Central Company from developing the air rights over its terminal, worked a
taking of private property for which compensation was required.
In finding no taking and hence no need for compensation, Justice
Brennan punted on all questions of theory, reducing *Armstrong* to
a mere parenthetical phrase in an unruly and overgrown takings
universe. The following passage has exerted such power over the
subsequent course of the law that it is best to set it out in full:

> Before considering appellants' specific contentions, it will be
> useful to review the factors that have shaped the jurispru-
> dence of the Fifth Amendment injunction "nor shall private
> property be taken for public use, without just compensation."
> The question of what constitutes a "taking" for purposes
> of the Fifth Amendment has proved to be a problem of
> considerable difficulty. While this Court has recognized that
> the "Fifth Amendment's guarantee . . . [is] designed to bar
> Government from forcing some people alone to bear public
> burdens which, in all fairness and justice, should be borne
> by the public as a whole," *Armstrong v. United States*, 364
> U.S. 40, 49 (1960), this Court, quite simply, has been unable
> to develop any "set formula" for determining when "justice
> and fairness" require that economic injuries caused by public
> action be compensated by the government, rather than
> remain disproportionately concentrated on a few persons.
> Indeed, we have frequently observed that whether a particu-
> lar restriction will be rendered invalid by the government's
> failure to pay for any losses proximately caused by it depends
> largely "upon the particular circumstances [in that] case."
> *United States v. Central Eureka Mining Co.*, 357 U.S. 155, 168
> (1958).
>
> In engaging in these essentially ad hoc, factual inquiries, the
> Court's decisions have identified several factors that have
> particular significance. The economic impact of the regula-
> tion on the claimant and, particularly, the extent to which
> the regulation has interfered with distinct investment-backed
> expectations are, of course, relevant considerations. So, too,
> is the character of the governmental action. A "taking" may
> more readily be found when the interference with property

[14] 438 U.S. 104 (1978).

> can be characterized as a physical invasion by government, than when interference arises from some public program adjusting the benefits and burdens of economic life to promote the common good.[15]

Several features of this passage cry out for attention. *Armstrong's* clarion call, not to mention its deep linkage to the structure of the Takings Clause, is muffled in judicial confession of an incapacity to find any path through the Takings Clause thicket. There has "quite simply" been "no test" that allows one to reach coherent and predictable results in these cases. How then should one deal with these essentially "ad hoc" inquiries? Answer: by transforming the text. In isolating the relevant factors for analysis, we are told that the economic impact of the regulation—most particularly, "distinct investment-backed expectations"—are to count as relevant factors.

Here is where the trouble begins. Just what count as "distinct investment-backed expectations," which receive special emphasis in the analysis? This odd phrase appears *nowhere* in the Constitution; nor, unlike the disproportionate impact test, can it be derived by interpretive means either. By transforming the question from "whether private property has been taken" to "whether distinct investment-backed expectations have been interfered with," we move from language familiar to the Framers to catchy words that carry no discernible meaning at all. Most property is not held for investment purposes, of course; yet, it hardly follows that the government can take it without paying compensation. Nor does it make sense to say that property that has been purchased is entitled to one level of protection while property that has been received as a gift is entitled to a different, lower level of protection. It is doubtful that Brennan meant to capture either of those two senses.

From the context, it looks like Brennan's test protects *existing* but not *prospective* uses—or, indeed, existing uses if done only prospectively. But that dichotomy clearly confounds any sensible or traditional definition of property, which is a bundle of rights that covers both present and future development. To say that taking future rights is not compensable is like saying that you can void a stock option when it is not in the money (for example, when the stock is

---

[15] *Id.* at 124 (citations omitted).

below the option price, with time yet to run), even when that option is trading at a positive value.

Unfortunately, Brennan's appeal to investment-backed expectations reduces the stability of property holdings, creating a perverse incentive to rush to build to perfect one's development rights. Indeed, one difficulty in dealing with moratoria stems from this simple question: Just what loss do they cause to any particular property owner? Many people in the Tahoe basin, for example, purchased property long before they intended to build on it. Some, with relatively short-term plans, were devastated by the moratoria; others, who were holding for the long term, were less hard hit. Do we give large compensation to the former group and little or none to the second; or do we just ignore the differences and award all owners a sum equal to the diminution of market value on the ground that the government faces the same overall liability either way?[16] The latter is the usual takings standard, which tends to undercompensate in most cases by ignoring subjective-use values in total takings situations. But either standard produces a hefty charge that should induce TRPA to rethink its regulatory strategy, for it cares more about how much it pays than it does about which claimants get which amounts. All such complexities of valuation, however, are swept under the carpet by speaking about investment-backed expectations instead of property rights. The upshot is that the terminological shift to "investment-backed expectations" works, *sub silentio*, to remove development rights from the protection of the Takings Clause.

The second problem is as deep as the first. Once we abandon some per se rule, how do we perform the balancing tests that *Penn Central* contemplates? It is certainly proper for a court to say that some form of balancing is needed to resolve difficult constitutional questions. Indeed, the Takings Clause *requires* that some explicit account be given of the justification the government puts forward to explain why the disproportionate effects disfavored in *Armstrong* should be allowed in some cases. On that score, the phrase "police power" has long been the preferred term of art to point to the set

---

[16] *See Dodd v. Hood River County*, 136 F.3d 1219, 1230 (9th Cir. 1998), in which delays in the intention to build were held to negate any losses from a temporary taking. For a perceptive discussion of the issue, see Judge Reed's opinion below in *Tahoe*, 34 F. Supp. 2d, at 1241–42.

of government interests that in principle justify some takings. In its usual formulation, the police power speaks about the government's role in promoting "health, safety, morals, and the general welfare." But, that comprehensive phrase was not crafted to insulate *every* government activity from the compensation requirement of the Takings Clause. The appeal to investment-backed expectations, however, gives us no guide about when no compensation is due, because the government is acting under the police power.

What, then, does the police power cover? In ordinary interactions between private individuals, the rights of property are never "absolute," if by that is meant that anyone can do with his property whatever he wants. That crude view is no better than equating liberty with the right of all individuals to do whatever they want whenever they want. In both cases, the law of tort, with its prohibitions on force and fraud, limit one's natural freedom of action. In the land-use case, the law of nuisance—which regulates noises, smells, pollution, and similar forms of nontrespassory invasions—hems in what one property owner can do to another. It would be odd in the extreme if government had no power to prevent one property owner from creating a nuisance to the detriment of another, or no power to act on behalf of many individuals who might not be able to coordinate a private suit against one or many polluters. Figuring out the proper limits of the police power is a large job because it requires an assessment of the legitimate purposes for government action, and some assessment of whether the means chosen are reasonably related to those purposes.

If *Penn Central* were trying to voice some reasoned view on the scope of the police power, then we might have some clue as to how its "ad hoc" balancing should proceed. But in fact the quoted passage makes no effort to address that question nor to show how the police power elements fit into the overall picture. Rather, it refers to only two points: the importance of economic impact, with those elusive investment-backed expectations; and the critical distinction between physical takings (e.g., the occupation of land) and regulatory takings (e.g., the restriction on land-use or disposition when the owner retains possession). Any theory of takings has to take both points into account to circumvent the intellectual tar pit created in *Penn Central*.

In a sustained attack on my argument in *Takings*, Margaret Radin praises *Penn Central's* balancing act as a proper use of a "pragmatic" approach—that is, one that self-consciously distances itself from my (barren) "conceptual approach."[17] But her use of such epithets as "pragmatic" and "conceptual" rings hollow without any explanation of how that "pragmatic" system works. In this instance, it is easy to see that Brennan's two factors cannot ground a coherent account of the Takings Clause. For, the "economic impact" of any regulation is surely a matter of degree, and that, generally speaking, does not lend itself to answering the yes/no question of whether one party has, or has not, an obligation to compensate another. No one would suggest, for example, that the dollar amount of Armstrong's lien (the measure of its economic impact) had anything to do with Justice Black's holding that its negation counted as a taking by the United States. Logically, economic impact goes to the number of dollars the government has to pay, conditioned on liability being found on independent grounds. The bigger the lien, the larger the obligation. But Brennan intends something different in *Penn Central*, yet no one knows precisely what. At the least, his rule complicates litigation because evidence of value is now relevant both to liability and to damages.

The situation gets no clearer when Brennan notes that a taking may be "more readily" found when the action counts as a physical invasion versus one designed to regulate the benefits and burdens of our common economic life in ways intended to promote the general good. On which side of that line does the *Armstrong* case lie? Here the government acted pursuant to a general policy on financing public improvements. Its removal of the boat from Maine waters could, with some verbal artistry, be characterized as a physical invasion of the would-be lien. But nothing in Black's general proposition attaches any weight to this purported distinction. He would have found for the boat owner even if the government's action were characterized as part of a policy for military financing.

Penn Central's articulation of this mushy framework was done, however, for a specific purpose—namely, to create a complete separation between the robust law of property that governs relations between private individuals and the feeble law of property that binds the state. If the private model were used, then *Penn Central*

---

[17] *See, e.g.*, Margaret Jane Radin, *The Liberal Conception of Property: Cross Currents in the Jurisprudence of Takings*, 88 Colum. L. Rev. 1667, 1668–78 (1988).

17

would have been decided for the landowner in a walk. Air rights are recognized interests in land that are freely bought and sold. In this case, those air rights were eliminated, at least for the duration of the regulation. More concretely, Brennan argued that the mere fact that the city of New York offered Penn Central air rights over other structures in the city helped the city under his pragmatic approach. But this maneuver only obfuscates a simple dilemma. Why offer any compensation at all if no property was taken? And if Penn Central's air rights were taken, then why should partial in-kind compensation discharge its obligation?

Perhaps, then, Penn Central's plans should be thwarted because their use would constitute a nuisance. That factor is not on Brennan's list, of course. If it were, then the air rights offered over another parcel would create a second nuisance as it removes the first. What is needed is some account of why certain high buildings should be regarded as nuisances when others (like the Pam Am building next door) are not. No private law precedent eases that burden, for the traditional view treats the ordinary use of air rights as perfectly legitimate.[18] Finally, there is no alternative source of in-kind compensation for the landowner who has been stripped of his development rights. The upshot is that the landmark designation board may take Penn Central's air rights, but only by paying for them, a conclusion that Brennan brushed aside as simply untenable.

Once the new pragmatic—read, "muddled"—framework is introduced, the landmark designation program goes through without a hitch. The questions of physical takings, just compensation, and nuisance all get mushed together. Out of this intellectual stew comes the wrong conceptual maneuver: *never* look at the rights that have been taken; *always* look at the larger holdings of the owner.

> "Taking" jurisprudence does not divide a single parcel into discrete segments and attempt to determine whether rights in a particular segment have been entirely abrogated. In

---

[18] *Fontainebleu Hotel Corp. v. Forty-Five Twenty-Five, Inc.*, 114 So. 2d 357 (Fla. Dist. Ct. App. 1959), is right on principle as well as authority. If blocking the views of an existing building were to count as a nuisance, then no one could build after the first builder, for the first would be allowed to enjoin the second. That would also mean, of course, that the initial builder takes development rights from the second. And, it would encourage a race to develop. The correct rule says either both or neither can build. The former choice yields the higher output.

deciding whether a particular governmental action has effected a taking, this Court focuses rather both on the character of the action and on the nature and extent of the interference with rights in the parcel as a whole—here, the city tax block designated as the "landmark site."[19]

That passage was meant to deal with the objection that the air rights could be regarded as a property interest distinct from the ground rights below them, a maneuver that Professor Radin denounces as a formalistic "conceptual severance."[20] Brennan feared that if the air rights were considered as a separate unit of property, their elimination by the state would be seen as wiping out an owner's "entire" interest in that property. At that point, even he would be hard-pressed to deny that some taking had occurred, given that the plaintiff had nothing left. But by linking the air rights to the ground rights, he could say that Penn Central was still able to use its existing facility as it had before. Because that current use was its only firm investment-backed expectation, in the odd sense noted previously, it followed that the partial loss—the loss of the air rights—did not rise to the dignity of a taking. This philosophical obfuscation has paid large dividends. It has shifted the balance of advantage to the government in individual taking cases that fall short of total dispossession.

Regulatory and Temporary Takings

But these clever philosophical maneuvers render incoherent the entire body of takings law. Four years after the Supreme Court handed down *Penn Central*, it decided *Loretto v. Teleprompter Manhattan CATV Corporation*.[21] There the issue was whether New York had effected a taking by requiring the owner of an apartment complex to place its small cable box and wiring on the roof of her building.

[19] *Penn Cen.* 438 U.S. at 131.

[20] "'Conceptual severance' consists of delineating a property interest consisting of just what the government action has removed from the owner, and then asserting that that particular whole thing has been permanently taken. Thus, this strategy hypothetically or conceptually 'severs' from the whole bundle of rights just those strands that are interfered with by the regulation, and then hypothetically or conceptually construes those strands in the aggregate as a separate whole thing." *Radin, supra* note 17, at 1676.

[21] 458 U.S. 419 (1982).

There was no restriction on land-use, just the physical occupation of a small fraction of the overall parcel. Did that piddling entry count as a taking? In *Loretto*, Justice Marshall took the opposite tack of Brennan: physical occupation cases, no matter how large or small, lent themselves to the application of a clear per se rule: pay for the space you have occupied.

What, then, of a regulation that leaves a person in possession of his land but refuses him permission to develop? The Court faced that question in *Lucas v. South Carolina Coastal Comunication*,[22] and again it opted for a per se rule requiring compensation, but only in those cases in which the restriction in value amounted to a loss of *all* viable economic use. At this point the overall doctrine is able to provide answers for only two polar extremes. First, if there is some viable existing use, then the government can ban any new uses of the property: future development rights are not protected. That is the message of *Penn Central*. Second, if use of the property is allowed, the government must compensate for the total loss of the property. That is the message of *Lucas*.

The identification of those two endpoints, however, offers no clue about what should be done with the countless variations that fall in the middle. Most conspicuously, the Court has never addressed any case in which a landowner's future right to build is subject to manifold restrictions—setbacks, height restrictions, volume restrictions, density restrictions, grading restrictions—that may well eliminate all or most of the value of the land. But in *First English Lutheran Church v. Los Angeles*,[23] the most direct precedent for *Tahoe*, the Court did consider whether a party should receive compensation for the temporary loss of use of its property when a local interim flood control ordinance blocked it from constructing or reconstructing any building or structure within the boundaries of the flood plane area.

In *First English*, the Court came to the sensible conclusion that the temporary taking of property was prima facie compensable, even if the state removed its restrictions after they were challenged in court. It then noted, almost in passing, that the rule it announced would not apply to "normal delays in obtaining building permits, changes

---

[22] 505 U.S. 1003 (1992).
[23] 482 U.S. 304 (1987).

in zoning ordinances, variances, and the like."[24] *First English* invites three comments.

First, it is not clear on which side of the physical invasion line the *First English* case falls. Was this a case in which there was only a total temporary restriction on use, and thus not a physical invasion, or was it a case in which the state had taken the disputed land for indefinite future use as a flood easement?[25] In my view, that difference is relevant only on the question of valuation, if at all. But under *Penn Central*, it must receive far greater weight.

Second, the police power issue, not mentioned in *Penn Central*, does place a strong crimp on the plaintiff's claim. The protection of health and safety seems to offer a strong justification for preventing the church from rebuilding a camp for disabled children in the midst of a flood plain, as was held when the case was remanded.[26]

Third, the issue of normal delays requires some explication of why it is included and how it ought to be treated. Those questions are addressed below.

In principle, *First English* was correctly decided. A term of years is surely an interest in property, and numerous Supreme Court cases have made it clear that the government cannot just occupy someone's premises for an indefinite time without paying compensation for the use.[27] But in *Tahoe*, we do not have a direct occupation by government, only a temporary (but total) restriction on use. Still, is there any reason to think that the government should be able to exclude me from my house for a period of years and then deny its obligation to pay on the ground that it never entered the premises itself? The logic of *First English* is, or at least should be, that *total* temporary restrictions on land-use count as takings even if the government does not enter the land. Why, then, don't *partial* temporary restrictions count as takings for which compensation is required as well? The soft underbelly of *Penn Central* is exposed. There is simply no categorical distinction that separates a partial use restriction on one hand from a total occupation on the other. Of course, there are

---

[24] 482 U.S. 321, *quoted in Tahoe*, 122 S. Ct. 1484.

[25] *See* Frank Michelman, *Takings, 1987*, 88 COLUM. L. REV. 1600, 1619–21 (1988).

[26] 210 Cal. App. 3d 1353 (1989).

[27] *See, e.g.*, United States v. Petty Motor Co., 327 U.S. 372 (1946); United States v. Gen. Motors Corp., 323 U.S. 373 (1945).

differences of degree between the two, but those go to the amount of compensation that is presumptively owed, not to whether any compensation is owed at all.

Numerators and Denominators

How then does one wiggle out of this problem? The linchpin of *Penn Central* is commonly known as the numerator/denominator problem.[28] In any routine private suit, the amount of damages that a defendant owes the plaintiff depends on what the defendant took from the plaintiff, not what the plaintiff has left after the taking is completed. The more one takes, the more one pays. In *Penn Central* proper, the Court compared the amount that was taken with the total amount that was initially owned. The relevant denominator was the "parcel as a whole," the numerator was the air rights. The easy configuration of the parcel gave this test an appearance of objectivity, but later cases have exposed the conceptual (or pragmatic) barrenness of the test. Thus, suppose that the landowner has acquired adjacent plots of land at different times (and perhaps through trusts or other entities), some of which have been sold off before the state imposes a moratorium on building. The question then arises, which acreage counts as "the parcel" that has been subjected to regulation. If all the lands ever owned by the plaintiff are included, then the sale of any one of them could be deemed to prevent the total wipeout of his investment-backed expectations. But if some fraction of that larger agglomeration counts as "the" parcel, then it increases the chance that compensation should be paid.

In *Tahoe*, Justice Stevens explains at great length why some balancing test should be used, and so it should for dealing with police power issues. But consider a person who owns uplands and wetlands, the latter subject to building restrictions, the former not. If the wetlands were considered separate from the uplands, the restriction on their use could be regarded as total. But if the two are considered together, then the restriction might be regarded as partial. What tells us, then, whether those lands should be regarded as a

---

[28] Keystone Bituminous Coal Ass'n v. DeBenedictis, 480 U.S. 497 (1987) (quoting Frank I. Michelman, *Property, Utility, and Fairness: Comments on the Ethical Foundations of 'Just Compensation' Law*, 80 HARV. L. REV. 1165, 1192 (1967)). For my earlier criticism of this doctrine, see Richard A. Epstein, *Takings: Descent and Resurrection*, 1987 SUP. CT. REV. 1, 14–15.

single parcel or as separate parcels? In some cases, as in *Palazzolo*, the uplands could be sold off before the time that the state restricts filling in the wetlands. Do we treat the two parcels as one, or separately? Does it make a difference that they were acquired at the same time? From the same seller? By the same deed? Does it matter whether they are held by the same family members, and in the same proportions? Those details sound like irrelevancies to any serious inquiry about when regulation requires compensation, but after the decision in *Penn Central* they are the stuff of everyday concern. They were evident in *Palazzolo* and in other cases as well.[29]

The denominator has no role *whatsoever* to play in *any* takings case. The correct answer is simple: Across the board, the loss from regulation is measured by the value of the interests taken. On one hand, the landowner should not be allowed or encouraged to sell off parts of his land to increase the odds of receiving compensation. But on the other hand, neither should the government be allowed to duck its obligation to compensate by showing the sale of some tract of land in a prior unrelated transaction. There are important issues to balance in wetlands cases—whether, for example, proposed development on sensitive waterfront lands constitutes a public nuisance. But those issues should be faced head-on, not by digressing into obscure discussions of numerators and denominators. Takings law does not have to be ad hoc.

Tahoe-Sierra Up Close

We have now covered sufficient ground to address the *Tahoe* moratoria directly. In dealing with that issue, Justice Stevens was surely correct to insist that a per se approach was inappropriate. But here again, the right questions are these: Was private property taken? Was it taken for a public use? Was the taking justified under the police power to prevent nuisances? Was just compensation required? Stevens came out with the wrong answers on those questions because he refused to break the case down into its component parts.

Instead, he simply noted that a per se rule would cover not only permits, variances, and zoning changes, but

---

[29] *See* K & K Construction, Inc. v. Mich. DNR, 217 Mich. App. 56 (1996).

orders temporarily prohibiting access to crime scenes, businesses that violate health codes, fire-damaged buildings, and other areas that we cannot now foresee. Such a rule would undoubtedly require changes in numerous practices that have long been considered permissible exercises of the police power. As Justice Holmes warned in *Mahon*, "[g]overnment hardly could go on if to some extent values incident to property could not be diminished without paying for every such change in the general law." 260 U.S., at 413. A rule that required compensation for every delay in the use of property would render routine government processes prohibitively expensive or encourage hasty decision-making. Such an important change in the law should be the product of legislative rulemaking rather than adjudication.[30]

That passage is equal parts of common sense and intellectual panic. Note his mixing of categories. The last examples involve clear police power restrictions pertaining to health and safety. With those, the nature of the necessity limits the duration of the intrusion, and the grounds for intrusion certainly do not favor those who have built over those who have not. Police power cases like those are a far cry from the 20-year-plus moratoria at issue in this case.

The sensible way to approach this case is to break it down into its constituent parts. First, there is little doubt that the moratoria count as a taking of property. Surely that would be the case if one landowner were able to prevent his neighbor from building for a like period of time: the state therefore stands in no better position. As a prima facie matter, we don't have to ask whether 32 months is long enough to matter. That delay could easily eat up 10 to 15 percent of the total value of the property. But that figure is relevant only in setting damages, not in determining liability.

Second, we ask whether the taking is for a public use. Here, the protection of Lake Tahoe preserves a valuable public resource. Thus, the answer is yes.

Third, did the landowners who were shut out from development receive any compensation for their loss? In fact, TRPA offered them a set of transferable development rights. If accumulated in sufficient amounts, those rights would allow the aggrieved owner to build

---

[30] *Tahoe*, 122 S. Ct. 1465.

somewhere else.[31] But the rights were hedged in with so many limitations that they were largely worthless.[32] Thus, the answer on this question is easy: the owners received no compensation.

Fourth, and this is the only real point of dispute, did the Tahoe Planning Authority have a police power justification for preventing additional homes from being built? That question involves the subtle interaction between the *Armstrong* principle of disproportionate impact and the law of nuisance. To see how those two factors interact, begin with the obvious point that all of the eutrophication of Lake Tahoe is attributable to the actions of those who have already built along the lake. One obvious question, to which the district court rightly devoted extensive time, is whether those actions were tortious in themselves. In answering that question, it should be noted at the outset that if the lake damage were caused in any degree by leakage—say, from septic tanks or other storage facilities built on the lands—then the answer is an unequivocal yes.

The question of tortious responsibility is much more complex if we assume that the only source of eutrophication of Lake Tahoe is from the increased run-off of organic matter created by the extensive construction of homes, driveways, patios, and other hard surfaces that prevent ground absorption of the water. California tort law does not extend this far, so the owners' conduct could well be regarded as lawful.[33] To date, the law of nuisance has not covered cases of clearing one's own land and allowing weeds and other organic growth to take root, thereby causing damage to nearby lands.[34]

Tahoe, of course, presents a borderline case. Yet we do not have to resolve the nuisance question authoritatively to decide its outcome.

---

[31] *See* Suitum v. TRPA, 520 U.S. 725, 745–49 (1997) (Scalia, J. concurring).

[32] In Williamson County Regional Planning Commission v. Hamilton Bank, 473 U.S. 172 (1985), the Court held that a judicial challenge could take place only after a final agency determination of proper land use. In Suitum, the Court rejected TPRA's argument that the transferable development rights would suffice as compensation, for the final land use decision would be made only years later, when the value of the TDRs would be sorted out.

[33] *See, e.g.,* Rylands v. Fletcher L.R. 3 H.L. 330 (House of Lords, England, 1868), *affirming,* Fletcher v. Reynolds, L.R. 1 Ex. 265 (1866).

[34] Such actions are generally allowed under common law. *See, e.g.,* Robinson v. Whitelaw, 364 P.2d. 1085 (Utah 1961); Giles v. Walker, 24 Q.B.D. 656 (1890) (thistles). Statutes have imposed duties on railroads to keep down weeds. *See* Chicago, T. H. & S. E. R. Co. v. Anderson, 234 U.S. 283 (1916).

What we must do, however, is apply the tort law consistently to early and latecomers alike. Thus, suppose we decide that the run-off in question does not constitute tortious behavior even if it leads to eutrophication of the lake. Now the incumbent owners could not be required to pay for the cleanup of damage that had already occurred, which would be chalked up to an act of God. (I will not dwell on the irony of environmentalists adopting narrow definitions of pollution.) But once that step is taken, what is the justification for preventing later builders from building? The state cannot argue that their future actions would constitute a nuisance if the actions of the current owners of built-up plots did not. If the first group should be able to build, then the second group should be able to build as well. Lake Tahoe is a common resource. If the question were riparian use—that is, the limited rights vested in people who own waterfront property—then the earlier arrivals to the water's edge would have to cut back on their use to make room for the subsequent riparians when and if they started to make the same demands on the water. The rule in question is doubtless motivated by the inability to decide which landowners along the water's edge arrived there first,[35] and by the fear that a first-user rule would induce people to make premature development of their lands in order to preserve their fractional rights in the common.

The same principle applies to pollution of the lake as to the removal of water from it. It may well be more efficient to stop all new construction along the edge of Lake Tahoe; but if so, then the newcomers should be compensated because they have been denied the identical rights the earlier comers enjoyed. Once that compensation is required, moreover, it could easily lead planning officials to make a healthy reexamination of its damage-control policies for the lake. Suppose that much of the concrete and asphalt poured in the earlier days is of little value relative to that of building an additional house. Under Justice Stevens's rule, the incentive to reconsider past investments is weak. But if the ability to build were worth say $100,000 per plot, then the incumbents might decide to rip out some old hard surfaces if that would increase the level of absorption from built-up plots. The payment of compensation could thus introduce a responsible reexamination of dubious past practices.

---

[35] *See* RESTATEMENT (SECOND) OF TORTS, § etc.

But what if the asphalt and concrete do constitute a tort? Now the existing owners are in a worse position than the owners of unbuilt plots because only they should be fined for the harm that their building alone has caused the lake. That money could then be used to clean up the lake. The holders of unbuilt plots of land have done nothing wrong and hence should not be required to contribute to this pool.

Moving forward, however, raises different considerations. Here all landowners should be subject to parallel regulations to the extent that they choose to maintain their old construction or add new construction. If the incumbents are allowed to continue with their activities, without any payment, then newcomers who are in the same relative position should be allowed to build to the same extent. Stated otherwise, the principle in *Armstrong* should prevent a disparate impact whereby heavier sanctions are applied to latecomers to the lakefront than to the established arrivals, without compensation. Either way, the same regime has to be applied going forward to early and latecomers. What is striking about Stevens's opinion is that he never once addresses such issues: his rejection of a per se rule is followed by a narrow view of what issues are relevant to the disposition of the case.

But what of the one issue that he did discuss: the question of normal delays for permits and the like. One approach is to adopt a general rule that would allow all local governments one year to consider routine applications before starting the clock. That approach would have several effects.[36] First, it would rid the dockets of minor takings suits. Second, it would favor neither incumbents nor outsiders because the individuals who are inconvenienced by the delays in one case are benefited from the delays imposed on other individuals in the next. Third, this position conforms with the moratoria rules of most states. California, for example, allows moratoria to go into effect for an initial period for 45 days, with extensions of up to 2 years.[37] Minnesota allows for an initial 6-month period with extensions of up to 8 months. Oregon allows for a 120-day period with one 6-month extension. Colorado and New Jersey

---

[36] See the Amicus Curiae Brief of the Institute for Justice in *Tahoe*, http://www.ij.org/index.shtml.

[37] See the dissent of Rehnquist, C.J., in *Tahoe*, 122 S. Ct. at 1490.

allow for single 6-month periods. The 1-year automatic pass is certainly within the range of common practice. Fourth, that 1-year period could be extended to cover cases that fall within the traditional scope of the police power, such as Stevens's horror stories relating to public health and crime prevention measures.

Given this modest alternative, Stevens has failed to make out any case for rolling moratoria without compensation. His ultimate claim is that local governments have to be given wide discretion to avoid "rushing through" the planning process. Unfortunately, his failure to impose any limitation on local government dawdling creates larger error in the opposite direction. TPRA can now take forever to decide how to plan for future development. At root, Stevens's opinion immunizes every land-use planning decision from constitutional review under the Takings Clause.

Beyond the Rule of Law?

Tahoe has not left us with a pretty picture. Until this decision, a fragile majority of the Supreme Court was prepared to make cautious inroads on the unlimited ad hoc approach of *Penn Central*. The results of that effort were mixed. *First English* treated temporary occupations of indefinite duration by the same standards as permanent occupations. *Lucas* meant that at least some regulatory takings required payment of compensation. *Palazzolo* stood for the important proposition that an owner who takes title after the passage of some land-use regulation does not lose his right to compensation merely because he had "notice" of the regulation. Yet that rule is now in doubt. The point of the rule in *Palazzolo* was not that the transfer of title from a corporation to its sole stockholder immunized his development plans from public review. Rather, the rule was meant only to ensure that a transfer of title did not upset the balance of power one way or the other. On that narrow question, a per se rule makes perfectly good sense, even if many takings cases, such as *Tahoe*, require balancing property interests against environmental claims.

The numbing ad hoc nature of *Penn Central* and its progeny is in fact symptomatic of a larger problem that has afflicted the Court in recent years—its refusal to think that rules of law are capable of articulation in any of today's countless regulatory settings. Instead, the Court has offered a full-throated endorsement of various kinds of procedural devices and balancing tests. These sound learned, even pragmatic, in the abstract, but in practice they introduce endless confusions and uncertainty. This trend manifested itself in *Tahoe* on at least four critical points.

First, the narrow interpretation of the question presented on the writ of certiorari allowed Stevens to fragment the set of relevant issues presented for analysis. Second, the ringing endorsement of the ad hoc balancing approach of *Penn Central* perpetuated the numerator/denominator problem when what is needed is the rejection of any categorical distinction between physical and regulatory takings. Third, *Tahoe* undermined *Palazzolo's* firm conclusion that allows the subsequent owner of property to stand in the shoes of his predecessor in takings cases. Finally, *Tahoe* adhered to the proposition that "it is the interest in informed decisionmaking that underlies our decisions imposing a strict ripeness requirement on landowners asserting regulatory takings claims."[38]

That approach might make sense in a legal universe in which all government agencies act with dispatch and in good faith, and all landowners seeking development act in bad faith. But that division of good and evil does not remotely square with the realities of land-use planning in which all parties, public and private, have strong political agendas. The legal rules have to take into account the risk of misbehavior from both sides. They can do so only if they cabin administrative discretion and allow for prompt and effective judicial review on all matters of principle. Procedural dodges and substantive ad hoc tests always increase deference to administrative bodies. Holding back judicial review until final judgment is an open invitation for savvy administrators to stall by choking landowners with endless procedural hurdles. It is no accident that 20-year delays are the norm in cases like *Tahoe*, *Suitum*, and *Palazzolo*. The more planning bodies back and fill, the longer they delay judicial review. The cumulative effect of these strategies is to choke off all takings claims, even in cases of egregious imbalance, such as *Tahoe*. Justice delayed is justice denied is an old theme that has found a new home in the *Tahoe* view of the Takings Clause.

---

[38] *Tahoe*, 122 S. Ct. 1488 (citing *Palazzolo*, 533 U. S. 620–21).

When State Dignity Trumps Individual Rights

Federal Maritime Commission v. South Carolina State Ports Authority

Robert A. Levy

Introduction

Sovereign immunity is the legal doctrine that forecloses litigation against the government without its consent. In *Federal Maritime Commission v. South Carolina State Ports Authority*[1] (*FMC*), the Supreme Court extended the doctrine to preclude suits by private parties against a state in a federal administrative agency. Justice Thomas wrote for a five-member majority that included Chief Justice Rehnquist and Justices O'Connor, Scalia, and Kennedy. Justice Breyer filed a dissenting opinion joined by Justices Souter, Ginsburg, and Stevens, who also filed a separate dissent. *FMC* was "the term's most important federalism case."[2]

The constitutional foundation for sovereign immunity rests in the Eleventh Amendment, which bars suits in federal court against a nonconsenting state by citizens of another state, and thereby limits the "Judicial power of the United States." By holding that the South Carolina State Ports Authority (Ports Authority) did not have to defend itself before the Federal Maritime Commission (Commission), the Supreme Court broadened the reach of sovereign immunity for the first time to cover adjudication by executive branch agencies, which are not ordinarily regarded as a component of the U.S. judicial power.

Here's how the case unfolded. South Carolina Maritime Services (Maritime), a private company, had repeatedly asked the Ports

---

[1] 122 S. Ct. 1864 (2002).

[2] Linda Greenhouse, *Justices Expand States' Immunity in Federalism Case*, N.Y. TIMES, May 29, 2002, at A1.

Authority for permission to berth a cruise ship at state-owned port facilities in Charleston, South Carolina. On each occasion, the Ports Authority denied permission, allegedly because the primary purpose of the cruise ship was gambling. Maritime filed a complaint with the Commission, arguing that the Ports Authority's refusal of berthing space violated the Shipping Act of 1984.[3] The complaint asserted that the Ports Authority had implemented its policy in a discriminatory fashion by providing a berth to two Carnival Cruise Line vessels that also offered gambling.

As its remedy, Maritime asked the Commission to (1) seek a temporary restraining order and preliminary injunction in federal court that would prohibit the Ports Authority from discriminating against Maritime; (2) issue an order commanding the Ports Authority to stop violating the Shipping Act; and (3) direct the Ports Authority to pay reparations, plus interest and attorneys fees, to compensate Maritime for its losses.

After rejecting Maritime's charges, the Ports Authority filed a motion to dismiss the complaint on the ground that a South Carolina state agency is entitled to Eleventh Amendment immunity. The Commission's administrative law judge (ALJ) agreed that Maritime's complaint should be dismissed. He relied on *Seminole Tribe of Fla. v. Florida*,[4] in which the Supreme Court held that Congress, enacting legislation authorized under Article I of the Constitution, cannot abrogate state sovereign immunity. The ALJ inferred from *Seminole*, "if federal courts . . . must respect States' 11th Amendment immunity and Congress is powerless to override the States' immunity under Article I of the Constitution, it is irrational to argue that an agency like the Commission, created under an Article I statute, is free to disregard the 11th Amendment or its related doctrine of State immunity."[5]

Maritime did not appeal the ALJ's dismissal of its case. But the Commission on its own motion reversed the ALJ decision, concluding that "the doctrine of state sovereign immunity . . . is meant to

---

[3] 46 U.S.C. app. §1701 *et seq.* (1994 & Supp. V).

[4] 517 U.S. 44 (1996). *Seminole* overruled *Pennsylvania v. Union Gas Co.*, 491 U.S. 1 (1989), which had held that Congress is empowered to abrogate state sovereign immunity when legislating under the Commerce Clause of Article I.

[5] *Quoted in Fed. Mar. Comm'n* at 1869.

cover proceedings before judicial tribunals, whether Federal or state, not executive branch administrative agencies like the Commission."[6] That conclusion, in turn, was reversed when the Ports Authority appealed to the U.S. Court of Appeals for the Fourth Circuit, which held that "any proceeding where a federal officer adjudicates disputes between private parties and unconsenting states would not have passed muster at the time of the Constitution's passage nor after the ratification of the Eleventh Amendment. Such an adjudication is equally as invalid today whether the forum be a state court, a federal court, or a federal administrative agency."[7]

The Court of Appeals reasoned that the proceeding before the Commission "walks, talks, and squawks very much like a lawsuit" and that "[i]ts placement within the Executive Branch cannot blind us to the fact that the proceeding is truly an adjudication."[8] Accordingly, the court instructed that the case be dismissed. The Commission then sought and obtained review by the Supreme Court, which affirmed the holding of the Court of Appeals. The high Court's decision is the latest in a series of sovereign immunity opinions, split 5–4 along conservative-liberal lines, that have evolved during the Rehnquist era.

Indeed, the Court's expanding doctrine of sovereign immunity is the most notable component of a Rehnquist-led reinvigorated jurisprudence of federalism. Because the constitutional pedigree for sovereign immunity is the Eleventh Amendment, I will begin with a discussion of that amendment and the major sovereign immunity cases that it spawned. Then I will summarize the majority and dissenting views in the *FMC* case, focusing mainly on disputes over constitutional text and the overriding purpose of state immunity. Finally, I will offer a few comments from a libertarian perspective on the legitimacy, value, and proper interpretation of the immunity doctrine.

In brief, I will argue that federalism—by which I mean a system of checks and balances based on dual sovereignty—was intended by the Framers as a method of protecting individual rights against excessive power in the hands of federal or state government. When

---

[6] *Id.*

[7] S.C. State Ports Auth. v. Fed. Mar. Comm'n, 243 F. 3d 165, 173 (4th Cir. 2001).

[8] *Id.* at 174.

sovereign immunity is invoked, purportedly to reinforce the doctrine of federalism, it belies the Framers' design and constricts rather than enlarges personal liberty. That proposition is especially pertinent when immunity is expanded to cover cases outside the textual bounds of the Eleventh Amendment.

More specifically, I offer these observations: First, the Constitution would be a more liberating document if the Eleventh Amendment, notwithstanding its common law roots, had never been ratified. Second, the scope granted to sovereign immunity by the Rehnquist Court has effectively denied redress for many injuries suffered by individuals at the hands of government. Third, the textualist approach to constitutional interpretation, supposedly favored by conservatives on the Court, provides no support for *FMC* or its precursors. Fourth, a proper understanding of the role of government dictates that sovereign immunity be construed narrowly, in accordance with the specific text of the Eleventh Amendment.

The reach of federal power is reduced when states are immunized from litigation brought by private citizens suing under federal statutes. That outcome is most appealing to those of us who believe in a federal government of delegated, enumerated, and, therefore, limited powers. But the correct means of accomplishing that end is to rein in federal powers directly, rather than misappropriate a potentially pernicious doctrine like sovereign immunity.

Background

The Eleventh Amendment provides that "[t]he Judicial power of the United States shall not be construed to extend to any suit in law or equity, commenced or prosecuted against one of the United States by Citizens of another State, or by Citizens or Subjects of any Foreign State." That provision, narrowly construed in accordance with its express text, bars suits against state governments in federal court brought by anyone other than citizens of the state sued, the federal government, or another state.[9] For purposes of the Eleventh Amendment, "state" includes state agencies, like the Ports Authority, but not political subdivisions such as municipalities and school boards.[10]

[9] For a summary of case law interpreting the Eleventh Amendment in the wider context of federalism, see Ronald D. Rotunda, *The New States' Rights, the New Federalism, the New Commerce Clause, and the Proposed New Abdication*, 25 OKLA. CITY U. L. REV. 869 (2000).

[10] *See, e.g.*, Mt. Healthy City Sch. Dist. Bd. of Educ. v. Doyle, 429 U.S. 274 (1977).

States can and do waive their Eleventh Amendment immunity.[11] Moreover, the Amendment does not bar suits brought against state officials in their personal capacities, even if those officials are acting under color of state law. That is, if a state official acts as a representative of his state and violates the Constitution, he is not immune from damages or a federal court order to cease and desist his unconstitutional acts.[12] In practice, that means the state, through its officials, can be prevented from abridging constitutional rights, but the state cannot be compelled to reimburse an official for damages he is directed to pay out of his own pocket.[13]

Notwithstanding those avenues still open to private litigants, the Eleventh Amendment places meaningful restrictions on the ability of citizens to sue states for money damages. And those restrictions, expanded by the Supreme Court, now apply to cases that are not covered by the text of the Amendment. For example, in *Hans v. Louisiana*,[14] the Court concluded that the Eleventh Amendment, by implication, extends state immunity to include suits in federal court by citizens of the *same* state. More important, in *Seminole*, the Court rejected the notion that sovereign immunity applies to suits involving diversity jurisdiction[15] but not to suits involving federal question jurisdiction.[16]

That distinction is explained as follows: Federal courts are empowered to hear and decide cases if the subject matter concerns either

---

[11] *See, e.g.*, Ports Auth. Trans-Hudson Corp. v. Feeney, 495 U.S. 299 (1990).

[12] *Ex parte Young*, 209 U.S. 123 (1908).

[13] A state may, however, be required to pay the *future* costs of complying with an injunction issued against an official by a federal court. Edelman v. Jordan, 415 U.S. 651, 668 (1974). Further, the state may, on its own volition, agree to reimburse an official for past damages that a federal court directs the official to pay.

[14] 134 U.S. 1 (1890).

[15] *Seminole* involved a Florida citizen suing the state of Florida. Technically, therefore, the case did not fall within the text of the Eleventh Amendment. Nevertheless, citing *Hans*, the Court invoked a broader version of sovereign immunity that barred suits against a state by its own citizens. *Seminole* at 54.

[16] *Seminole* also narrowed the *Ex parte Young* doctrine, which might otherwise have permitted suit against individual state officials to prohibit future violations of federal law. The Court reasoned that the Indian Gaming Regulatory Act, at issue in *Seminole*, prescribed a detailed but modest set of sanctions against a state. In contrast, an *Ex parte Young* action would expose a state official to a federal court's full remedial powers, thus rendering the prescribed sanctions largely irrelevant. *Seminole* at 74–75.

a federal question[17]—that is, one arising under the U.S. Constitution, a federal statute, or a treaty—or diversity jurisdiction[18]—that is, a suit between citizens of different states or between a state and a foreign citizen. By its text, the Eleventh Amendment applies to suits "against one of the United States by Citizens of another State, or by Citizens or Subjects of any Foreign State." That would seem to immunize states against diversity lawsuits but not federal question lawsuits.[19] Yet the Supreme Court held in *Seminole* that Congress cannot use its enumerated powers under Article I of the Constitution—specifically, the Commerce Clause in Article I, section 8—to circumvent state sovereign immunity. In other words, the Eleventh Amendment and sovereign immunity were construed to encompass federal question as well as diversity suits—an issue that we will revisit below.

There is, however, an important exception to *Seminole*'s holding concerning federal question lawsuits. When Congress enacts legislation, not under the Commerce Clause but under section 5 of the Fourteenth Amendment, private lawsuits brought against a state in federal court to enforce that legislation are sometimes not subject to sovereign immunity. In relevant part, the Fourteenth Amendment prohibits states from "depriv[ing] any person of life, liberty, or property, without due process of law; [or denying] to any person within its jurisdiction the equal protection of the laws."[20] Section 5 of the Amendment authorizes Congress to enforce those prohibitions by appropriate legislation. Chronologically, the Fourteenth Amendment, which was designed to limit state power, trumps the earlier ratified Eleventh Amendment.

[17] *See* U.S. CONST., art. III, § 2; 28 U.S.C. §1331.

[18] *See* U.S. CONST., art. III, § 2; 28 U.S.C. §1332.

[19] Chief Justice John Marshall apparently agreed. Twenty-six years after ratification of the Eleventh Amendment, he wrote in *Cohens v. Virginia*, 19 U.S. (6 Wheat.) 264, 382 (1821), that the judicial department "is authorized to decide all cases of every description, arising under the constitution or laws of the United States. From this general grant of jurisdiction, no exception is made of those cases in which a State may be a party."

[20] The Fourteenth Amendment also bars a state from "abridg[ing] the privileges or immunities of citizens of the United States." But the Supreme Court somehow eliminated that clause from the Constitution in the *Slaughter House Cases*, 83 U.S. (16 Wall.) 36 (1873). *See* Kimberly C. Shankman & Roger Pilon, *Reviving the Privileges or Immunities Clause to Redress the Balance Among States, Individuals, and the Federal Government*, CATO INST. POL. ANALYSIS, no. 326, Nov. 23, 1998.

Still, section 5 does not give Congress carte blanche to negate state immunity. In *City of Boerne v. Flores*,[21] a case not directly involving sovereign immunnity, the Supreme Court ruled that Congress exceeded its section 5 powers when it enacted the Religious Freedom Restoration Act (RFRA). That case arose when the historical Landmark Commission in Boerne, Texas, denied a permit to Archbishop Flores to enlarge his church. Flores sued under the RFRA, which provided that a state could not substantially burden the free exercise of religion unless it had a "compelling governmental interest" and adopted the "least restrictive means of furthering" that interest. The Court concluded that the RFRA was unconstitutional because it was an attempt by Congress to define the Free Exercise Clause. That job, said the Court, belongs to the Court itself.

Under section 5, the Court explained, Congress can enforce a constitutional provision but cannot define it. The RFRA was not merely prophylactic or remedial. It was meant to delineate the scope of the Free Exercise Clause. In determining whether a section 5 statute is actually an enforcement provision or an effort at altering substantive law, the Court demanded a direct connection between the remedy chosen by Congress and alleged Fourteenth Amendment violations by the states. As the Court put it, "There must be a congruence and proportionality between the injury to be prevented or remedied and the means adopted to that end."[22]

In the wake of the *Boerne* case, the Court rejected four attempts by Congress to use section 5 as a means to bypass sovereign immunity. The first case, *Florida Prepaid Postsecondary Education Expense Board v. College Savings Bank*,[23] involved an alleged patent infringement by a state agency. The patentee sued in federal court, relying on the Patent Remedy Act, in which Congress had declared its intent to revoke the states' Eleventh Amendment immunity. The Court held that the revocation was unconstitutional. Although the Fourteenth Amendment protects property, including patents, the state of Florida already provided an adequate remedial process through a takings or conversion claim. Because Congress had not identified a pattern of uncompensated patent infringements by the state, section 5 of

[21] 521 U.S. 507 (1997).
[22] *Id.* at 520.
[23] 527 U.S. 627 (1999).

the Fourteenth Amendment could not be used to remove Florida's immunity from suit in federal court.[24]

The second case in the post-*Boerne* series was a companion case involving the same two Florida litigants.[25] College Savings Bank claimed that the state agency had printed misstatements about the bank's product in brochures and annual reports. The bank sued under section 43(a) of the federal Lanham Act, and the Court observed that Congress, in its Trademark Remedy Clarification Act, had subjected the states to such suits despite sovereign immunity. Still, said the Court, the Lanham Act claim had to be dismissed for lack of federal jurisdiction. Even if Florida had wrongly disparaged the bank's product, that did not intrude on any property right protected by the Fourteenth Amendment. One's right to be free from false advertising is not "property" in the Fourteenth Amendment context. Accordingly, any attempt by Congress to abrogate state immunity pursuant to section 5 of the Amendment was null and void.

---

[24]Congress, in the Patent Remedy Act, did not cite the Takings Clause of the Fifth Amendment as its rationale for revoking state immunity. Presumably, if a state infringed a private patent, then pleaded immunity to a takings claim in federal court, the state would be in violation of the just compensation requirement of the Fifth Amendment. But Congress cited procedural Due Process, not the Takings Clause, when it enacted the Patent Remedy Act. Because Florida provided an adequate process, there was no Fourteenth Amendment Due Process violation for Congress to remedy.

That raises an interesting question, however, regarding takings claims and sovereign immunity. The federal government, under the Tucker Act, has waived its immunity from takings claims. Some states have not done so. Are those states immune from such claims absent a federal statute revoking their immunity? No, said Boston University law professor Jack M. Beermann, *Government Official Torts and the Takings Clause: Federalism and State Sovereign Immunity*, 68 B.U. L. REV. 277 (1988). Beermann insisted, first, that the Eleventh Amendment does not proscribe federal question claims. *Id.* at 337. Second, he argued that the Takings Clause of the Fifth Amendment, applied to the states by the Fourteenth Amendment, overrides any immunity that might otherwise bar just compensation for a taking. *Id.* at 339. The Supreme Court has not conclusively resolved that question. But it has stated that the Takings Clause, "*of its own force*, furnish[es] a basis for a court to award money damages against the government." First English Evangelical Lutheran Church of Glendale v. County of Los Angeles, 482 U.S. 304, 316 n.9 (1987) (emphasis added).

[25]Coll. Sav. Bank v. Fl. Prepaid Postsecondary Educ. Expense Bd., 527 U.S. 666 (1999).

The following year, in *Kimel v. Florida Board of Regents*,[26] the Court tackled the question whether the Eleventh Amendment bars private suits against the states under the Age Discrimination in Employment Act (ADEA). A fractured Court held that Congress's attempted abrogation of state immunity—although clearly stated in the ADEA—exceeded congressional authority to enforce the Equal Protection Clause under section 5 of the Fourteenth Amendment. Unlike race and religion, age is not a "suspect class" for Equal Protection purposes. That means states have more leeway to discriminate by age under the ADEA than they would have to discriminate by, say, race under Title VII of the 1964 Civil Rights Act (amended in 1972 to cover public employers). In *Kimel*, the Court held that the ADEA imposed restrictions on state governments that were disproportionate to any unconstitutional conduct targeted by the Act. Moreover, said the Court, the ADEA's legislative history showed that Congress never identified a pattern of age discrimination by the states. Accordingly, Congress could not use section 5 of the Fourteenth Amendment to quash state immunity from private suits under the ADEA.

The same fate soon awaited Congress's attempt to authorize private lawsuits against the states under the Americans with Disabilities Act (ADA). Thirteen months after *Kimel*, the Court decided *Board of Trustees of the Univ. of Alabama v. Garrett*[27]—again holding that the Eleventh Amendment can trump a federal statute enacted under section 5. Applying the *Boerne* criteria, the Court reiterated that private individuals may not recover money damages against nonconsenting states in federal court unless Congress (a) identifies a pattern of discrimination by the states that violates the Fourteenth Amendment, and (b) adopts a remedy that is congruent and proportional to the targeted violation. Those requirements were not met in *Garrett*. Disability, like age, is not a suspect class, so the Court employed so-called rational basis—that is, minimal—scrutiny[28] to

[26] 528 U.S. 62 (2000).

[27] 531 U.S. 356 (2001).

[28] Rational basis scrutiny requires only that there be some reasonably conceivable set of facts, even if unstated, that might justify the state's policy. For example, said the Court, "it would be entirely rational (and therefore constitutional) for a state employer to conserve scarce financial resources by hiring employees able to use existing facilities [even if] the ADA requires employers to 'make existing facilities used by employees readily accessible to and usable by individuals with disabilities.'" *Id.* at 372.

determine if the state could justify its discrimination. Congress would be permitted to override state immunity only if the discrimination was irrational and pervasive. It was not.

Next term, beginning in October 2002, the Court will have yet another opportunity to hear a major state-immunity case.[29] This time the alleged discrimination is based on gender—a class that does not rise to "suspect" status like race and religion, but does receive from the courts an intermediate level of review that exceeds the rational basis scrutiny that is applied when discrimination is based on age (*Kimel*) or disability (*Garrett*). In *Nevada Dept. of Human Resources v. Hibbs*,[30] the Court will resolve whether Congress can set aside the Eleventh Amendment by means of the Family and Medical Leave Act. Passed in 1993, that Act was designed to address lingering gender discrimination in the workplace. Congress found that women were disproportionately burdened by having to take care of sick family members.

Meanwhile, as the Court consistently expands the doctrine of sovereign immunity by contracting Congress's powers under section 5 of the Fourteenth Amendment, a separate chapter in the history of federalism has unfolded. Under the Fair Labor Standards Act (FLSA), passed in 1938, Congress authorized private parties to sue their employers in federal or state court for minimum wages and overtime. Until the FLSA was amended in 1966, "employer" excluded states and state agencies. Two years after the amendment, the more expansive definition was tested in *Maryland v. Wirtz*.[31] The Supreme Court held that the FLSA's application to state entities was permissible under the Commerce Clause. Justice Douglas, in dissent, warned that the Court had seriously compromised state sovereignty.

Douglas's view prevailed, temporarily, when the Court overruled *Wirtz* in *National League of Cities v. Usery*.[32] "One undoubted attribute of state sovereignty," wrote then Justice Rehnquist, "is the States' power to determine the wages which shall be paid to those whom

---

[29] *See* Linda Greenhouse, *Justices to Hear a Major State-Immunity Case*, N.Y. TIMES, June 25, 2002, at A21.

[30] No. 01-1638.

[31] 392 U.S. 183 (1968).

[32] 426 U.S. 833 (1976).

they employ."[33] That modest limitation on Congress's authority under the Commerce Clause didn't last long. In 1985, the Court reconsidered *Usery* and overruled it as well.

The new view, set out in *Garcia v. San Antonio Metropolitan Transit Authority*, was that "the attempt to draw the boundaries of state regulatory immunity in terms of 'traditional government function' is not only unworkable but is also inconsistent with established principles of federalism."[34] Instead, the Court relied on "[t]he structure of the federal Government itself . . . to insulate the interests of the States."[35] Justice Blackmun, for a five-member majority, explained that the states are equally represented in the U.S. Senate, and numerous federal laws operate to benefit the states. The dissenters vigorously disputed Blackmun's structural rationale and predicted that *Garcia* would someday be reversed.

After 17 years, *Garcia* has not been reversed. But private FLSA rights of action against the states for money damages have effectively been abolished. First, in *Seminole*, the Court said that the Eleventh Amendment trumped the Commerce Clause. That meant private parties could no longer pursue their FLSA claims against a state in *federal* court. Then, in *Alden v. Maine*,[36] the Court held for the first time that states are immune from private FLSA suits in *state* courts also. Acknowledging that the text of the Eleventh Amendment would not support such a holding, the *Alden* Court turned instead to the Constitution's structure and history as well as the Court's own precedent enlarging the sovereign immunity doctrine.

Justice Souter, in dissent,[37] rejected the majority's version of constitutional history and challenged the Court's assertion that state immunity vests even when the state is not itself the source of the law at issue. He insisted that no substantial—let alone dominant— body of thought at the time of the Constitution's framing conceived of sovereign immunity as an inherent right of statehood. According to Souter, the majority's newly formed concept of federalism ignored the time-honored authority of Congress to enforce federal rights in

[33] *Id.* at 845.
[34] 469 U.S. 528, 531 (1985).
[35] *Id.* at 551.
[36] 527 U.S. 706 (1999).
[37] *Id.* at 760–814 (Souter, J., dissenting).

state court. Without a private right of damages in either federal or state court, the Secretary of Labor alone would have to enforce the FLSA; and that enforcement, concluded Souter, would not prove adequate.

Adequate or not, that was the law as the Supreme Court considered this year's *FMC* case, to which we turn next. *FMC* is but the latest aggrandizement of the sovereign immunity doctrine. From this point forward, according to the Court, that doctrine embraces adjudication before federal administrative agencies, not just courts. In fleshing out the Court's *FMC* opinion, I will discuss the dispute over constitutional text and the meaning of "the Judicial power of the United States." Then I will examine the overriding purpose of sovereign immunity, the constitutionalization of common law, and remedies for state misbehavior.

Constitutional Text and Judicial Power

Justice Thomas, author of the *FMC* majority opinion, has been an outspoken proponent of textualism and originalism as approaches to constitutional interpretation. So too has Justice Scalia and, to a lesser extent, Chief Justice Rehnquist—both of whom joined the *FMC* majority. In a nutshell, textualism assigns overriding importance to the meaning of the words in the Constitution. Originalism is the variant of textualism that looks not to the contemporary meaning of the words but to their meaning at the time they were incorporated in law. If the meaning of the constitutional text is unambiguous, textualists adopt that meaning unless it would lead to absurd consequences. Only if the meaning is unclear will textualists consult the structure, purpose, and history of the Constitution.[38]

The text of the Eleventh Amendment is crystalline. In essence, it says that federal courts shall not entertain lawsuits against a state by citizens of another state. When the Constitution was ratified in 1789, Article III, which addresses the "judicial Power of the United

---

[38]Structure relates, first, to the internal relationship among the various provisions of the Constitution and, second, to the overall design or framework of government that the Constitution establishes. Purpose refers to the Framers' values and objectives when they enacted a particular provision. History involves the law or practices that preceded enactment, as well as early post-enactment interpretations. *See* Michael B. Rappaport, *Reconciling Textualism and Federalism: The Proper Textual Basis of the Supreme Court's Tenth and Eleventh Amendment Decisions*, 93 NW. U. L. REV. 819, 822–23 (1999).

States," provided that federal courts had jurisdiction over "Controversies between . . . a State and Citizens of another State." Four years later in *Chisholm v. Georgia*,[39] the Supreme Court held that Article III took precedence over common law sovereign immunity. The Court rejected the notion that Article III pertained only to federal litigation in which the state was the plaintiff. In *Chisholm*, the executor for a South Carolina merchant sued Georgia for the value of clothing supplied during the Revolutionary War. The states' broader concern, however, was their exposure to liability in federal court on all of their war debts, which were substantial.

Moving quickly to overturn *Chisholm*, Congress proposed and the states ratified the Eleventh Amendment in 1795. Because it was crafted for the limited purpose of reversing *Chisholm*, says Justice Thomas, "the Eleventh Amendment does not define the scope of the States' sovereign immunity; it is but one particular exemplification of that immunity."[40] That argument effectively concedes that the text of the Eleventh Amendment will not support the *FMC* holding. Thus, Thomas departs from the textualist approach, for which he is well known, and resorts to structure, purpose, and history, notwithstanding the unambiguous meaning of the Amendment.

Thomas justifies that departure from the plain meaning of the text by asserting a right to sovereign immunity that predated the Eleventh Amendment. Yet that assertion is belied by the 4-to-1 decision in *Chisholm*—rendered by a Court on which several of the Framers sat. Yes, *Chisholm* was later overturned by the Amendment itself. But in 1793, four out of five members of the Supreme Court concluded that, before the Eleventh Amendment, the law and the Constitution expressly granted federal court jurisdiction to lawsuits in which the defendant was a state and the plaintiff was a citizen of a different state.

To be sure, the Court's conservative *FMC* majority did not suddenly discover an expansive version of sovereign immunity lurking within the emanations and penumbras of the Eleventh Amendment. There were numerous precedents, ranging from *Hans* in 1890 to *Alden* in 1999. Still, Thomas availed himself of those precedents without apparent discomfort—even assuming "[f]or purposes of

---

[39] 2 U.S. (2 Dall.) 419 (1793).
[40] *Fed. Mar. Comm'n* at 1871.

this case . . . that in adjudicating complaints by private parties under the Shipping Act, the FMC does not exercise the judicial power of the United States,"[41] which means that the Commission failed the textual litmus test for Eleventh Amendment immunity.

That didn't matter, insisted Thomas. If the Framers of the Amendment considered it offensive to a state's dignity to be compelled to defend itself in a private lawsuit in federal court, they would also have found it unacceptable

> to compel a State to do exactly the same thing before the administrative tribunal of an agency, such as the FMC . . . . [I]t would be quite strange to prohibit Congress from exercising its Article I powers to abrogate state sovereign immunity in Article III judicial proceedings [as the Court did in *Seminole*], but permit the use of those same Article I powers to create court-like administrative tribunals where sovereign immunity does not apply.[42]

Indeed, the Supreme Court had previously held that the Tax Court, a special Article I entity, exercised a "portion of the judicial power of the United States,"[43] And the Supreme Court had also ruled that administrative law judges, like Article III judges, are "entitled to absolute immunity from damages liability for their judicial acts."[44] In that same case, the Court noted that administrative adjudications and judicial proceedings shared many common features. "[F]ederal administrative law requires that agency adjudication contain many of the same safeguards as are available in the judicial process."[45]

Although history and logic seem to have impressed Justice Thomas, he did not find it conclusive. In fact, he acknowledged that "[i]n truth, the relevant history does not provide direct guidance for our inquiry."[46] Still, Thomas reasoned that "[t]he Framers, who envisioned a limited Federal Government, could not have anticipated the vast growth of the administrative state."[47] He adds that

---

[41] *Id.* at 1871.

[42] *Id.* at 1874–75 (internal citations and quotation marks omitted).

[43] Freytag v. Commissioner of Internal Revenue, 501 U.S. 868, 890–91 (1991).

[44] Butz v. Economou, 438 U.S. 478, 514 (1978).

[45] *Id.* at 513.

[46] *Fed. Mar. Comm'n* at 1872.

[47] *Id.*

"the Constitution was not intended to raise up any proceedings against the States that were anomalous and unheard of when the Constitution was adopted."[48] Evidently, Thomas subscribes to Justice Scalia's rule of constitutional interpretation: When there is "disagreement as to how . . . original meaning applies to new and unforeseen phenomena . . . the Court must follow the trajectory of the [Constitution], so to speak, to determine what it requires."[49]

In this instance, however, there's a rather obvious answer to the Scalia-Thomas rule: The growth of the administrative state was an "unforeseen phenomena" because it was patently unconstitutional.[50] In plotting the "trajectory" of the Constitution, one would have thought that unconstitutional developments would be excluded. In fact, when Justice Breyer, in his *FMC* dissent, became a late convert to textualism—citing the Eleventh Amendment's limiting phrase, "the Judicial power of the United States," and stressing that federal administrative agencies do not exercise that power[51]—Justice Thomas quite properly admonished him for adopting "a textual approach in defending the conduct of an independent agency that itself lacks any textual basis in the Constitution."[52]

[48] *Id.* (internal quotation marks omitted).

[49] Antonin Scalia, A Matter of Interpretation: Federal Courts and the Law 45 (1997).

[50] Article I, section 1 of the Constitution states that "All legislative Powers herein granted shall be vested in . . . Congress." The so-called non-delegation doctrine flows from that provision. It holds that Congress may not delegate its legislative authority to other entities, such as administrative agencies in the executive branch. A major purpose of the non-delegation doctrine was to ensure that legislative, executive, and judicial powers be kept separate, so that each branch of government could serve as a check on possible abuse of authority by the other branches. Although Congress was not permitted to delegate its core legislative power, the Supreme Court long ago allowed Congress some leeway in assigning a partial policy role to the executive branch. The key requirement was that Congress first legislate "an intelligible principle to which the person or body authorized to [act] is directed to conform." J.W. Hampton, Jr. & Co. v. United States, 276 U.S. 394, 409 (1928). For a while, the intelligible principle requirement was sensibly enforced. *See, e.g.*, ALA Schechter Poultry Corp. v. United States, 295 U.S. 495 (1935); Pan. Ref. Co. v. Ryan, 293 U.S. 388 (1935). But the post-New Deal explosion of the regulatory state effectively nullified the intelligible principle requirement along with its parent, the nondelegation doctrine.

[51] *Fed. Mar. Comm'n* at 1883 (Breyer, J., dissenting).

[52] *Id.* at 1871 n.8.

In one breath, Justice Breyer criticizes the majority for reaching a decision lacking "any firm anchor in the Constitution's text."[53] In the next breath, his born-again textualism somehow morphs into support for a living Constitution "designed to provide a framework for government across the centuries, a framework that is flexible enough to meet modern needs."[54] Our constitutional system requires, says Breyer, "structural flexibility sufficient to adapt substantive laws and institutions to rapidly changing social, economic and technological conditions."[55]

That said, Justice Thomas appears to be no more consistent. His resort to "constitutional design"[56] and "plan of the convention"[57] in the face of explicit text leaves even his admirers somewhat perplexed. For example, Catholic University law school dean Douglas Kmiec, a self-described "pretty strong advocate of federalism" and unabashed Thomas fan, says that the *FMC* ruling is even harder to justify than previous enlargements of sovereign immunity. "I would have thought the words 'judicial power' in the 11th Amendment would have been a bright-line boundary," he observes, "but apparently that is not the case."[58]

With the majority of the Court selectively espousing textualism and condemning the living-document school, and the dissenters espousing the living-document school except when it serves their interests to espouse textualism, it is little wonder that court watchers are more than a little confused. They need not be. The text of the Constitution, as set out in the Eleventh Amendment, tightly circumscribes the sovereign immunity doctrine. And even if the text were ambiguous, which it is not, an analysis of the purpose of sovereign immunity leads us to the same end.

Purpose of Sovereign Immunity

In *FMC*, the federal government suggested that sovereign immunity should not apply to Commission proceedings because they do

---

[53] *Id.* at 1883 (Breyer, J., dissenting).

[54] *Id.* at 1885 (Breyer, J., dissenting).

[55] *Id.* at 1889 (Breyer, J., dissenting).

[56] *Id.* at 1879.

[57] *Id.* at 1870.

[58] *Quoted in* Marcia Coyle, *States Get New Shield from Suits*, NAT'L L.J., June 3, 2002, at A1.

not represent the same threat to the financial integrity of the states as do private lawsuits in court. For example, if the Commission were to issue a reparation order, as Maritime requested in the *FMC* case, and the state chose not to pay, that order could be enforced only by the private beneficiary in federal court, not by the federal government. Under those circumstances, because the state need not consent to the private suit, it would not be exposed to reparations.

The Supreme Court agreed that "state sovereign immunity serves the important function of shielding state treasuries,"[59] but the Court rejected the government's assertion that Commission proceedings could not deplete a state's coffers. If the state willfully and knowingly disobeyed a Commission-issued reparation order or injunction, the Commission could impose a civil penalty of up to $25,000 per day enforceable in court by the Justice Department. States are not immunized from suit when the plaintiff is the federal government.

That counterargument depends, however, on the notion that sovereign immunity legitimately exists to protect state treasuries. It does not—despite the Court's assertion to the contrary. Liberal societies traditionally place greater value on compensating injured parties and deterring state misbehavior than they do on safeguarding government bank accounts. Surely, if the government were to act illegally, it would be more equitable to spread the cost of any injury among all taxpayers than to compel the unfortunate injured party to bear the cost alone. In fact, the Supreme Court acknowledged that principle in the takings context when it stated that "[t]he Fifth Amendment's guarantee that private property shall not be taken for a public use without just compensation was designed to bar Government from forcing some people alone to bear public burdens which, in all fairness and justice, should be borne by the public as a whole."[60]

If the states' financial integrity is not the primary purpose of sovereign immunity, what is? "[T]he doctrine's central purpose," said the Court, "is to accord the States the respect owed them as joint sovereigns."[61] The Court continued, "Sovereign immunity does not merely constitute a defense to monetary liability or even to all

---

[59] *Fed. Mar. Comm'n* at 1877.

[60] Armstrong v. United States, 364 U.S. 40, 49 (1960).

[61] *Fed. Mar. Comm'n* at 1877 (internal quotation marks omitted).

types of liability. Rather, it provides an immunity from suit."[62] Thus, the preeminent reason for immunity is to extend to the states the dignity that their sovereign status entails.

The government's answer to the "states' dignity" rationale is that no state is compelled to appear before the Commission. That's because the Commission's orders are not self-enforcing. They can only be enforced by a federal court, in which case the usual rules regarding immunity would apply. The Supreme Court rejects that contention. Absent immunity, notes the Court, the states would have to defend themselves against private parties in Commission actions, or else compromise their later defense in court. A party sanctioned by the Commission may not litigate the merits of its position in a federal court enforcement suit. At that point, the only relevant issue is whether the Commission order "was properly made and duly issued."[63]

Moreover, if the dignity of the states is the paramount justification for sovereign immunity, what can explain the numerous exceptions that have been carved out? Municipalities, which are creations of the state, can be sued without the state's consent. The federal government or another state can sue a nonconsenting state. A state can be sued in an enforcement action under section 5 of the Fourteenth Amendment, or when the defendant is an official of the state rather than the state itself. None of those exceptions has had a palpable effect on the ability of states to perform their sovereign functions.

The dignity rationale appears to be based more on tradition than necessity. State immunity—grounded in respect for sovereign dignity and derived from English common law—has existed in one form or another throughout American history. Yet that begs the central question, says University of Southern California law professor Erwin Chemerinsky. Is the tradition one that should continue? After all, he notes, "Slavery, enforced racial segregation, and the subjugation of women were also deeply embedded traditions."[64]

---

[62] *Id.*

[63] *Id.* at 1876.

[64] Erwin Chemerinsky, *Symposium: Shifting the Balance of Power? The Supreme Court, Federalism, and State Sovereign Immunity: Against Sovereign Immunity*, 53 STAN. L. REV. 1201, 1223 (2001).

A doctrine derived from the English law premise that "the King can do no wrong" is an "anachronistic relic [that] should be eliminated from American law," continues Chemerinsky.[65] America rejected monarchy, disavowed royal prerogatives and, in their place, established a system of enumerated and separated powers, checks and balances that recognized this fundamental reality: Governments and government officials can and will do wrong. They must be held accountable; and sovereign immunity is antithetical to that goal.

Chemerinsky has it right. "Sovereign immunity is inconsistent with a central maxim of American government: no one, not even the government, is above the law. The effect of sovereign immunity is to place the government above the law and to ensure that some individuals who have suffered egregious harms will be unable to receive redress for their injuries."[66] In essence, by enlarging the scope of the Eleventh Amendment beyond any conceivable reading of its text, our courts have allowed a common law doctrine to trump the laws duly enacted by the federal legislature. Never mind that the "Framers feared judicial power over substantive policy and the ossification of law that would result from transforming common law into constitutional law."[67]

Because the common law of sovereign immunity has been constitutionalized, attempts by Congress to override sovereign immunity by statute will usually be invalidated. Consequently, the common law rights of state government will supersede the statutory rights of individuals. That astonishing—some might say, "un-American"— development flies in the face of the Supremacy Clause of Article VI. There, the Constitution provides that "the Laws of the United States ... shall be the supreme Law of the Land ... any Thing in the Constitution or Laws of any State to the Contrary notwithstanding." The hierarchy laid out in Article VI places the laws of the United States above the laws of any state—even above a state constitution. Yet, sovereign immunity, which is mostly a state common law doctrine, is accorded a status above that of a federal statute. As for individuals, they are relegated by judicial ukase to the bottom of the pecking order.

---

[65] *Id.* at 1201–02.

[66] *Id.* at 1202.

[67] Seminole Tribe of Fla. v. Florida 517 U.S. 44, 165 (1996) (Souter, J., dissenting).

Article VI is not the only constitutional provision that is incompatible with sovereign immunity. In Article I, section 9, the Framers provided that "No Title of Nobility shall be granted by the United States." One purpose of that prohibition was to establish a government obligated to follow the rule of law as established by the people. Indeed, the First Amendment guarantees "the right of the people . . . to petition the Government for a redress of grievances." According to University of Illinois law professor James Pfander, "the Petition Clause guarantees the right of individuals to pursue judicial remedies for government misconduct."[68] That right, says Pfander, is "historically calculated to overcome any threshold government immunity from suit."[69] The Fifth and Fourteenth Amendments prevent states from depriving any person "of life, liberty, or property, without due process of law." Chemerinsky points to numerous cases in which the Supreme Court recognized that due process requires a judicial forum in which individuals can obtain redress for losses at the hands of government.[70]

In *Alden*, the majority suggested that redress for injuries was available through one or more of the various exceptions to the sovereign immunity doctrine that the Court has fashioned.[71] For instance, the Commission could itself have initiated an investigation into Ports Authority and sued the state of South Carolina. But practicing attorneys are skeptical of that alternative. Eric Glitzenstein of Washington, D.C.'s Meyer & Glitzenstein calls the prospect of agency action "laughable." Agencies "depend heavily on private parties," he says. "That's why Congress crafted those laws to permit private actions."[72] David Vladek of Public Citizen Litigation Group adds that it's "a leap of faith completely unwarranted" to think that agencies "have

---

[68] James E. Pfander, *Sovereign Immunity and the Right to Petition: Toward a First Amendment Right to Pursue Judicial Claims Against the Government*, 91 Nw. U. L. REV. 899, 906 (1997).

[69] *Id.* at 980.

[70] Chemerinsky at 1215. *See, e.g.*, McNary v. Haitian Refugee Ctr., Inc., 498 U.S. 479, 491–95 (1991); Webster v. Doe, 486 U.S. 592, 599–600 (1988); United States v. Mendoza-Lopez, 481 U.S. 828, 835 (1987); Johnson v. Robison, 415 U.S. 361, 368–70 (1974); Oestereich v. Selective Serv. Sys. Local Bd. No. 11, 393 U.S. 233, 244 n.6 (1968) (Harlan, J., concurring).

[71] Alden v. Maine, 527 U.S. 706, 755–57 (1999).

[72] *Quoted in* Coyle, supra note 58.

the ability to investigate and bring enforcement proceedings against the states. . . . It turns a blind eye to the serious lack of resources of these agencies."[73]

Although injunctive relief may be available when state officials are sued under the fiction of *Ex parte Young*, that relief is limited to preventing future violations. It does not compensate for past injuries. Nor are suits for money damages against individual officers likely to be successful. Some officers—for example, judges and legislators—are themselves immune from suit. Other officers have qualified immunity unless they violate a clearly established right about which a reasonable officer should have known.[74] Finally, suits that circumvent sovereign immunity under section 5 of the Fourteenth Amendment have been sharply curbed in recent years by the Supreme Court.

Without adequate recourse for harms caused by the state, the dual principles of government accountability and popular sovereignty are trivialized. The first words of the Constitution, "We the People," are stripped of meaning. Lincoln's model of a government "of the people, by the people, and for the people" is discredited. And James Madison's cautionary words in *Federalist* 46 are flouted: "The federal and State governments are in fact but different agents and trustees of the people, constituted with different powers, and designed for different purposes [but] the ultimate authority . . . resides in the people alone."

The states should be "subservient to the people who created them," says Evan Caminker, law professor at the University of Michigan. Instead, the Supreme Court, by means of its sovereign immunity jurisprudence, has "exalt[ed] states as having a status superior to individuals. . . . [T]he prioritization of states' dignitary interest over individuals' competing interest in compensation for injuries . . . expresses a message that individuals are subordinate to states rather than the other way around."[75]

Yale law professor Akhil Reed Amar agrees. He argues that popular sovereignty and constitutional government mandate that victims

---

[73] *Id.*

[74] Harlow v. Fitzgerald, 457 U.S. 800 (1982).

[75] Evan H. Caminker, *Judicial Solicitude for State Dignity*, 574 ANNALS AM. ACAD. POL. & SOC. SCI. 81, 86 (2001).

of unconstitutional acts by government must be accorded a means of relief.[76] Amar amasses historical evidence that the Framers did not intend to immunize states from constitutional claims.[77] The Eleventh Amendment, he concludes, should be limited in accordance with its text to foreclosing common law suits against states in federal courts by citizens of another state.

Justice Stevens, in his *FMC* dissent, also offers an interesting historical perspective on the Eleventh Amendment.[78] *Chisholm*, the holding of which was overturned by the Amendment, had decided two issues relevant to federal court jurisdiction. First, federal courts had *personal* jurisdiction authorizing them to serve process on the state of Georgia. Second, the courts had *subject matter* jurisdiction because, according to Article III of the Constitution, the judicial power extended to suits "between a State and Citizens of another State." Both of those jurisdictional components had to be satisfied before a federal court could decide *Chisholm*.

The House of Representatives' draft of the Eleventh Amendment overruled the first jurisdictional component, but not the second: "[N]o state shall be liable to be made a party defendant, in any of the judicial courts . . . established under the authority of the United States." That draft, which would have nullified service of process, was not adopted. In its place, the Senate version, almost verbatim, became the Eleventh Amendment: "The Judicial Power of the United States shall not extend to any Suits in Law or Equity commenced or prosecuted against any one of the United States by Citizens of another State or by Citizens or Subjects of any foreign State." The Senate version said nothing about immunizing a state from federal court process, but it expressly overruled Article III's subject-matter jurisdiction on the basis of diversity of citizenship.

From that, Stevens reasonably deduces, "If the paramount concern of the Eleventh Amendment's framers had been protecting the so-called 'dignity' interest of the States, surely Congress would have endorsed the first proposed amendment granting the States immunity from process, rather than the later proposal that merely delineates the subject-matter jurisdiction of courts."[79] Perhaps the Framers

---

[76] Akhil Reed Amar, *Of Sovereignty and Federalism*, 96 YALE L.J. 1425, 1491–95 (1987).

[77] *Id.* at 1444–55.

[78] *Fed. Mar. Comm'n* at 1880 (Stevens, J., dissenting).

[79] *Id.*

objected to the House draft because it foreclosed process even if the federal government were itself the plaintiff. If so, they could have modified the draft to that extent. But they did not. Instead, they left personal jurisdiction intact and crafted the text of the Eleventh Amendment to cover just one aspect of subject-matter jurisdiction—diversity of citizenship—leaving states exposed to federal court litigation whenever a controversy arose under the Constitution, a treaty, or a federal statute.

A Proper Understanding of Sovereign Immunity

Despite the clear text of the Eleventh Amendment and compelling historical evidence of the Amendment's narrow purpose, most conservative legal analysts celebrate the Rehnquist Court's sovereign immunity jurisprudence. They insist that sovereign immunity, by respecting the dignity of the states, promotes federalism, a centerpiece of the Constitution. Perhaps so. But only if federalism equates to states' rights—in which case, because states occasionally enact repressive laws, federalism will sometimes constrict rather than enlarge personal liberty.[80] Yet if federalism ever stood for states' rights, that notion was dispelled in 1868 when the Fourteenth Amendment was ratified. Designed to guard against state repression, the Fourteenth Amendment fundamentally altered the relationship between the federal and state governments. Clearly, the touchstone of the new federalism was dual sovereignty, not states' rights. Dual sovereignty entails checks and balances intended to promote liberty by limiting excessive power in the hands of either state or federal government.

---

[80] In that regard, it is interesting to contrast Justice Thomas's *FMC* opinion with his provocative concurrence a month later in *Zelman v. Simmons-Harris*, 122 S. Ct. 2460 (2002), the Cleveland school choice case. *FMC* promoted an extratextual reading of the sovereign immunity doctrine, supposedly to advance states' dignitary interests. Ironically, that version of federalism subordinates individual rights to states' rights—a principle that Thomas appeared to rebuff in *Zelman*. There, he argued that actions by the federal government to incorporate rights against the states through the Fourteenth Amendment "should advance, not constrain, individual liberty." *Id.* (LEXIS at *66; S. Ct. pagination not available) (Thomas, J., concurring). One would think, therefore, that Thomas would favor actions by the federal government to ensure that an individual right, like the right of redress for injury, could be asserted against the states. But that is not his position in *Fed. Mar. Comm'n*.

Oddly, Justice Thomas in *FMC* seems to adopt the concept of federalism as dual sovereignty—but then, although citing dual sovereignty, he resolves the immunity issue as if states' rights were all that mattered. Dual sovereignty, Thomas writes, represents the "constitutionally mandated balance of power between the States and the Federal Government [that] was adopted by the Framers to ensure the protection of our fundamental liberties."[81] So far so good. Inexplicably, he follows that accurate characterization with this non sequitur: "By guarding against encroachments by the Federal Government on fundamental aspects of state sovereignty . . . we strive to maintain the balance of power embodied in our Constitution and thus to reduce the risk of tyranny and abuse from either front."[82] Somehow Thomas equates sovereign immunity with a reduced risk of government abuse.

At root, state sovereign immunity is incompatible with dual sovereignty federalism. The federal government cannot fully redress state violations of individual rights if it cannot abrogate state immunity from private litigation. That said, even opponents of sovereign immunity comprehend that the Eleventh Amendment is incontrovertibly part of our Constitution. And it does confer limited immunity on the states. Specifically, the Eleventh Amendment immunizes states against private suits in federal court when jurisdiction is based on diversity of citizenship. But that is all it does. The Supreme Court, not the text of the Eleventh Amendment, has extended sovereign immunity to include nondiverse citizens (*Hans*), federal question jurisdiction (*Seminole*), suits in state court (*Alden*), and now private actions before federal administrative agencies (*FMC*). At the same time, the Court has steadily circumscribed Congress's power to abrogate sovereign immunity under section 5 of the Fourteenth Amendment (*Florida Prepaid, College Savings Bank, Kimel*, and *Garrett*).

Essentially, the court has constitutionalized the common law of sovereign immunity, thereby forbidding Congress to create many private causes of action against the states. In its defense, the Court has engaged in that process with the best of intentions—to rein in an unrestrained Congress that has made a mockery of the doctrine of enumerated powers and limited government. In establishing a

---

[81] *Fed. Mar. Comm'n* at 1879 (internal quotation marks omitted).

[82] *Id.* (internal quotation marks omitted).

pervasive regulatory and redistributive state, Congress has stretched the Commerce Clause, the General Welfare Clause and the Necessary and Proper Clause beyond recognition. The federal government can now regulate virtually anything and everything. It can exact tribute from anyone for almost any purpose, then dispense the proceeds to anyone else. At last, the Rehnquist Court has taken a few ministeps to curtail Congress's seemingly boundless power. That curtailment is long overdue. But it has been accomplished in the wrong manner.

Here's how Chapman University law professor John C. Eastman summarizes the Court's treatment of federalism and sovereign immunity:

> [T]he Court's enthusiasm for federalism has sometimes caused it to forget the other half of the founders' vision, namely, that the federal government was to be supreme within the spheres assigned to it. Several of the decisions . . . interpret the Eleventh Amendment in a way that is arguably contrary to that vision. That is not necessarily to disagree with the outcome of these cases, only with their reasoning. In *Seminole Tribe*, for example, the correct holding from the view of the framers would have been that Congress had exceeded the scope of its authority under the Indian Commerce Clause. . . . By relying instead on a nontextual reading of the Eleventh Amendment, the Court essentially erected an artificial barrier to an artificial power—producing the correct outcome in the case but creating real analytical problems for future cases where a power clearly given to Congress was at issue.[83]

In pursuit of legitimate ends—limited federal government—the Supreme Court has adopted illegitimate means—sovereign immunity that denies to individuals full recourse for injuries they may have suffered at the hands of the states. Yes, the Court should press ahead with a full and vigorous frontal assault to restore a federal government of delegated, enumerated, and thus limited powers. In doing so, however, the Court must not forget that preservation of personal liberty is the quintessential ingredient of the American experience. In a free society, the "dignity" of state governments cannot be permitted to trump the rights of individual Americans.

[83]John C. Eastman, *Restoring the 'General' to the General Welfare Clause*, 4 Chap. L. Rev. 63 n.4 (2001).

Until a more apprehensive electorate repeals the Eleventh Amendment, the reach of state sovereign immunity must extend no further than the Amendment's unambiguous text.

Registering Publius: The Supreme Court and the Right to Anonymity

Jonathan Turley

I. Introduction

One of the most interesting facts about George Orwell, author of *1984* and *Animal Farm*, is that he was not George Orwell.[1] The man who created a society of total transparency and observation chose to conceal his own name, Eric Blair.[2] Authors like Blair, Mary Ann Evans (George Eliot),[3] and Samuel Clemens (Mark Twain) adopted noms de plume for a variety of reasons ranging from persecution to prejudice to privacy.[4] The practice of publishing anonymously was once the norm among literary and political thinkers. There was nothing strange about a Framer adopting a name like Publius to espouse fundamental principles in *The Federalist Papers*. Today, this practice is viewed with greater suspicion and prompts endless efforts to uncover the true identity of historical figures like Deep Throat[5]

---

[1] *See* Jonathan Turley, *Anonymous Advocacy at Risk*, NAT'L L. J., Apr. 1, 2002, at A20.

[2] Orwell is indicative of someone who risked social and political (if not legal) backlash for some of his views. A former police officer in Burma, Orwell was a socialist who developed contrarian views during service in the Spanish Civil War. *See* Lewis C. Mainzer, *Orwell: The Authorized Biography*, 30 SOC'Y. 89 (1993).

[3] *A Class Act*, TORONTO STAR, Apr. 23, 2000, at 1 ("the female authors known as George Sand and George Eliot, published under male pseudonyms to ensure a fair reading from a public that assumed no woman could write great literature.").

[4] Another author who employed a pseudonym was Amandine Auror Lucie Dupin (George Sand).

[5] The search has never waned for the most mysterious figure of Watergate. *See, e.g.*, Ron Grossman, *Deep Throat Mystery Over, Students Say; U. of I. Team Feels Buchanan Is Watergate Figure*, CHI. TRIB., June 15, 2002, at 8.

or literary figures like "Anonymous," the author of *Primary Colors.*[6] Yet, anonymity has never been more important, with a trend against privacy and confidentiality interests in the United States. With the diminishment of the expectation of privacy has come a diminishment of the expectation of anonymity. Like the right to distribute thoughts, the right to anonymous thoughts is an essential component of free speech. It is a right that protects the most valuable speech in a free nation: those views that challenge the status quo and question both the government and most of its citizens. The question of the "right" to anonymity in public expression was put squarely before the Supreme Court last term. In *Watchtower Bible Society v. Village of Stratton,*[7] the Court reviewed an ordinance that required a permit for any door-to-door solicitation. This case was only the latest round in a long and uncertain debate over the relative importance of anonymity in the shifting balance between speech rights and governmental interests.

For the Framers and their contemporaries, anonymity was the deciding factor between whether their writings would produce a social exchange or a personal beating. Obviously, before and during the war, anonymity was used to disguise the identity of a writer who might be subject to British punishment. The pamphleteer was a vital element of the American resistance movement, and the greatest of this diverse group, Thomas Paine, would significantly influence both the war and its underlying cause. Even after the war, anonymity was an accepted and widely used practice. Early American politics produced severe divisions between Federalist and anti-Federalists. Later, with the establishment of political parties, the division between Federalists and Jeffersonian Republicans emerged. These were not mere parlor debates. Jefferson would refer to the rule of the Federalists as the "reign of the witches."[8] Each side accused the other of treasonous intentions and engaged in violent attacks against their opponents. Even the First Army was involved

---

[6] Despite repeated public denials, the author proved to be Joe Klein, a political columnist for Newsweek. Klein was uncovered by handwriting on the manuscript and writing analysis. This outing of the author not only stripped him of his desired anonymity but, at a professional cost, forced him to admit that he had lied to other journalists and friends. Elisabeth Bumiller, *A No-Apologies, Sometimes No-Name Author,* N.Y. TIMES, March 13, 1998, at B2.

[7] ___ U.S.___, 122 S. Ct. 2080 (2002).

[8] Letter from Thomas Jefferson to John Taylor (June 1, 1798), *reprinted in* 7 THE WRITINGS OF THOMAS JEFFERSON 263, 265 (P. Ford ed. 1892–1899).

in widespread attacks on Republicans and Anti-Federalists under John Adams,[9] who also used the Sedition Act to punish critics criminally. Anonymity in this period was not simply a charming diversion but a matter of personal survival.

Our history as a republic was shaped by essays written by anonymous authors.[10] Federalist essays appeared under fictitious names like "Americanus,"[11] "An American Citizen,"[12] "Caesar," "A Countryman,"[13] "Fabius,"[14] "Landowner,"[15] and "Publius."[16] Anti-Federalists responded with writings under names like "An Old Whig," "Brutus,"[17] "Cato,"[18] "Centinel,"[19] "Cincinnatus,"[20] and "Federal

[9] *See* Jonathan Turley, *The Military Pocket Republic*, 97 Nw. U. L. Rev. 1 (2002).

[10] Some of these authors like "Caesar," "An Old Whig" and "Aristocratis" remain uncertain as to their actual identities.

[11] *See* Americanus No. 7 (John Stevens Jr.), *A Refutation of Governor Edmund Randolph's Objections*, Daily Advertiser (N.Y.), Jan. 21, 1788, *reprinted in* 2 The Debate on the Constitution: Federalist and Anti-Federalist Speeches, Articles, and Letters During the Struggle Over Ratification 58, 60 (Bernard Bailyn ed., 1993).

[12] James Wilson is believed to have used the name "An American Citizen."

[13] Roger Sherman wrote under the name "A Countryman." *See* 16 The Documentary History of the Ratification of the Constitution 290 n.15 (John P. Kaminski & Gaspare J. Saladino eds., 1986) at 172. Sherman also wrote under the pseudonym "Citizen of New Hampshire."

[14] "Fabius" was the pseudonym of John Dickinson. *See* Letters of Fabius (1788), *reprinted in* Pamphlets on the Constitution of the United States 178 (Paul L. Ford ed., 1888).

[15] This name was used by Federalist Oliver Ellsworth. *See* 3 The Documentary History of the Ratification of the Constitution 513 (M. Jensen ed. 1976) at 490; Ellsworth, *Landholder, No. 7* (Dec. 17, 1787), *reprinted in* 4 The Founders' Constitution 639, 639–40 (P. Kurland & R. Lerner eds., 1987).

[16] Publius was used by James Madison, Alexander Hamilton, and John Jay.

[17] Brutus was used by Robert Yates. "Brutus" was a powerful counterbalance to Publius and the publication of sixteen essays in "Letters of Brutus," was highly influential at that time. *See* Essays of Brutus, *in* 2 The Complete Anti-Federalist 214, at 358, 369, 379–80 (H. Storing ed., 1981).

[18] Cato was the name used by pre-Revolutionary era pamphleteers John Trenchard and Thomas Gordon, as well as George Clinton, though there remains some debate on the latter. *See* 2 Debate on the Constitution at 102.

[19] Samuel Bryan also wrote under the fictitious name "Centinel." *See, e.g.*, Reply to Wilson's Speech: "Centinel" (1787), *in* 1 Debate on the Constitution *supra* note 11, at 77; *Letters of Centinel, in* 2 The Complete Anti-Federalist at 130, 142 (H. Storing ed., 1981).

[20] Cincinnatus was a name attributed to Arthur Lee. *See, e.g., Reply to Wilson's Speech: "Cincinnatus"* (1787), *in* 1 Debates, *supra* note 11, at 114. Some of these essays may

Farmer."[21] Alexander Hamilton and James Madison shared the famous moniker "Publius." When they disagreed over George Washington's neutrality policies, they simply spawned new identities as "Helvidius"[22] and "Pacificus."[23] Because of this historical record, the use of anonymity was firmly ingrained in American society and, as noted by the Supreme Court, "under our Constitution, anonymous pamphleteering is not a pernicious, fraudulent practice, but an honorable tradition of advocacy and of dissent."[24]

This is not to say that there was no opposition to anonymous speech. Not surprisingly, many leaders resented the ability of writers to criticize the government or its policies behind the protection of anonymity. The Continental Congress tried to uncover the identity of the writer known as "Leonidas" after he accused Congress of corruption and ineptitude.[25] The writer was, in fact, Dr. Benjamin Rush, but various members rose to defend the right of the author to anonymity and free speech. These members viewed the effort to expose the author as inimical to the "freedom of the press."[26] Likewise, irritated legislators in New Jersey sought to uncover the identity of "Cincinnatus," to allow a possible charge of sedition. The printer of this work, Isaac Collins, refused to disclose the identity with the declaration: "Were I to comply ... I conceive I should betray the trust reposed in me, and be far from acting as a faithful guardian of the Liberty of the Press."[27] In some cases, anonymity was used to defend anonymous speech. Such was the case with William Livingston who wrote as "Scipio" in defense of anonymous speech as both necessary to prevent retaliation and as an element

---

also have been written by his brother Richard Henry Lee. 6 THE COMPLETE ANTI-FEDERALIST, *supra* note 19, at 5,6 & n.2.

[21] "The Federal Farmer" is believed to have been Richard Henry Lee.

[22] Alexander Hamilton, *Pacificus No. 1*, June 29, 1793, *in* 15 PAPERS OF ALEXANDER HAMILTON 33–43 (H. Syrett ed., 1969).

[23] James Madison, *Helvidius No. 1*, Aug. 24, 1793, in 15 PAPERS OF JAMES MADISON 66–73 (T. Mason, R. Rutland, J. Sisson eds. 1985); James Madison, *Helvidius No. 4*, Sept. 14, 1793, in 6 THE WRITINGS OF JAMES MADISON 171, 174 (Gaillard Hunt ed., 1906).

[24] McIntyre v. Ohio Elections Comm'n, 514 U.S. 334, 357 (1995).

[25] *McIntyre*, 514 U.S. at 361–362. Justice Thomas recounts this history (and the various examples below) in his concurrence to *McIntyre*.

[26] *Id.* at 362.

[27] R. HIXON & ISAAC COLLINS: A QUAKER PRINTER IN 18TH CENTURY AMERICA 95 (1968), quoted in *McIntyre*, 514 U.S. at 362.

of freedom of the press.[28] Not surprisingly, it was the Federalists who proved most hostile to anonymity and were the most frequent targets of anonymous attacks. Nevertheless, anonymous speech flourished and ultimately shaped aspects of our early constitutional and political debates.

II. Anonymity, Spontaniety, and Ambiguity: The Court's Uncertain Treatment of the Identification of Speakers and Solicitors

The historical use of anonymous speech strongly suggests that the Framers originally viewed anonymity as a vital part of free speech and freedom of the press. This relative historical clarity has been met with persistent judicial ambiguity over the place of anonymous speech in the First Amendment. Indeed, the right to anonymity is a subject that the Supreme Court has treated with almost coquettish regard, neither formally establishing the right nor allowing its abrogation. While the Court has repeatedly struck down laws that stripped citizens of anonymous speech, it has also permitted the abridgement of this right under certain circumstances. This has led to continual debate as to whether this is a true "right" that triggers the strictest scrutiny or some lesser type of constitutional value that informs but does not control a constitutional interpretation.[29] This uncertainty can be traced to Court decisions that often note the dangers of compelled identity disclosure but actually decide the merits on a more general First Amendment theory or an alternative constitutional provision. This was the case in *Lovell v. Griffen*[30] in which Alma Lovell was imprisoned for failing to pay a $50 fine for distributing a magazine entitled *Golden Age*, which contained religious material proselytizing Jehovah's Witnesses. The city of Griffen had an ordinance requiring a license to distribute any printed material. The Court viewed the issue as a restriction on the right to circulate or distribute literature as central to the First Amendment. The Court specifically noted the failure of the city to tailor the restrictions so as not to prohibit unlicensed distribution "of any kind

---

[28] *McIntyre*, 514 U.S. at 363.

[29] This ambiguity has been carried over to appellate and district court opinions that refer to anonymity as "an aspect of free speech." Wasson v. Sonoma County Junior Coll., 203 F.3d 659, 663 (9th Cir. 2000).

[30] 303 U.S. 444 (1938).

at any time, at any place, and in any manner."[31] While noting the danger of licensing schemes in history and the importance of every type of publication in "defense of liberty," the Court avoided a direct establishment of a right to anonymity.

In later cases the Court repeatedly confronted unconstitutional statutes restricting anonymous speech and repeatedly avoided the issue in favor of alternative constitutional theories. In *N.A.A.C.P. v. Alabama*,[32] such a case presented itself when Alabama sought to force the NAACP (National Association for the Advancement of Colored People) to reveal the names and addresses of its members—a disclosure that could have resulted in beatings and lynchings in 1958.[33] The Court viewed the disclosure requirement as impinging on freedom of association. Protecting the "privacy" interests of the members, the Court noted that it is "hardly a novel perception that compelled disclosure of affiliation with groups engaged in advocacy may constitute [an] effective restraint on freedom of association."[34] Anonymity was a question relevant to the maintenance of "[e]ffective advocacy"[35] and meaningful association rather than a concern in its own right. The Court again avoided a direct reliance on the right to anonymity in *Bates v. City of Little Rock*,[36] in which the NAACP violated a membership disclosure requirement under a different ordinance. The Court focused on the right of association and membership disclosure ordinances as simply a "more subtle [form of] governmental interference" with that right.[37]

This ambiguity might have come to an end in 1960, in *Talley v. California*,[38] when the Court considered an ordinance that prohibited the distribution of anonymous handbills in Los Angeles. The handbill in question was on behalf of the "National Consumers Mobilization" and sought a boycott of named businesses that would not

---

[31] *Id.* at 451.

[32] 357 U.S. 449 (1958).

[33] *Id.* at 462 (noting that "on past occasions revelation of the identity of its rank-and-file members [had] exposed these members to economic reprisal, loss of employment, threat of physical coercion, and other manifestations of public hostility.").

[34] *Id.* at 462.

[35] *Id.* at 460.

[36] 361 U.S. 516 (1960).

[37] *Id.* at 486.

[38] 362 U.S. 60 (1960).

"offer equal employment opportunities to Negroes, Mexicans, and Orientals." It also solicited members for the organization. Talley's failure to include the required names and addresses of the author, printer, and distributor resulted in a conviction and a $10 fine. *Talley* was in some respects the perfect anonymous speech case with all of the elements that concern those supportive of this right. First, the case involved both speech and association components. Second, the anonymous advocacy was the work of an organization and a cause that was intensely unpopular in some quarters in the 1960s. Third, the content of the speech could pose a social and economic risk for the authors, printers, and distributors if identified. Finally, the case involved a state interest that is characteristically broad in barring anonymity to prevent "fraud, deceit, false advertising, negligent use of words, obscenity, and libel." The fact that the speech dealt with racial discrimination at the height of the Civil Rights period magnified these concerns. Perhaps for this reason, the Court voted 6–3 to strike down the law as facially unconstitutional. However, the Court failed to embrace the notion of a free-standing right to anonymity and instead employed what would become a characteristic (and maddening) level of ambiguity. Justice Hugo Black seemed to studiously avoid recognizing a right of anonymity while strongly defending anonymity as a condition needed for free speech. The Court crafted its language to refer to restrictions that would harass or deter speech. The Court simply held that

> [t]here can be no doubt that such an identification requirement would tend to restrict freedom to distribute information and thereby freedom of expression. Liberty of circulating is as essential to that freedom as liberty of publishing; indeed, without the circulation, the publication would be of little value.[39]

As in later cases, the Court went on to recognize the historical role of anonymous speech but it did so to reinforce the importance of its holding and not as the specific right abridged. The Court observed that "[i]t is plain that anonymity has sometimes been assumed for the most constructive purposes."[40] Nevertheless, the Court stressed

---

[39] *Id.* at 64.
[40] *Id.*

the "important role in the progress of mankind"[41] played by anonymous publications. Black noted that "persecuted groups and sects from time to time throughout history have been able to criticize oppressive practices and laws either anonymously or not at all."[42] In this way, *Talley* established that the mandatory disclosure of identity as a prerequisite for speech runs afoul of the First Amendment—as a restriction generally on speech as opposed to a right to speak anonymously.

Despite the ambiguity of such cases, the Supreme Court has repeatedly identified anonymity as a vital component to both free speech and association. If this were the extent of the Court's precedent, it would leave a strong presumption, at minimum, that the statutes barring anonymous speech were unconstitutional. However, the Court verged sharply away from this position in *Buckley v. Valeo*[43] in which it upheld reporting and disclosure requirements for political contributors in the Federal Election Campaign Act of 1971. There, the Court accepted that the federal law requiring disclosure of contributors would chill some speech. Nevertheless, it found the statute to be constitutional given the strong governmental interests in detecting and deterring corruption.[44] Despite its holdings in cases like *NAACP v. Alabama*,[45] the Court insisted that the countervailing interest in the "free functioning of our national institutions" could outweigh such rights.[46] As for the right to anonymity, the Court was silent and gave only passing reference to *Talley*. Once again, the fate of the anonymous speech seemed uncertain, if not dim.

The fortunes of this fledging right were reversed roughly 20 years later in the Court's decision in *McIntyre v. Ohio Elections Commission*.[47] While lingering in the darkness of past cases, anonymity was directly at issue in the question before the Court: "whether and to what

---

[41] *Id.* at 65.

[42] *Id.* at 64.

[43] *424 U.S. 1 (1976).*

[44] *Id.* at 67; *see also id.* at 68 ("disclosure requirements ... appear to be the least restrictive means of curbing the evils of campaign ignorance and corruption that Congress found to exist.").

[45] 357 U.S. 449 (1958); *see also* Brown v. Socialist Workers '74 Campaign Comm. (Ohio), 459 U.S. 87 (1982).

[46] *Id.* at 66.

[47] 514 U.S. 334 (1995).

extent the First Amendment's protection of anonymity encompasses documents intended to influence the electoral process."[48] The specific controversy involved an Ohio statute requiring that writings used in elections bear the name and address of the individual or individuals responsible for the communication. Margaret McIntyre's advocacy was the prototypical example of anonymous and spontaneous speech. Opposed to a new school tax levy, she prepared a leaflet on her home computer and passed out copies of it at various meetings. After a long fight over the levy, a school official who supported the levy filed a charge against McIntyre that resulted in a $100 fine.

Justice Stevens placed anonymity at the heart of the controversy and stressed its importance as a prerequisite for speech in some cases. Stevens noted that the motivation for anonymous speech may be to avoid social ostracism, to prevent retaliation, or to protect privacy. It may also be used by an unpopular individual "to ensure that readers will not prejudge her message simply because they do not like its proponent."[49] It is anonymous speech that shields individuals "from the tyranny of the majority . . . [It] protect[s] unpopular individuals from retaliation—and their ideas from suppression—at the hand of an intolerant society."

In *McIntyre*, the Supreme Court magnified the significance of *Talley* as a case defending anonymous speech. Although Stevens recognized that the Court had limited anonymous speech in *Buckley*, a distinction was drawn between the regulation of candidate elections versus issues like a school tax. Stevens noted that "[t]hough such mandatory reporting undeniably impedes protected First Amendment activity, the intrusion is a far cry from compelled self-identification on all election-related writings. A written election-related document—particularly a leaflet—is often a personally crafted statement of a political viewpoint."[50]

Despite the powerful language, however, the most that Stevens would say about anonymous speech as a constitutional matter is that "an author's decision to remain anonymous, like other decisions concerning omissions or additions to the content of a publication,

[48] *Id.* at 344.
[49] *Id.* at 343.
[50] *Id.* at 445.

is an aspect of the freedom of speech protected by the First Amendment."[51] In this way, Justice Stevens fell just short in *McIntyre* of recognizing a right to anonymity—a fact not missed by Justice Clarence Thomas. Thomas concurred in the decision but objected to the ambiguity in the Court's treatment of anonymous speech. Thomas placed the real question in sharp relief and offered a refreshing and long-overdue recognition of the right to anonymity. "Instead of asking whether 'an honorable tradition' of anonymous speech has existed throughout American history or what the 'value' of anonymous speech may be," Thomas wrote, "we should determine whether the phrase 'freedom of speech, or of the press,' as originally understood, protected anonymous political leafleting. I believe that it did."[52] Thomas viewed the issue as one of original meaning and, although there is no record of any discussion of anonymity in the First Congress, the original meaning of terms like "press" appear to include anonymous publishing. Thomas correctly noted that the Framers referred to a variety of independent publishers and pamphleteers as "the press," including those who published anonymous writings.[53] Detailing this historical record, including thwarted attacks on anonymous writing, Thomas criticized the majority for failing to directly deal with the question as one of original meaning.

Thomas's view was answered in an equally strong and well-written dissent by Justice Scalia (and joined by Chief Justice William Rehnquist). Scalia objected to relying on historical practice as a misleading and uncertain basis for protecting anonymity either as a right or as a dominant value under the First Amendment. Scalia noted that "to prove that anonymous electioneering was used frequently is not to establish that it is a constitutional right."[54] Scalia further noted that earlier anonymous speech cases involved questions of punishing speech in which anonymity was a mere collateral issue.[55] Noting that every state except California had legislation similar to Ohio's, Scalia denounced the imposition of a new constitutional

[51] *Id.* at 342.
[52] *Id.* at 359.
[53] *Id.* at 360.
[54] *Id.* at 374.
[55] *Id.* at 375.

"value" that would undo a widely accepted view of the First Amendment. In Scalia's view, the decision effectively created a right to anonymity and "[t]he silliness that follows upon a generalized right to anonymous speech has no end."[56] Finally, discussing *Buckley*, Scalia observed that the Court had not adopted inherently conflicting positions on anonymity and had avoided this conflict by ignoring the extent of the loss of anonymity under its prior holding.[57] Ultimately, Scalia concluded that the decision to strike down the Ohio law "on the ground that all anonymous communication in our society is traditionally sacrosanct, seems . . . a distortion of the past that will lead to a coarsening of the future."[58]

Whether *McIntyre* created a de facto right to anonymity would remain a question for academic debate.[59] However, it was clear that the Court viewed anonymity as a critical component of speech under the First Amendment. This was clear in the Court's 1999 decision in *Buckley v. American Constitutional Law Foundation.*[60] In this case, the Court struck down provisions of Colorado's law governing ballot initiatives and specifically the signature-gathering process. Writing for the majority, Justice Ginsburg reaffirmed the Court's view that petition circulation is a "core" element of political speech. The Court relied on *McIntyre* to invalidate the badge requirement provision in the law as inimical to anonymity. The Court distinguished between an affidavit submitted to the agency and a badge identifying an individual who is interacting with other citizens:

> Unlike a name badge worn at the time a circulator is soliciting signatures, the affidavit is separated from the moment the circulator speaks. As the Tenth Circuit explained, the name badge requirement "forces circulators to reveal their identities at the same time they deliver their political message," . . . it operates when reaction to the circulator's message is immediate and "may be the most intense, emotional, and unreasoned." The affidavit, in contrast, does not expose the circulator to the risk of "heat of the moment" harassment.

[56] *McIntyre*, 514 U.S. at 381 (Scalia, J. dissenting).

[57] *Id.* at 384.

[58] *Id.*

[59] *See* Jonathan Turley, *Anonymous Advocacy at Risk*, NAT'L L. J., April 1, 2002, at A20.

[60] 525 U.S. 182 (1999).

> [T]he restraint on speech in this case is more severe than
> was the restraint in *McIntyre*. Petition circulation is the less
> fleeting encounter, for the circulator must endeavor to per-
> suade electors to sign the petition. . . . The injury to speech
> is heightened for the petition circulator because the badge
> requirement compels personal name identification at the pre-
> cise moment when the circulator's interest in anonymity is
> greatest.[61]

Much like the analysis of *Watchtower* discussed below, the Court
was ambiguous on the level of scrutiny or its application to specific
provisions in invalidating the provisions. The Court used a maddening array of expressions that studiously avoided a clear standard.
It was Justice Thomas who identified this problem in his concurrence
and argued that the Court should have applied a strict scrutiny
standard when a state imposed such "severe burdens" on speech.
The only indication that the Court was in fact applying such a
standard came in a footnote in response to Thomas, but (perhaps
to maintain its precarious alliance of justices) the Court left the
matter intentionally ambiguous.[62]

These cases offered advocates of anonymous speech a sense of
protection while clearly recognizing the place of anonymity in the
core rights of speech, religion, and association. Given the strong
combination of *Talley* and *McIntyre*, it was long predicted that the
Court was close to establishing a "right to anonymity" and, when
the Court accepted *Watchtower v. Village of Stratton*, it appeared that
this constitutional value might finally ripen into a constitutional
right.

III. *Watchtower v. Village of Stratton*: Protecting the Exercise of, if Not the Right to, Anonymous Speech

The two greatest contributors to constitutional interpretation in
our history may be Chief Justice John Marshall and the Jehovah's

---

[61]*Id.* at 199–200.

[62] As in other speech cases, the majority was met with a strong dissent from Chief
Justice Rehnquist. Rehnquist contested the majority's statistical studies indicating
that such rules discourage participation in the political system and further questioned
the constitutional significance of such a finding.

Witnesses. The latter have actively and successfully resisted restrictions on their rights of speech, religion, and association for decades.[63] Many of these struggles produced important precedent that has benefited the entire population to a degree that most laypersons are entirely unaware.[64] Mention the Jehovah's Witnesses,[65] and most people immediately think of preachers visiting our homes at inconvenient hours. For the Jehovah's Witnesses, proselytizing door-to-door is not simply to advance their faith but the very article of faith. Founded by Charles Taze Russell in 1875,[66] Jehovah's Witnesses read various biblical passages[67] to require such individual preaching, particularly passages like Matthew 28:19–20, where Jesus went house-to-house to preach.[68] For that reason, Jehovah's Witnesses often refer to themselves as "publishers."[69] Biblical passages also prevented the Jehovah's Witnesses from participating in oaths of allegiance and other forms of patriotic expression. This belief led to well-known acts of repression in the United States. However, the

---

[63] *See generally* WILLIAM KAPLAN, STATE AND SALVATION: THE JEHOVAH'S WITNESSES AND THEIR FIGHT FOR CIVIL RIGHTS (1989); William Shepard McAninch, *A Catalyst for the Evolution of Constitutional Law: Jehovah's Witnesses in the Supreme Court*, 55 U. CINN. L. REV. 997 (1987).

[64] *See, e.g.,* Thomas v. Review Bd. of Ind. Employment, 450 U.S. 707 (1981); 430 U.S. 705 (1977); Murdock v. Pennsylvania, 319 U.S. 105 (1943); Jones v. City of Opelika, 316 U.S. 584 (1942); Cantwell v. Connecticut, 310 U.S. 296 (1940).

[65] The term Jehovah's Witnesses was not actually adopted by the church until 1931. Before that date, they were known variously in 1884 as "Zion's Watch Tower Society"; in 1896 as 'Watch Tower Bible and Tract Society"; or more generally as "Russellites." *See* McAninch, *supra*, at 1004. The term is based on the repeated reference to Jehovah in the Bible and the passage in John 18:37 where Jesus Christ tells Pontius Pilate: "To this end was I born, and for the cause came I into the world, that I should bear witness unto the truth." *See generally* Gabriele Yonan, *Spiritual Resistance of Christian Conviction in Nazi Germany: The Case of the Jehovah's Witnesses*, 41 J. CHURCH & STATE 307 (1999). They also rely on the passage of Isaiah in which God states "Ye are my witnesses, said Jehovah."

[66] There remains some debate on this point since Russell technically established the "Bible Students" in 1872 and many Russell followers split off from the church after his death and the establishment of Joseph Rutherford as president. *See* Kenneth Rawson, *Pastor Charles Taze Russell*, JERUSALEM POST, Jan. 6, 1993. It was Rutherford in 1931 who created the term Jehovah's Witnesses.

[67] These include Isaiah 43:9–12; Matthew 10:7, 12; Acts 20:20; 1 Peter 2:21 and 1 Corinthians 9:11.

[68] *Watchtower*, 122 S. Ct. at 2085 n.7.

[69] McAninch, *supra*, at 1005.

Jehovah's Witnesses faced even worse treatment at the hands of the Nazi and Imperial Japanese governments. Refusing to say "Heil Hitler" or even to bow to the Emperor Hirohito led to the torture and killing of thousands of Jehovah's Witnesses.[70] The religion's apocalyptic predictions,[71] anti-Catholic statements,[72] and neutral position in the major wars led to direct oppression by the U.S. government.[73] Despite this persecution, including recent hostile acts by governments,[74] the church has grown to include millions around the world.[75]

When the Village of Stratton, Ohio, enacted Ordinance No. 1998-5, the Jehovah's Witnesses found it all too familiar, including evidence of specific hostility against their faith by the mayor.[76] The ordinance required that anyone "going in and upon" any private residence for any "cause" would have to obtain a "solicitation permit." Although there was no charge for the permit, the "solicitor" was required to fill out a "Solicitor's Registration Form" that included identification information as well as the names of residents who would be visited. The solicitor was then required to carry the permit and produce it when asked. Although modified by the district

---

[70] *See generally* Carolyn R. Wah, *Jehovah's Witnesses and the Empire of the Sun: A Clash of Faith and Religion During World War II*, 44 J. CHURCH & STATE 45 (2002); Gabriele Yonan, *Spiritual Resistance of Christian Conviction in Nazi Germany: The Case of the Jehovah's Witnesses*, 41 J. CHURCH & STATE 307 (1999).

[71] Russell had predicted the "end of the Gentile times" would come in 1914. McAninch, *supra*, at 1006. Armageddon was again predicted for 1925 and then 1975. *Id.*

[72] The Roman Catholic Church was "pictured as a semiclad harlot reeling drunkenly into fire and brimstone." McAninch, *supra*, at 1006.

[73] This included widespread arrests and seizure of property. McAninch, *supra*, at 1006.

[74] This includes the decision of the French government that the Jehovah's Witnesses do not constitute a true religion but rather a "dangerous sect." Larry Witham, *Jehovah's Witnesses Fight Taxes in France; Probe Decided Sect Is Not Religion*, WASH. TIMES, July 1, 1998, at A1.

[75] *See* Linda Tagliaferro, *Jehovah's Witnesses Hold Forth at Coliseum*, N.Y. TIMES, July 11, 1999, at 2. The Jehovah's Witnesses claim roughly 15 million members worldwide. Wiham, *supra* note 74, at A1.

[76] *Watchtower*, 122 S. Ct. at 2085. (noting that evidence was introduced "that the ordinance was the product of the mayor's hostility to their ministry, but the District Court credited the mayor's testimony that it had been designed to protect privacy rights of the Village residents.").

court, the ordinance also prohibited solicitation after 5:00 P.M.[77] Like many of the laws addressed earlier, the Stratton ordinance was expressly based on broad justifications of protecting citizens from "fraud and undue annoyance" and criminal violations.

A split panel of the United States Court of Appeals for the Sixth Circuit found this basis to be sufficient.[78] Judge Cornelia G. Kennedy viewed the regulation as subject to standard time, place, and manner analysis. As a content neutral regulation, the court applied an intermediate standard.[79] Judge Ronald Lee Gilman dissented. Although Gilman viewed the intermediate standard to be the appropriate standard, he disagreed with its application to these facts. In Gilman's view the "ordinance violates the First Amendment by burdening substantially more speech than is necessary to further the Village's legitimate interests."[80] As it turns out, the appellate court paid far greater attention to methodology and standards than would be the case before the Supreme Court.

Justice Stevens wrote for the majority of eight justices.[81] Stevens traced the Court's protection of door-to-door canvassing and pamphleteering over the prior 50 years. Remarkably, Stevens, the author of *McIntyre*, spent little time discussing the protection of anonymous speech. Referring to "anonymity interests" under the First Amendment, Stevens cited this intrusion as one of three "examples" of the "pernicious effect of such a permit requirement."[82] In the one paragraph committed to this interest, Stevens expressly noted that such interests can be abridged, but that the ordinance "sweeps more

---

[77] The district court ordered that this be changed to "reasonable hours of the day" and also removed the requirement that every resident be listed. It then found the ordinance to be constitutional in a rather curious interpretation. It is hard to see how these small modifications would cure the constitutional violation recognized by the court.

[78] Watchtower Bible and Tract Society v. Vill. of Stratton, 240 F.3d 553 (6th Cir. 2001).

[79] *Watchtower*, 240 F.3d at 561 ("our review of the ordinance leads us to conclude it is content neutral and of general applicability . . . [a] law is content neutral and of general applicability if on its face and in its purpose it does not make a distinction between favored and disfavored speech.").

[80] *Id.* at 570.

[81] This included a concurrence by Justice Breyer, joined by Justices Souter and Ginsburg, and a concurrence by Justice Scalia, joined by Justice Thomas.

[82] 122 S. Ct. at 2089.

broadly, covering unpopular causes unrelated to commercial transactions or to any special interest in protecting the electoral process."[83] It was the lack of tailoring in the ordinance that was the most cited reason for its downfall. Indeed, in a strong signal for the next case in this area, Stevens notes that "[h]ad this provision been construed to apply only to commercial activities and the solicitation of funds, arguably the ordinance would have been tailored to the Village's interest in protecting privacy of its residents and preventing fraud."[84] Although vague on the specific constitutional standard and basis used to reach this result, the majority found the ordinance to be "offensive—not only to the values protected by the First Amendment, but to the very notion of a free society."[85] Both speech and religion concerns are implicated by such ordinances. Moreover, in the area of speech rights, Stevens notes that one interest is not simply anonymity but spontaneity. The ordinance is cited as barring the most genuine forms of neighbor-to-neighbor political speech by requiring a trip to a village office and the completion of an application for a permit.

The two concurring opinions did not significantly add to the majority decision. A concurrence by Justice Breyer (with Justices Souter and Ginsburg) is only a one-page response to the sole dissenter, Chief Justice Rehnquist. Breyer criticized Rehnquist for relying heavily on a crime prevention justification that was not advanced by the village. "In the intermediate scrutiny context," Breyer stated, "the Court ordinarily does not supply reasons the legislative body has not given."[86] The concurrence by Justice Scalia (with Justice Thomas) was even more pointed. Scalia objected to the language that some individuals "would prefer silence to speech licensed by a petty official."[87] Such language, according to Scalia, only suggests protection for fringe beliefs over otherwise valid regulations:

---

[83] *Id.* at 2090.

[84] *Id.* at 2089.

[85] *Id.*

[86] *Id.* at 2091 (Breyer, J., concurring).

[87] *Id.* at 2092 (Scalia, J., concurring). It is telling that the specific importance of anonymity is not emphasized by either the majority or the concurring justices to any significant degree. The fact that Scalia and Thomas (the combatants in the *McIntyre* decision) joined in a concurrence indicates that no "right to anonymity" was seen as established by the majority decision.

> If a licensing requirement is otherwise lawful, it is in my view not invalidated by the fact that some people will choose, for religious reasons, to forgo speech rather than observe it. That would convert an invalid free-exercise claim . . . into a valid free-speech claim—and a more destructive one at that. Whereas the free-exercise claim, if acknowledged, would merely exempt Jehovah's Witnesses from the licensing requirement, the free-exercise claim exempts *everybody*, thanks to Jehovah's Witnesses.
>
> As for the Court's fairy-tale category of "patriotic citizens" . . . who would rather be silenced than licensed in a manner that the Constitution (but for their "patriotic" objection) would permit: If our free-speech jurisprudence is to be determined by the predicted behavior of such crackpots, we are in a sorry state indeed.[88]

As he had in cases like *Buckley v. American Constitutional Law Association* and *McIntyre*, Chief Justice Rehnquist dissented over the sweep of the Court's holding in uprooting long-standing state interests and laws. Rehnquist emphasized what he viewed as a clear crime prevention interest behind the ordinance and took judicial notice of a recent murder of two Dartmouth College professors. The professors, Rehnquist noted, were killed by teenagers posing as door-to-door canvassers conducting an environmental survey for school. Rehnquist objected that the Court was ignoring a long line of cases that explicitly or implicitly recognized the right of a state to regulate solicitation in the interests of crime prevention. Rehnquist correctly brings the majority up short on the same failure that was evident in *Buckley v. American Constitutional Law Association*: the failure to state a clear standard for review of such violations. Rehnquist insists that such regulations should be handled under the Court's prior holdings relating to time, place, and manner regulations. As such, Rehnquist argued that "[t]here is no support in our case law for applying more stringent than intermediate scrutiny to the ordinance."[89] Rehnquist notably does not view the case as turning on anonymity, a subject on which he had previously expressed strong opposition in his dissent with Scalia in *McIntyre*. Rather, the issue was for Rehnquist a simple application of intermediate scrutiny and

[88] *Id.* (internal citations omitted).

[89] *Id.* at 2094 (Rehnquist, C.J., dissenting).

the rule that "[a] discretionless permit requirement for canvassers does not violate the First Amendment."[90]

There was much in these decisions to encourage those who advocate the right of anonymity and those who believe in a robust protection of speech and association. However, *Watchtower* is more notable in maintaining a trend of ambiguity over the standard protecting the "interest" in anonymity. As will be discussed, this trend appears quite intentional —a by-product of the politics of the Court rather than legal theory or philosophy.

IV. The Importance of Being Anonymous: A Right in Search of a Rationale

Anonymity is a value that is often viewed with considerable suspicion today. Privacy and anonymity are under attack in a society that is increasingly subject to a variety of governmental and private tracking and surveillance systems. The use of the Social Security number as an effective national identifier has led to massive data banks and the potential for real-time tracking systems.[91] Private and governmental surveillance cameras have become commonplace and can be found on highways, convenience stores, workplaces, and virtually every destination outside of the home.[92] As we develop a type of fishbowl society, the expectations of citizens regarding privacy and anonymity have diminished sharply. Given the centrality of the "reasonable expectation of privacy" in protecting citizens, this trend may have significant effects in the criminal area. In the area of speech, the expectation of anonymity has eroded under the same pressures as the expectation of privacy. The one exception has proven to be the Internet where anonymous communications are one of the great draws of users. This produces an increasing conflict among young citizens on the question. When *Watchtower* was still

---

[90] *Id.* at 2097.

[91] This subject was discussed recently in the context of the proposed national identification card. *See Oversight Hearing on National Identification Cards Before the Subcomm. on Government Management, Information, and Technology of the House Committee on Government Reform*, 107th Cong. (Sept. 16, 2002) (testimony of Professor Jonathan Turley); *see also* Jonathan Turley, *National ID: Beware What You Wish For*, L.A. TIMES, January 9, 2002, at A11.

[92] *See* Lisa Guernsey, *Living Under an Electronic Eye*, N.Y. TIMES, Sept. 27, 2001, at 1 (discussing various new surveillance measures in society).

under consideration, the case was debated in my *The Supreme Court and the Constitution* class. Many law students expressed skepticism over the value of door-to-door solicitation and seemed willing to curtail anonymous speech for the least showing of government interest. Yet, when the question turned to the Internet, students argued strongly in favor of a right to anonymity. This argument reflects a shift in the center of gravity for speech in the United States from in-person advocacy to a type of virtual democracy. The solicitor who goes door-to-door is viewed as an annoyance, if not an anachronism, by many students. The effect of this generational shift is difficult to gauge. However, regardless of the forum, there remain compelling interests that are protected by a right to anonymity.

1. Protection from Persecution. Anonymity allows speech where identification would chill or deter speech for some citizens.[93] Persecution may come from associating with an unpopular group like socialists or from advocating an unpopular cause like opposition to a war. The Court has recognized that "anonymity is a shield from the tyranny of the majority."[94] Putting aside the social benefit of such speech (discussed below), this protection guarantees the very conditions needed for speech.

2. Preventing Disenfranchisement. Many citizens in history have faced marginalization in society because of their religious beliefs, race, social standing, or political viewpoints. For such citizens, participation in public debate is severely limited by social stereotyping or unpopularity. Anonymity becomes the avenue through which they can continue to enjoy the most cherished element of citizenship: participation in social and political debates. For a socialist or an anti-war protester, an anonymous flier allows their views and ideas to be considered without the heavy baggage of an unpopular identification. Such a right protects the general speech and association rights of such individuals by assuring them that unpopular stands will not necessarily cut off their access to participatory politics. It also increases the ideas and values that are offered in public debate;

---

[93] This need for anonymity was stressed by Justice Hugo Black who noted that "persecuted groups and sects from time to time throughout history have been able to criticize oppressive practices and laws either anonymously or not at all." Talley v. California, 362 U.S. 60, 64 (1960).

[94] *McIntyre*, 514 U.S. at 357.

allowing worthy ideas to work through the filter of personalities. For example, in the 1930s and 1940s, socialists in the United States argued for many policies that are now considered mainstream like worker safety laws and minimum wage statutes. Yet, associating with a socialist organization was viewed as so stigmatizing that such identification limited the reach of any proposal in society. Anonymity untethers such ideas from their sources and prevents some individuals from being rendered effectively inactive in the exercise of their speech rights.

3. *Encouraging Pluralistic Values and Thoughts.* American society is rich precisely because it is pluralistic and diverse. From the very founding of the Republic, this nation was established to allow and foster a variety of faiths and views. Although other nations viewed such diversity and heterogeneity as a weakness, we viewed it as a strength. Moreover, it is easy for those in the majority to belittle the need for anonymity of some people to express their views fully to other citizens. Although Justice Scalia has characterized as "crackpots" those people who would rather be silenced than licensed in some circumstances, today's social crackpots often turn into tomorrow's political prophets.

4. *Protecting Spontaneity.* One of the least appreciated interests in the area of free speech is spontaneity. In some ways, spontaneous speech is a barometer of the condition of free speech rights in a society. The degree to which an individual feels free to speak in a spontaneous and unrehearsed manner is a good measure of a society's success in protecting the expression of ideas. Moreover, spontaneous speech is often the most genuine. It is the type of speech that occurs between neighbors. It is the type of speech involved in the first-time expression of political views. It is the impulse to suddenly speak out on a question of personal import. Spontaneous speech is often anonymous. When people feel an urge to oppose a policy or law, they often act in the heat of the moment. They are people, like Ms. McIntyre, who quickly run off a flier venting their anger against a new tax or local decision. It is this spontaneous speech that may be the greatest bulwark against government abuse—petty and grand. It is the ability of a citizen to mount a one-person campaign that guarantees that contemporary debates are not controlled exclusively by the institutional press or the political system.

5. Enhancing Privacy Values. Anonymous speech is also tied to the privacy interests of citizens. Privacy is often perceived as the security of a home from invasion or as the confidentiality of communications. There is also an element of privacy in free speech despite the apparent contradiction. Obviously, people who advocate a public position expose themselves to the world, or at least a small part of it. Yet, some citizens withhold a part of their privacy in the form of their names. This may be due to the fear of reprisals. However, it may be due to a desire to separate their personal home life from their public advocacy. Moreover, the fear of identification in joining public debates undermines the more general notions of privacy. The attacks on the expectations of anonymity chill speech in the same way as attacks on the expectations of privacy.

6. Protecting Internet Speech. Anonymity has a particularly direct relationship to the most important avenue for speech invented since the printing press—the Internet. If Thomas Paine were alive today, the Great Pamphleteer would most likely turn to the Internet rather than the mainstream press to express his ideas. Internet speech is now the virtual town hall for individual public expression. Individuals who would once take a soapbox to London's Hyde Park would now go online to seek those of like minds. It is on the Internet that a lone wolf may become a pack leader. However, it is anonymity that gives this powerful form of unregulated speech such appeal. Anyone perusing the Internet will find every type of thought—some half-formed, others presented in detail. Missing, until recently, has been the threat of government surveillance. Even with such threats as the government's Carnivore system and surveillance,[95] it remains raw and uninhibited—and largely anonymous. The Internet is the one major development that runs against the trend toward greater control and surveillance over communications. It is a vital resource that must be protected as a form of individual expression. The protection of anonymity is the single most valuable factor in fostering

[95] Carnivore is an intelligence system that allows the government to intercept e-mail systems. This system has an obvious chilling effect on Internet speech as do other governmental efforts to tap into the Internet. Anick Jesdanun, *Privacy, Security, Censorship Among Upcoming Net Challenges*, SAN DIEGO UNION-TRIB., Dec. 26, 2000, at 7. Ironically, whatever value Carnivore would offer to the government has been limited by serious failures in its use. Dan Eggen, *Carnivore Glitches Blamed for FBI Woes*, WASH. POST, May 29, 2002, at A7.

Internet speech, and fostering Internet speech may be the single most valuable factor in the protection of free speech in the twenty-first century.

These interests were significantly advanced by the decision in *Watchtower*. Certainly, *Watchtower* strengthens the notion that identification requirements "extend beyond restrictions on time and place—they chill discussion itself."[96] However, the Court intentionally left anonymity as an "interest" that is clearly protected but poorly defined. The Court has repeatedly suggested that this interest will trigger a strict scrutiny analysis. In *Buckley v. American Constitutional Law Foundation*, the Court made passing reference to the higher standard in response to the challenge by Justice Thomas.[97] In *Watchtower*, Chief Justice Rehnquist noted that the Court suggested that "Stratton's regulation of speech warrants greater scrutiny" than intermediate scrutiny.[98] Although the appellate court in *Watchtower*, was, in my view, mistaken, it was far more methodical in identifying and explaining its application of intermediate scrutiny of a time, place, and manner regulation. The Court's reluctance to expressly establish this standard may reflect a box of its own creation. While seemingly applying the higher standard, the Court does not want to trigger an open confrontation with these cases. As a result, the Court simply rules on the outcome of these cases without articulating a clear justification.

In the area of anonymous speech, the Court's confused analysis over the relevant constitutional standard also reflects a coalition that comprises justices with wildly different views. This produces a judicial variation of "cycling majorities" that depend on the shifting facts and order of cases. Anonymous speech is highly illustrative of the problem. The coalition has comprised justices like Thomas and Scalia who take diametrically opposed views of a right to anonymity. These justices often agree only on the outcome of cases. In the absence of a clear constitutional interpretative position, these rulings appear to be instinctive judgments that border on legislative choices as to the value of and alternatives to state regulations. Of course, the area of anonymous speech is hardly unique. The division of the Court

[96] Hynes v. Mayor of Oradell, 425 U.S. 610, 628 (1976).

[97] *Id.* 525 U.S. at 192 n.12.

[98] *Id.* S. Ct. at 2094 (Rehnquist, C.J., dissenting).

has routinely produced decisions that contain maddening gaps and ambiguities. These opinions reflect the same phenomenon seen in legislative decisionmaking. It is common for Congress to knowingly leave gaps in legislation to secure the passage of a bill. Faced with opposition over a provision, the compromise is often to simply remove it without answering the underlying dispute. Often members hope that courts will gap-fill and remove the painful political choices from the legislative branch. However, the divided Court increasingly has used the same technique to secure its own slim majorities and pluralities. This is one of the reasons that I have criticized the current structure of a nine-justice Court.[99] The relatively small number of justices increases the likelihood of such tight votes and artificially elevates the importance of "swing" justices like O'Connor and Kennedy.[100] I have suggested increasing the size of the Court to as many as 19 members.[101] There are a variety of reasons for such an expansion,[102] but one of the most important is to diminish the political cycling systems of a small majority court.

The Court's ambiguous treatment of the relevant standard leaves uncertain whether mandatory identification requirements can be reviewed under a time, place, and manner precedent, as suggested by Chief Justice Rehnquist in *Watchtower*. This uncertainty leaves state and municipal officials confused over whether they must support such regulations under an intermediate or strict standard. Of course, protecting a right to anonymity may come at a social price.

---

[99] *See* Jonathan Turley, *Justice O'Connor Wields a Mighty Vote*, L.A. TIMES, July 4, 2002, at A17; *see also* Jonathan Turley, *Undoing a Stitch in Time: The Expansion of the Supreme Court in the Twenty-First Century*, Symposium on The Supreme Court and the Rule of Law, Perspectives on Political Science.

[100] The anonymity cases have not turned on 5–4 splits to the same extent as some other areas like the religion clause cases. *See* Zelman v. Simmons-Harris, ___ U.S.___, 122 S. Ct. 2460 (2002). However, the anonymity cases often reflect the highly generalized and uncertain language that has come to characterize decisions on this divided court.

[101] Such expansion of the Court's membership would be staggered over years to prevent a single president or Congress from stacking the Court.

[102] In addition to the problem of swing voting and cycling majorities, there are practical reasons for this expansion. It seems inevitable that we will increase the number of federal circuits in time. It is likely that we will end up with 16 to 18 circuits with a possible splitting of the Ninth Circuit. Increasing the size of the Supreme Court to 19 members would allow each circuit to have a single assigned justice without the current "doubling" the number of circuits assigned to each justice.

For example, some states have prohibited the wearing of masks or hoods to combat the hateful activities of the Ku Klux Klan. Here, courts like the Georgia Supreme Court have held that "when individuals engage in intimidating or threatening mask-wearing behavior, their interest in maintaining their anonymity . . . must give way to the weighty interests of the State."[103] A state cannot outlaw racist speech generally without violating the First Amendment. In the same fashion, it should not be able to criminalize the concealing of an identity while engaging in such protected speech. The fact that the Ku Klux Klan is an infamous and despicable organization does not alter the fact that citizens are allowed to engage in racist speech. In fact, protecting this type of speech is the main purpose of the First Amendment; there is less need to protect speech that is popular or valued. If protected expression is "the transcendent value to all society,"[104] anonymity is the prerequisite for much of this expression. It would obviously be a great social benefit to be rid of the type of hateful and ignorant views associated with groups like the Ku Klux Klan. However, the removal of such views from society will occur, if at all, through social debate and not governmental restrictions. Restrictions on anonymous speech only force some views underground where they fester and grow more extreme or violent. Of course, nothing prevents citizens from calling for advocates of hate speech to reveal themselves and not to hide behind hoods. Nor does anything prevent citizens from refusing to hear or consider any views that are offered anonymously. However, the decision to listen and the value of listening to anonymous speech are choices for individual citizens to make in carrying out their First Amendment activities. Hoods are threatening because they are tied to the content of the speech itself. They are a powerful symbol for both the wearer and the observer. The same may be true of cross-burning, which will be before the Court in the next term.[105] Such facts, however, only bring the expression closer to the core of the First Amendment.

[103] State v. Miller, 398 S.E.2d 547, 553 (Ga. 1990).

[104] Los Angeles Police Dep't v. United Reporting Publg. Corp., 528 U.S. 32, 38 (1999).

[105] In *Virginia v. Black*, No. 01-1107, the Court will consider Virginia's law prohibiting the burning of a cross with the intent to intimidate. Various states have similar such laws.

Both the abridgment of the right of anonymity and the use of content-based restrictions on speech are implicated in such cases.

It is quite likely that we will see another round of anonymity cases after *Watchtower*. The Court clearly indicated that some limitation of anonymous speech would be acceptable to the majority. If Stratton narrowly tailors its ordinance to commercial speech, the Court is poised to accept such a restriction as justified by a showing of a governmental interest to prevent fraud and abuse. The more worrisome possibility is an ordinance that restricts speech more broadly but is based more clearly on crime prevention. Justice Breyer's concurrence suggests that some members did not review the ordinance under this justification and criticized Chief Justice Rehnquist for his assuming such a rationale.[106] Justice Breyer noted that "[b]ecause Stratton did not rely on the crime prevention justification, because Stratton has not now 'present[ed] more than anecdote and supposition,' . . . and because the relationship between the interest and the ordinance is doubtful, I am unwilling to assume that these conjectured benefits outweigh the cost of abridging the speech covered by the ordinance."[107] Although there appears to be a strong majority that would have overturned the ordinance even with such a suggested governmental purpose, the exchange between Chief Justice Rehnquist and Justice Breyer leaves a lingering question as to whether an ordinance based on crime prevention would have garnered more support. Clearly, any such attempt will be met with some skepticism if the ordinance touches on political or religious speech.[108] Yet, there is enough in this opinion to give hope to those who either oppose the right to anonymity or desire to curtail door-to-door advocacy. For that reason, *Watchtower* may be the prelude

---

[106] Justice Breyer noted that the rationales advanced below were described by the district court and appellate court as deterring "flim-flam con artists" and "protecting residents from fraud and undue annoyance." Watchtower, 122 S. Ct. at 2091 (Breyer, J., concurring).

[107] *Id.* at 2092.

[108] Justice Breyer noted that both the scope and purpose of such an ordinance would be closely scrutinized:"It is . . . intuitively implausible to think that Stratton's ordinance serves any governmental interest in preventing such crimes. As the Court notes, several categories of potential criminals will remain entirely untouched by the ordinance. . . . And as to those who might be affected by it, "[w]e have never accepted mere conjecture as adequate to carry a First Amendment burden." *Id.* (internal qoutations and citations omitted).

to a more fundamental showdown over the status of anonymous speech.

V. Conclusion

For those who believe in a right to anonymity, *Watchtower* can only be viewed as a significant and positive development. The combination of *Watchtower, Buckley,* and *McIntyre* offer strong and relatively consistent support for the practice of anonymous speech. What is missing is a clear foundational principle and standard as advocated by Justice Thomas in his concurrence to *McIntyre.* Anonymous speech is an example of the realpolitik that has reigned on this Court during its years of 5–4 divisions. Majorities are often secured on the conclusions rather than the principles of a case. It is clear that the majority of justices do not want to undermine anonymous speech. The isolation of Chief Justice Rehnquist as the sole strong dissent in *Watchtower* reflects this general agreement. However, this unified façade is misleading. Chief Justice Rehnquist was correct in his criticism of the imprecision in the language and standards used by the Court. He saw a majority that was bound only by the loose convenience of a decision that strived to reach the "right outcome." The failure of the Court to be clearer on the foundations and standard for a right to anonymity leaves a dangerous ambiguity when privacy and confidentiality are under increased attack. Just as the Court succeeded recently in reinforcing the long-neglected right of association,[109] it was hoped that it would draw a bright line of protection around anonymous speech. It may still do so. With the combination of these cases, the Court is inching closer to a clear and unambiguous recognition of anonymity, not as an "aspect" or a "condition," but as a right of free speech and freedom of the press.

Anonymity is an issue for our time. As we increasingly yield to the countless demands for increased surveillance and monitoring, the fight over anonymity reminds us of what we may have lost in the crush of technology and modern life. One of the greatest liabilities of a democracy is the danger that majoritarian authority will coerce citizens into silence or acquiescence. Forcing some people into the

---

[109] Boy Scouts of America v. Dale, 530 U.S. 640 (2000) (allowing the Boy Scouts to bar a gay scoutmaster); Jonathan Turley, *Of Boy Scouts and Bigots,* CHICAGO TRIB., June 30, 2000, at A27 (supporting the Court's holding in *Boy Scouts of America v. Dale*).

light may just force many ideas into the darkness. This could come at considerable cost for society. History has shown that it is sometimes those individuals on the very edge of our society who possess the greatest insights or clearest perspective of contemporary problems. In some ways, by protecting the right to anonymity, a society maximizes the likelihood that its collective decisions will be challenged and tested. As counterintuitive as that may seem for some countries, it is the very essence of the American experiment with democratic rule.

Judicial Elections and the First Amendment: Freeing Political Speech

James L. Swanson

Introduction

In *Republican Party of Minnesota v. White*,[1] an important but under-reported case,[2] the Supreme Court protected freedom of political speech by ruling that candidates campaigning for election possess a constitutional right to announce their views on "disputed legal and political issues." Such a result might seem obvious, an unlikely topic for disagreement, and one hardly in need of judicial affirmation more than two centuries after the Bill of Rights, including the First Amendment, became law.[3] Thus, the opinion of the Court provokes the obvious question: Prior to *Republican Party of Minnesota*, didn't

---

[1]122 S. Ct. 2528 (2002).

[2]Several cases from the October Term 2001 involving highly publicized issues including school choice (*Zelman v. Simmons-Harris*, 122 S. Ct. 2460), child pornography (*Ashcroft v. Free Speech Coalition*, 122 S. Ct. 1389), obscenity (*Ashcroft v. ACLU*, 122 S. Ct. 1700), takings (*Tahoe-Sierra Preservation Council Inc. v. Tahoe Regional Planning Agency*, 122 S. Ct. 1465), high school drug testing (*Board of Education v. Earls*, 122 S. Ct. 2559), execution of the mentally retarded (*Atkins v. Virginia*, 122 S. Ct. 2242), civil rights (*Correctional Services v. Malesko*, 122 S. Ct. 515), criminal law (*Harris v. United States*, 122 S. Ct. 2406, among others), and federalism (*Federal Maritime Commission v. S.C. State Ports Authority*, 122 S. Ct. 1864) attracted significant attention from the media that overshadowed *Republican Party of Minnesota v. White*. A handful of stories did appear. *See, e.g.*, George F. Will, *Minnesota Speech Police*, Washington Post, January 3, 2002, at A17; Robert S. Greenberger, *Supreme Court to Decide on Judicial Candidates' Speech*, Wall St. J., March 12, 2002, at A28; Paul Rosenzweig, *Protecting Speech in Bench Elections*, Wash. Times, July 1, 2002, at A18; Mark Kozlowski, *Robed and Running*, Legal Times, July 8, 2002, at 35.

[3]The Virginia legislature ratified the first ten amendments to the Constitution on December 15, 1791, and was the last of the necessary eleven states to ratify the Bill of Rights. For that history, see Robert Allen Rutland, The Birth of the Bill of Rights, 1776–1791 (1955); Leonard W. Levy, Origins of the Bill of Rights (1999).

political candidates *already* have the right to discuss controversial issues?

For some candidates—those running for office in the legislative or executive branches of government—the answer is, "of course." But for another class of candidates—those running in state elections for office in the judicial branch—the answer was "no." The citizens of Minnesota elect their state court judges, but the government regulates what candidates are allowed to tell the voters.[4] Intentionally or not, Minnesota's censorship regime effected three anti-democratic results: elections without politics, campaigns without controversy, and candidates without free speech.

On June 27, 2002, the Supreme Court struck down the Minnesota prohibition barring judicial candidates from expressing their views on controversial legal and political issues, concluding that it violated the First Amendment. The decision represents a victory for freedom of speech, liberty, and democratic elections. The Court affirmed that in America we cannot have elections without politics, and we cannot have politics without robust and unfettered speech. Minnesota's attempt to sanitize its elections by gagging candidates deprived them of their right to express their views to the voters, and voters of the right to hear the views that would otherwise have been expressed. From a policy perspective, electing judges might be a bad idea. But once a state has chosen to elect its judges, candidates cannot be muzzled.

Although the Court reached the correct result, the opinion is troubling for several reasons that must give pause to First Amendment devotees. In what should have been an easy choice favoring free speech over censorship, the decision was a close 5–4 vote. In other words, the Court was one vote away from ruling that a candidate in a democratic election may not discuss disputed issues with the public. Even more troubling than the fact of the narrow majority is the content and tone of the dissent. Justice Ruth Bader Ginsburg, joined by Justice John Paul Stevens, who also wrote a separate dissent, simply ignores the Court's vast literature on the vital importance of political speech in American life. Both Ginsburg and Stevens

---

[4] The so-called "announce clause" prohibits a judicial candidate from "announc[ing] his or her views on disputed legal or political issues." MINN. CODE OF JUDICIAL CONDUCT, Canon 5(A)(3)(d)(i)2000. Candidates are also barred from holding office in political organizations, attending political party events, seeking party endorsements, or soliciting funds for a political organization. Canon 5(1)(a), (d), (e).

promote their favored policy, trumping the First Amendment in the process. Also troubling, Justice Antonin Scalia's opinion for the majority, although grounded solidly on core First Amendment principles, suggests that, in other contexts not before the Court in this case, some speech by candidates might be regulated. A more expansive opinion might have better served the principles of limited government and the First Amendment. As we shall see, Justice Anthony Kennedy's concurrence points the way.

Republican Party of Minnesota v. White is not, therefore, the simple case that at first blush it might appear to be. Instead, it resurrects disturbing issues from the history of political speech in America; it illuminates disagreement among the justices about the central meaning of the First Amendment; it suggests the hidden motives of those who seek to regulate campaign speech; and it foreshadows how the Court might apply the First Amendment to the next great political speech case on its horizon, the recently enacted and immediately challenged regime of campaign finance regulation.

The significance of *Republican Party of Minnesota* can be understood best by placing the case in the context of what has gone before it. Therefore, Part I of this essay revisits briefly how American history, the scholarly commentary, and the Supreme Court have treated political speech during the past two-hundred years. Part II explains the origins of the relatively recent conflict between judicial elections and the First Amendment. Part III analyzes how the Supreme Court resolved that conflict correctly in *Republican Party of Minnesota*, and then criticizes the dissent. Part IV explains that campaign speech regulation, in addition to violating the First Amendment, is also bad policy because it is impractical and anti-democratic. The essay concludes by arguing for a constitutional bulwark against campaign speech regulation even stronger than the Court has been willing to erect.

Part I: The Curious History of Political Speech

"Congress shall make no law . . . abridging the freedom of speech, or of the press; or of the right of the people peaceably to assemble, and to petition the Government for a redress of grievances."[5] The text is brief. Rarely in American history have so few words inspired

---

[5] U.S. CONST. amend. I.

the writing of so many. During the last two-hundred years the First Amendment has inspired hundreds of significant judicial opinions, a few thousand books, and countless law journal, magazine, and newspaper articles. A literature so vast suggests that the First Amendment has always occupied a central place in American law and life. If Americans know nothing else about constitutional law, they know that the First Amendment guarantees them freedom of speech. Or does it? History tells a different story.

A. Legacy of Suppression?

The First Amendment has had a precarious history. Flouted at the close of the 18th century by the Sedition Act,[6] and ineffective through most of the 19th century, the Amendment attained significance only in the modern era, from about 1919.[7] Scholars of the Constitution and the Bill of Rights have disagreed on what those documents meant during the founding era. In a path-breaking book Leonard Levy argued that it was a time of suppression, not classical liberalism, and that our modern understanding of freedom of speech and the press would have seemed alien to the late 18th century American mind.[8] The long-neglected and surprising story of free speech in 18th and 19th century America reveals that the right to political expression, which we take for granted today, was often in jeopardy and even dangerous to exercise.

---

[6] Act for the Punishment of Certain Crimes, 1 Stat. 596 (July 14, 1798). Passed by the House of Representatives on July 11, the Sedition Act became law when signed by President John Adams on July 14. For more on the Act, see JOHN C. MILLER, CRISIS IN FREEDOM: THE ALIEN AND SEDITION ACTS (1951); DONALD H. STEWART, THE OPPOSITION PRESS OF THE FEDERALIST PERIOD (1969); Walter Berns, Freedom of the Press and the Alien and Sedition Laws: A Reappraisal, 1970 SUP. CT. REV. 109; James P. Martin, When Repression is Democratic and Constitutional: The Federalist Theory of Representation and the Sedition Act of 1798, 66 U. CHI. L. REV. (1999).

[7] See, e.g., ALBERT W. ALTSCHULER, LAW WITHOUT VALUES: THE LIFE, WORK, AND LEGACY OF JUSTICE HOLMES 71 (2000) ("Three prosecutions for violation of the Espionage Act of 1917 during World War I . . . commonly are seen as marking the beginning of modern First Amendment jurisprudence."). Altschuler summarizes the consensus, but of course disputes over free speech preceded modern First Amendment jurisprudence. See, e.g., DAVID RABBAN, FREE SPEECH IN ITS FORGOTTEN YEARS (1997).

[8] LEONARD W. LEVY, LEGACY OF SUPRESSION: FREEDOM OF SPEECH AND PRESS IN EARLY AMERICAN HISTORY (1960). For Levy's second look back on the subject see, LEONARD W. LEVY, EMERGENCE OF A FREE PRESS (1985).

The Bill of Rights became law in 1791, but just seven years later the First Amendment was under attack. Partisan feuding between the Federalists, the party of George Washington and John Adams, and the Republicans, the Jeffersonian faction (also called Democrats derisively by their foes), resulted in the passage in 1798 of the Sedition Act. That statute made it a crime to "write, print, utter, or publish . . . any false, scandalous, and malicious writing or writings, against the government of the United States, or either house of the congress of the United States, or the president of the United States, with intent to defame . . . or to bring them . . . into contempt or disrepute; or to excite against . . . any of them, the hatred of the good people of the United States."[9] A Vermont congressman was convicted under the act, sentenced to 18 months in prison and fined; several Republican newspaper editors were prosecuted. Indeed, the raucous press was the true target of the Sedition Act, and many newspapers were put out of business.[10] Timed to expire when John Adams left the presidency, the act died in 1800.

In his important history of free speech from 1791 to 1868, Michael Kent Curtis documents not only the Sedition Act of 1798 but later efforts to suppress political speech from the antebellum era through the end of the Civil War.[11] The increasingly bitter sectional conflict over slavery provoked a series of free speech crises. From the 1830s on, the South tried to suppress the rising abolitionist crusade. Proslavery leaders lobbied the United States Post Office to ban abolitionist newspapers and publications from the mails, put bounties on anti-slavery leaders, forced the U.S. House of Representatives to ban the acceptance or discussion of anti-slavery petitions, and enacted laws in Southern states that punished anyone who spoke against slavery. Southerners schemed to "extradite"—in other words, kidnap—abolitionists for trial for the capital crime of fomenting slave insurrections. In attempts to silence William Lloyd Garrison, he was "hanged in effigy, censored, jailed, sued, hunted by mobs, threatened with assassination and almost lynched. The State of Georgia offered a $5000 bounty to anyone who kidnapped Garrison and brought

[9] Act for the Punishment of Certain Crimes, 1 Stat. 596 (July 14, 1798).

[10] *See* MILLER and STEWART, *supra* note 4.

[11] MICHAEL KENT CURTIS, FREE SPEECH, "THE PEOPLE'S DARLING PRIVILEGE": STRUGGLES FOR FREEDOM OF EXPRESSION IN AMERICAN HISTORY (2000).

him to the state for trial on charges of seditious libel."[12] At the U.S. Capitol a senator was nearly caned to death by an enraged Southerner. Mobs attacked abolitionist newspaper presses in several cities and murdered editor Elijah Lovejoy in Alton, Illinois. But the pro-slavery powers failed in their quest to manipulate the federal government into suppressing the national debate over slavery. That debate made possible the rise of a new Republican party and lifted Abraham Lincoln to the presidency.

Ironically, once in power the Republicans also suppressed speech. In a time of national crisis, free speech was a casualty of Lincoln's effort to win the war and preserve the Union. In 1862 Lincoln issued a proclamation stating that "during the existing insurrection and as a necessary measure for suppressing same . . . all persons discouraging volunteer enlistments, resisting militia drafts, or guilty of any disloyal practice . . . shall be subject to martial law and liable to trial and punishment."[13] Lincoln then suspended the writ of habeas corpus; thousands of people were arrested; a former congressman was seized for making an anti-war speech in Dayton, Ohio; Congress tried to expel a member who spoke against the war; and the *Chicago Times* newspaper was suppressed.[14] And of course from Reconstruction until the 1960s, the political speech of African Americans was suppressed widely throughout the South. In all of these controversies from the 1790s through the 1860s, political speech was suppressed because its opponents claimed that the speech was dangerous, undermined the social order, and threatened the stability of the government.

The era of modern repression began in 1917, during the First World War and the Russian Revolution. To isolate America from the bacilli of socialism and communism, many anti-war protestors

---

[12] James L. Swanson, *The Great Crusader: The Life and Times of Slavery's Most Fiery Foe, William Lloyd Garrison*, CHI. TRIB., Jan. 31, 1999, § 14, at 4 (reviewing HENRY MAYER, ALL ON FIRE: WILLIAM LLOYD GARRISON AND THE ABOLITION OF SLAVERY (1998)).

[13] THE COLLECTED WORKS OF ABRAHAM LINCOLN 429–32 (Roy Basler ed. 1956), *quoted in*, CURTIS, *supra* note 11, at 306.

[14] CURTIS, *supra* note 11, at 300–356. For the definitive treatment on free speech and liberty in the North during the Civil War, see MARK E. NEELY JR., THE FATE OF LIBERTY: ABRAHAM LINCOLN AND CIVIL LIBERTIES (1991). See also, Michael Kent Curtis, *Lincoln, Vallandigham, and Anti-War Speech in the Civil War*, 7 WM. & MARY BILL RTS. J. 105 (1998).

were convicted under the Espionage Act and imprisoned. For speaking against the war Eugene Debs was sentenced to ten years in prison, and while incarcerated he received almost one million votes in the presidential election of 1920.[15] Looking back at these cases, constitutional scholar Steven Shiffrin wrote, "The whole line is simply depressing."[16] The suppression of political speech and dissent continued after the war ended in 1918. The story is so well known that there is no need to rehearse it at length here: the suppression of labor unions through "criminal syndicalism" laws; the criminalization of communist party membership; the establishment of patriotic loyalty oaths; the "Red Scare" of the 1950s; the suppression of the civil rights movement, and of dissenting speech, during the Vietnam War; and much more.[17] In 1791 the First Amendment proclaimed a glorious principle, but throughout our history a dark tradition of suppressing political speech has shadowed it.

B. Political Speech: The Central Purpose?

As in physics, where scientists seek the elusive unitary theory that will explain all things, the search in constitutional law for a grand theory of the First Amendment has obsessed scholars for half a

---

[15] Debs v. United States, 249 U.S. 211 (1919). For background on Debs see ZECHARIAH CHAFEE JR., FREE SPEECH IN THE UNITED STATES (1941); Harry Kalven, *Ernst Freund and the First Amendment Tradition*, 40 U. CHI. L. REV. 235, 237 (1973) ("To put the case in modern context, it is somewhat as though George McGovern had been sent to prison for his criticism of the [Vietnam] war.").

[16] STEVEN H. SHIFFRIN, THE FIRST AMENDMENT, DEMOCRACY, AND ROMANCE 73 (1990). The major W.W.I and postwar cases include *Schenck v. United States*, 249 U.S. 47 (1919); *Debs v. United States*, 249 U.S. 211 (1919); *Abrams v. United States*, 250 U.S. 616 (1919); *Gilbert v. Minnesota*, 254 U.S. 325 (1920); *Gitlow v. New York*, 268 U.S. 652 (1925).

[17] For several excellent texts, and for direction to all of the major cases, books, and articles, see for example, ZECHARIAH CHAFEE JR., FREEDOM OF SPEECH (1920); ZECHARIAH CHAFEE JR., FREE SPEECH IN THE UNITED STATES (1941); HARRY KALVEN JR., THE NEGRO AND THE FIRST AMENDMENT (1966); PATRICK S. WASHBURN, A QUESTION OF SEDITION: THE FEDERAL GOVERNMENT'S INVESTIGATION OF THE BLACK PRESS DURING WORLD WAR II (1986); HARRY KALVEN JR., A WORTHY TRADITION: FREEDOM OF SPEECH IN AMERICA (1988); STEVEN H. SHIFFRIN, THE FIRST AMENDMENT, DEMOCRACY, AND ROMANCE (1990); RODNEY A. SMOLLA, FREE SPEECH IN AN OPEN SOCIETY (1992); ARTHUR J. SABIN, IN CALMER TIMES: THE SUPREME COURT AND RED MONDAY (1999); PETER IRONS, A PEOPLE'S HISTORY OF THE SUPREME COURT (1999).

century.[18] Contrarians counter that no such general theory is possible—that case law has made First Amendment doctrine too particularized and inconsistent for that.[19] Some of the leading commentators on the Constitution have concluded that protecting political speech was the original and central purpose of the First Amendment. Alexander Meiklejohn, whom Archibald Cox once described as "perhaps the foremost American philosopher of freedom of expression,"[20] advocated this view in a series of books and articles.[21] Meiklejohn argued that freedom of speech is a precondition for self-government. According to his interpretation, the purpose of the First Amendment "is to give every voting member of the body politic the fullest possible participation in the understanding of those problems with

---

[18] For one of the major works, see, THOMAS I. EMERSON, TOWARD A GENERAL THEORY OF THE FIRST AMENDMENT (1966). This book, a revised version of an article that appeared in the Yale Law Journal, anticipated Emerson's magnum opus, THE SYSTEM OF FREEDOM OF EXPRESSION (1970), one of the most influential books ever written about the First Amendment. The literature on alternative theories of freedom of speech is vast, and I shall make no attempt to record its bibliography here. For some of the major articles, see, for example, David A. Richards, *A Theory of Free Speech*, 34 UCLA L. REV. 1837 (1987); Steven Shiffrin, *The First Amendment and Economic Regulation: Away From a General Theory of the First Amendment,*78 Nw. U.L. REV. 1212 (1983); Vincent Blasi, *The Pathological Perspective and the First Amendment*, 85 COLUM. L. REV. 449 (1985); Michael J. Perry, *Freedom of Expression: An Essay on Theory and Doctrine*, 78 Nw. U.L. REV. 1137 (1983); Alexander Meiklejohn, *The First Amendment is an Absolute*, 1961 SUP. CT. REV. 245; Daniel A. Farber, *Free Speech Without Romance: Public Choice and the First Amendment*, 105 HARV. L. REV. 554 (1991); William van Alstyne, *A Graphic Review of the Free Speech Clause*, 70 CALIF. L. REV. 107 (1982); Kenneth L. Karst, *Equality as Central Principle in the First Amendment*, 43 U. CHI. L. REV. 20 (1975); Ronald A. Cass, *The Perils of Positive Thinking: Constitutional Interpretation and Negative First Amendment Theory*, 34 UCLA L. REV. 1405 (1987). For some of the major books not heretofore cited in this article, see for example, WALTER BERNS, THE FIRST AMENDMENT AND THE FUTURE OF AMERICAN DEMOCRACY (1957); ALEXANDER M. BICKEL, THE MORALITY OF CONSENT (1975); MELVILLE B. NIMMER, FREEDOM OF SPEECH (1984); LEE C. BOLLINGER, THE TOLERANT SOCIETY (1986); FREDERICK SCHAUER, FREE SPEECH: A PHILOSOPHICAL ENQUIRY (1986); CASS R. SUNSTEIN, DEMOCRACY AND THE PROBLEM OF FREE SPEECH (1993); KENT GREENAWALT, FIGHTING WORDS: INDIVIDUALS, COMMUNITIES, AND LIBERTIES OF SPEECH (1995); MARK A. GRABER, TRANSFORMING FREE SPEECH: THE AMBIGUOUS LEGACY OF CIVIL LIBERTARIANISM (1991).

[19] *See, e.g.,* STEVEN H. SHIFFRIN, THE FIRST AMENDMENT, DEMOCRACY, AND ROMANCE (1990); HARRY KALVEN JR., A WORTHY TRADITION: FREEDOM OF SPEECH IN AMERICA (1998).

[20] ARCHIBALD COX, FREEDOM OF EXPRESSION 2 (1981).

[21] ALEXANDER MEIKLEJOHN, FREE SPEECH AND ITS RELATION TO SELF GOVERNMENT (1948); ALEXANDER MEIKLEJOHN, POLITICAL FREEDOM: THE CONSTITUTIONAL POWERS OF THE PEOPLE (1965); Alexander Meiklejohn, *The First Amendment is an Absolute*, 1961 SUP. CT. REV. 245.

which the citizens of a self-governing society must deal."[22] In a landmark article Judge Robert H. Bork pursued the Meiklejohnian thesis.[23] Interested initially in only political speech, Meiklejohn came to define the spectrum of speech related to self-government broadly. Ultimately he assigned First Amendment protection to "education . . . the achievements of philosophy and the sciences . . . literature and the arts."[24] The issues raised by Meiklejohn still occupy First Amendment scholars, who have promulgated and debated competing, sophisticated, and, frankly, sometimes confusing theories of the nature and purpose of the First Amendment.[25] An expansive interpretation of the First Amendment has been in vogue for decades, and today the view that it safeguards only political speech is considered narrow, quaint, and even dangerous to liberty.[26] Nevertheless, all leading constitutional scholars believe that the First Amendment, whatever its scope, affords a high level of protection for political speech.[27]

C. Political Speech in the Supreme Court

Since the days of *Schenck, Debs, Abrams,* and the rest, the Supreme Court has declared one free speech principle repeatedly, comprehensively, and passionately: Freedom of political speech is at the heart of democracy and merits the highest level of constitutional protection. So many justices have embraced this principle in so many cases that it would seem unnecessary, under normal circumstances, to quote them at length to prove the point. But because the dissenters

---

[22] ALEXANDER MEIKLEJOHN, POLITICAL FREEDOM: THE CONSTITUTIONAL POWERS OF THE PEOPLE 75 (1965).

[23] Robert H. Bork, *Neutral Principles & Some First Amendment Problems,* 47 IND. L.J. 1 (1971).

[24] Alexander Meiklejohn, *The First Amendment is an Absolute,* 1961 SUP. CT. REV. 245, 255.

[25] *See supra,* note 18.

[26] *See, e.g.,* STEVEN H. SHIFFRIN, THE FIRST AMENDMENT, DEMOCRACY, AND ROMANCE (1990).

[27] I leave for another day the discussion of various theories of the left which claim that the First Amendment is a source of oppression, not freedom. *See generally,* Bachmann, *The Irrelevant First Amendment,* 7 COMM. L.J. 3 (1985); Kairys, *Freedom of Speech, in* THE POLITICS OF LAW: A PROGRESSIVE CRITIQUE 253 (D. Kairys ed. 1982); Tushnet, *Corporations & Free Speech, in* THE POLITICS OF LAW: A PROGRESSIVE CRITIQUE 253 (D. Kairys ed. 1982).

in *Republican Party of Minnesota* dismissed them out of hand, it is important to note for the record exactly what the Supreme Court has said in defense of political speech. Many scholars identify the dissent of Justice Holmes in *Abrams* as the origin of modern First Amendment doctrine.

> But when men have realized that time has upset many fighting faiths, they may come to believe even more than they believe the very foundations of their own conduct that the ultimate good desired is better reached by free trade in ideas—that the best test of truth is the power of the thought to get itself accepted in the competition of the market, and that truth is the only ground upon which their wishes safely can be carried out. That at any rate is the theory of our Constitution. It is an experiment, as all life is an experiment.[28]

Eight years later, Justice Brandeis, writing in the notorious syndicalism case, *Whitney v. California*, justified freedom of political expression in what became one of the most celebrated passages in American law.

> Those who won our independence believed that the final end of the State was to make men free to develop their faculties; and that in its government the deliberative forces should prevail over the arbitrary. They valued liberty both as an end and as a means. They believed liberty to be the secret of happiness and courage to be the secret of liberty. They believed that freedom to think as you will and to speak as you think are means indispensable to the discovery and spread of political truth; that without free speech and assembly discussion would be futile; that with them, discussion affords ordinarily adequate protection against the dissemination of noxious doctrine; that the greatest menace to freedom is an inert people; that public discussion is a political duty; and that this should be a fundamental principle of the American government . . . the path of safety lies in the opportunity

---

[28] Abrams v. United States, 250 U.S. 616, 627–630 (1919) (Holmes, J., dissenting). The Holmes legacy is more ambiguous than his ringing pronouncement in *Abrams* might suggest. *Compare* ALBERT W. ALTSCHULER, LAW WITHOUT VALUES: THE LIFE, WORK, AND LEGACY OF JUSTICE HOLMES *with* RICHARD POSNER, THE ESSENTIAL HOLMES: SELECTIONS FROM THE LETTERS, SPEECHES, JUDICIAL OPINIONS, AND OTHER WRITINGS OF OLIVER WENDELL HOLMES JR. *See also,* James L. Swanson, *A Historical Look at Free Speech and a Critique of Oliver Wendell Holmes,* CHI. TRIB., May 13, 2001, § 14, at 4.

to discuss freely supposed grievances and proposed remedies; and that the fitting remedy for evil counsels is good
ones. Believing in the power of reason as applied through
public discussion, they eschewed silence coerced by law—
the argument of force in its worst form. Recognizing the
occasional tyrannies of governing majorities, they amended
the Constitution so that free speech and assembly should be
guaranteed.[29]

Another four years passed before Chief Justice Hughes wrote in
Stromberg v. California that "The maintenance of the opportunity for
free political discussion to the end that government may be respon-
sive to the will of the people and that changes may be obtained by
lawful means, an opportunity essential to the security of the Republic, is a fundamental principle of our constitutional system,"[30] and
more than a generation later Justice Brennan proclaimed in *Garrison
v. Louisiana* that "speech concerning public affairs is more than self-
expression; it is the essence of self-government."[31]

In *Wood v. Georgia*, a case involving a contempt-of-court order,
Chief Justice Warren wrote for the Court that "Men are entitled to
speak as they may please on matters vital to them; errors in judgment
or unsubstantiated opinions may be exposed, of course, but not
through punishment for contempt for the expression. Under our
system of government, counterargument and education are the
weapons available to expose these matters, not abridgement of the
rights of free speech and assembly."[32] And in *New York Times v.
Sullivan*, the most important case in the history of defamation law,
Justice Brennan wrote of "a profound national commitment to the
principle that debate on public issues should be uninhibited, robust,
and wide-open." That debate, he added, "may well include vehe-
ment, caustic, and sometimes unpleasantly sharp attacks on government and public officials."[33]

In *Cohen v. California*, the celebrated case involving the prosecution
of a man who wore a jacket bearing the motto "Fuck the Draft,"
Justice Harlan endorsed political speech.

[29] Whitney v. California, 274 U.S. 357, 375, 376 (1927).
[30] Stromberg v. California, 283 U.S. 359, 369 (1931).
[31] Garrison v. Louisiana, 379 U.S. 64, 66 (1964).
[32] Wood v. Georgia, 370 U.S. 375, 389 (1961) (citation omitted).
[33] N.Y. Times v. Sullivan, 367 U.S. 254, 270 (1964).

> The constitutional right of free expression ... is designed and intended to remove governmental restraints from the arena of public discussion, putting the decision as to what views shall be voiced directly into the hands of each of us, in the hope that use of such freedom will ultimately produce a more capable citizenry and more perfect polity and in the belief that no other approach would comport with the premise of individual dignity and choice upon which our political system rests ... That the air may at times seem filled with verbal cacophony is not a sign of weakness but of strength.[34]

And in *Buckley v. Valeo* the Court, although amenable to regulating financial contributions to candidates, emphasized the importance of allowing candidates to speak freely.

> The candidate, no less than any other person, has a First Amendment right to engage in the discussion of public issues and vigorously and tirelessly to advocate his own election and the election of other candidates. *Indeed it is of particular importance that candidates have the unfettered opportunity to make their views known* so that the electorate may intelligently evaluate the candidates' personal qualities and their positions on vital public issues before choosing among them on election day.[35]

Not only has the Supreme Court spoken repeatedly of the importance of political speech in general, it has stated specifically that judges are not immune from the democratic dialogue.

> The assumption that respect for the judiciary can be won by shielding judges from published criticism wrongly appraises the character of American public opinion. For it is a prized American privilege to speak one's mind, although not always with perfect good taste, on all public institutions. And an enforced silence, however limited, solely in the name of preserving the dignity of the bench, would probably engender resentment, suspicion, and contempt much more than it would enhance respect.[36]

[34]Cohen v. California, 403 U.S. 15, 24 (1971).
[35]Buckley v. Valeo, 424 U.S.1, 52–53 (1976).
[36]Bridges v. State of California, 314 U.S. 252 (1941).

Part II: Judicial Elections and the First Amendment: Origins of the Conflict

Judicial elections, like freedom of speech, are an established American tradition. Although the Constitution mandated that federal judges be nominated by the president and appointed by and with the advice and consent of the Senate, and not elected, the states were free to select judges as their citizens saw fit. Ultimately the majority of states, including Minnesota, rejected the federal model and chose to select judges by popular election. For a long time the speech of state judicial candidates was not regulated.[37] The idea of imposing a speech code on judicial candidates is a creature of the 20th century, characterized by overweening government working in concert with special interests. Unsuccessful in their efforts to abolish judicial elections, the special interests sought as their fallback position to undermine elections indirectly by gagging campaign speech.

A. Judicial Elections

The purpose of judicial elections is undeniable: to retain for the people the right to hold judges accountable in some fashion. What other purpose do popular elections serve? Animated by the spirit of Jacksonian democracy, and in some Northern states by the notorious *Dred Scott* decision,[38] "[b]y the time of the Civil War, the great majority of States elected their judges."[39] The origin of judicial elections in Minnesota is especially illuminating. "Minnesotans of both parties opted for an elected judiciary. Ultimately, they more feared the potential politics of an appointed bench and saw popular election as the proper remedy. Given the political climate, they desired more control over their judiciary. *That was the policy adopted by the people of Minnesota.* Minnesota's electorate has never since intimated a change in this policy."[40] Notably, both the court of appeals opinion upholding the "announce clause" in *Republican Party of Minnesota*, and the dissenting Supreme Court justices who would have upheld it, overlook that inconvenient history.

---

[37] Republican Party of Minn. v. White, 122 S. Ct. 2528, 2540 (2002).

[38] Dred Scott v. Sanford, 60 U.S. (19 How.) 1857.

[39] Republican Party of Minn. v. White, 122 S. Ct. 2528, 2540 (2002).

[40] Republican Party of Minn. v. Kelly, 247 F.3d 854, 889 (8th Cir. 2001) (Beam, J., dissenting) (emphasis in original).

The decision to elect judges was controversial. One delegate to the Minnesota convention opposed the method because he feared that judges chosen by the people might oppose slavery and be inclined to "Negro-worship."[41] An advocate for elections left no doubt as to their purpose: "We hear a great deal of talk about an Independent Judiciary. The phrase is in everybody's mouth. What does it mean? Independent of whom? Independent of what? Independent of the people . . . ? I say then that in order to correct the errors of Judges—and it may be important to correct them—the office should be made elective."[42]

B. Speech Codes

The American Bar Association (ABA) opposes judicial elections and wants to abolish them.[43] The ABA seeks to elevate state court judges to the federal plane, where trial, appellate, and Supreme Court judges preside above the fray, insulated from campaigns and elections. Elections, so says the ABA, just like the lawyer advertisements that it squelched for decades until the Supreme Court admonished otherwise, threaten to undermine public confidence in the profession.[44] The ABA also opposes straight political Appointments, preferring "merit" selection by "nonpartisan," ABA-approved elites who, naturally, will dominate the process. Unfortunately for the ABA, the citizens who need to be saved from judicial elections have shown little interest in saving themselves and in furthering the organization's agenda. In Minnesota, the people have resisted four attempts to amend their constitution and end judicial elections.

[41] *Id.* at 888.

[42] *Id.* at 889.

[43] MODEL CODE OF JUDICIAL CONDUCT Canon 5(C)(2), Cmt. (2000); AN INDEPENDENT JUDICIARY: REPORT OF THE ABA COMMISSION ON SEPARATION OF POWERS AND JUDICIAL INDEPENDENCE 96 (1997).

[44] Bates v. State Bar of California, 433 U.S. 350 (1977). The ABA also impeded the civil rights movement by prohibiting attorneys connected to political organizations from soliciting plaintiffs for lawsuits, until the Supreme Court said otherwise. NAACP v. Button, 371 U.S. 415 (1963). In 1978 the Supreme Court struck down an attempt by a state to discipline an attorney who sought litigants for the ACLU. *In re* Primus, 436 U.S. 412 (1978). Indeed, "[in] the space of fifteen years, the Supreme Court held ABA and state-sponsored provisions on solicitation to be in violation of the First Amendment to the Constitution on five separate occasions." Lloyd B. Snyder, *The Constitutionality and Consequences of Restrictions on Campaign Speech by Candidates for Judicial Office*, 35 UCLA L. REV. 207, 209 (1987).

"Thus, since first permitted to select its own judiciary, Minnesota has favored electorally-responsive judges."[45]

If it cannot abolish judicial elections then the ABA wants to sabotage them, purifying them of speech that the ABA considers unsavory. To promote its mission the ABA has drafted a series of model codes, or canons, which it lobbies the states to adopt. These canons, when adopted, are not approved by democratically elected state legislatures or by the people through popular vote. Instead, state supreme courts promulgate them unilaterally and declare all members of the state bar subject to their discipline. Since 1974, Minnesota lawyers have been subject to a canon that prohibits a "candidate for judicial office, including an incumbent judge," from "announc[-ing] his or her views on disputed legal or political issues."[46] The penalties for violating the speech canon are severe: incumbent judges may be suspended without pay, censured, or removed from office,[47] and lawyers are subject to probation, suspension, or disbarment.[48] Thus, although unable to ban elections, the ABA and the Minnesota Supreme Court were able to weaken them.

Part III: *Republican Party of Minnesota v. White*

The dispute that became *Republican Party of Minnesota v. White* began in 1996 when Gregory Wersal, a member of the state bar of Minnesota, ran for the post of associate justice of the Minnesota Supreme Court. His campaign literature criticized the court, including its past decisions on crime, welfare, and abortion. Subsequently, a complaint against Wersal was filed with the Office of Lawyers Professional Responsibility, the agency which, under the direction of the Minnesota Lawyers Professional Responsibility Board, investigates and prosecutes ethical violations of lawyer candidates for judicial office.[49] Although the Board dismissed the complaint, and even speculated whether the announce clause was constitutional, Wersal withdrew from the race, "fearing that further ethical complaints

---

[45] Republican Party of Minn. v. Kelly, 247 F.3d 854, 890 (8th Cir. 2001) (Beam J. dissenting).

[46] MINN. CODE OF JUDICIAL CONDUCT, Canon 5(A)(3)(d)(i)(2000).

[47] MINN. RULES OF BOARD ON JUDICIAL STANDARDS 4(a)(6), 11(d)(2002).

[48] MINN. RULES OF LAWYERS PROFESSIONAL RESPONSIBILITY 8–14, 15(a)(2002).

[49] Republican Party of Minnesota v. White, 122 S. Ct. 2528, 2531 (2002).

would jeopardize his ability to practice law."[50] When Wersal ran for associate justice again in 1998, he sought an advisory opinion from the Lawyers Board, inquiring whether it would enforce the announce clause. The Board demurred because he had failed to submit for approval a list of the announcements he wished to make. Wersal then filed suit in federal court seeking a declaration that the announce clause was unconstitutional. He complained that the clause chilled him from announcing his views to the press and the public. Other plaintiffs, including the Republican Party of Minnesota, joined his suit, arguing that without knowing Wersal's views, they could not decide whether to support him.

The district court ruled against Wersal,[51] and the Eighth Circuit affirmed.[52] In an attempt to save the announce clause, the court of appeals adopted what it claimed was a narrowing construction devised by the district court. The clause no longer barred candidates from announcing their views on disputed legal or political issues: it merely barred candidates from announcing their views on such issues likely to come before the court.[53] The court of appeals added its own gloss, concluding that candidates could discuss cases too. The Supreme Court of the United States granted certiorari to determine the constitutionality of the announce clause. Numerous other restrictions that Minnesota placed on judicial candidates were not before the Court.[54]

A. Opinion of the Court: The Primacy of the First Amendment

Justice Scalia's opinion for the Court, joined by Chief Justice Rehnquist and Justices O'Connor, Kennedy, and Thomas, began with first principles. The burden would not be on the petitioners to persuade the Court to create a First Amendment exception to a presumptively valid anti-speech policy promulgated by the Minnesota Supreme Court. Rather, the burden was on respondents to demonstrate that such a policy was a constitutionally permissible exception to the First Amendment. Scalia emphasized that this hurdle would be difficult to overcome. "We have never allowed the government

[50]*Id.*

[51]63 F. Supp. 2d 967.

[52]Republican Party of Minn. v. Kelly, 247 F.3d 854 (8th Cir. 2001).

[53]*Id.* at 881–882.

[54]Republican Party of Minn. v. White, 122 S. Ct. 2528, 2532 (2002).

to prohibit candidates from communicating relevant information to voters during an election."[55]

Scalia applied the same "strict scrutiny" test used by the Eighth Circuit to evaluate the constitutionality of the announce clause.[56] Under that test, the respondents must prove that the announce clause is narrowly tailored to serve a compelling state interest. "The Court of Appeals concluded that respondents had established two interests as sufficiently compelling to justify the announce clause: preserving the impartiality of the state judiciary and preserving the appearance of the impartiality of the state judiciary."[57] Scalia was dubious of how compelling such interests could be when they were so difficult to define. "Respondents are rather vague, however, about what they mean by 'impartiality.' Indeed, although the term is used throughout the Eighth Circuit's opinion, the briefs, the Minnesota Code of Judicial Conduct, and the ABA Codes of Judicial Conduct, none of these sources bothered to define it."[58] Does "impartiality" mean that judges should not be biased for or against actual, *individual* litigants in specific cases (friends, foes, family, former partners); biased against particular *classes* of litigants (African Americans, women, foreigners, all criminal defendants); biased for reasons of personal financial interest (as a stockholder, an investor, a beneficiary of fines); or biased against a legal theory or method of interpreting the law? Must judges' minds be blank slates unmarred by a judicial philosophy of any kind?[59]

---

[55] *Id.* at 2538.

[56] *Id.* at 2534–2535. "As the Court of Appeals recognized, the announce clause both prohibits speech on the basis of its content and burdens a category of speech that is 'at the core of our First Amendment freedoms'—speech about the qualifications of candidates for public office. 247 F. 3d, at 861, 863. The Court of Appeals concluded that the proper test to be applied to determine the constitutionality of such a restriction is what our cases have called strict scrutiny, *id.*, at 864; the parties do not dispute that this is correct. Under the strict-scrutiny test, respondents have the burden to prove that the announce clause is (1) narrowly tailored, to serve (2)–a compelling state interest. *E.G., Eu v. San Francisco County Democratic Central Comm.*, 489 U.S. 214, 222 (1989). In order for respondents to show that the announce clause is narrowly tailored, they must demonstrate that it does not 'unnecessarily circumbscrib[e] protected expression.' *Brown v. Hartlage*, 456 U.S. 45, 54 (1982)."

[57] *Id.*, at 2535.

[58] *Id.*

[59] *Infra*, notes 81–82.

Scalia concluded that the interests asserted by Minnesota were neither compelling or narrowly tailored, and that the real "purpose behind the announce clause is not openmindedness in the judiciary, but the undermining of judicial elections."[60] Waving off dissents by Ginsburg and Stevens as overwrought and off point, Scalia assuaged them by noting that "we neither assert nor imply that the First Amendment requires campaigns for judicial office to sound the same as those for legislative office. What we do assert, and what Justice Ginsburg ignores, is that, *even if* the First Amendment allows greater regulation of judicial election campaigns than legislative campaigns, the announce clause still fails strict scrutiny because it is woefully underinclusive, prohibiting announcements by judges (and would-be judges) only at certain times and in certain forms."[61]

Justice O'Connor's concurrence confesses her prejudice against judicial elections. "I am concerned that . . . the very practice of elect-ing judges undermines" an impartial judiciary.[62] Despite her per-sonal distaste for a judiciary that is vulnerable to public opinion and that engages in fundraising, she accepts that she is not a policy-maker, exercises restraint, shows deference to the states that choose to elect judges, and joins Scalia's opinion that the announce clause does not supersede the First Amendment. "[T]he State's claim that it needs to significantly restrict judges' speech in order to protect judicial impartiality is particularly troubling. If the State has a prob-lem with judicial impartiality, it is largely one the State brought upon itself by continuing the practice of popularly electing judges."[63] Like Scalia, she is skeptical about the unspoken subtext of the announce clause. At oral argument she wondered if its purpose might be to shield incumbents from challenge.

In his concurrence, Justice Kennedy agreed that Minnesota cannot have it both ways. "Minnesota may choose to have an elected judiciary. . . . What Minnesota may not do, however, is censor what the people hear as they undertake to decide for themselves which candidate is most likely to be an exemplary judicial officer. . . . The law in question here contradicts the principle that unabridged speech

---

[60]Republican Party of Minn. v. White, 122 S. Ct. 2528, 2538 (2002).

[61]*Id.* at 2539 (citation omitted).

[62]*Id.* at 2542 (O'Connor, J., concurring).

[63]*Id.* at 2544.

is the foundation of political freedom."[64] Kennedy's brief opinion does much more, however, than simply concur in the judgment of the Court. He advances a theory that, as I will soon suggest, may be the best solution to the conflict between judicial independence and free speech.

B. *The Dissent: In Policy's Thrall*

The dissenters' central theme is obvious: Justices Stevens and Ginsburg do not like judicial elections. But they do like policy. Therefore, if there must be elections, then "[j]udges are not politicians, and the First Amendment does not require that they be treated as politicians simply because they are chosen by popular vote."[65] In other words, judicial candidates are "different" and have second-class First Amendment rights. Therefore, the majority was "profoundly misguided" to suggest that all candidates in all American elections enjoy an equal right to free speech.[66] Indeed, the idea that candidates for the judiciary should possess an unfettered right to express themselves on issues of public importance is "seriously flawed."[67]

Free speech is dangerous, warn the dissenters. Election campaigns deform judges into vote-seeking politicians, enslave them as catspaws to the mob, and poison public confidence in the judiciary. Only by policing candidates' speech can we prevent them from pandering for votes by promising results in controversial cases after they take the bench. Only through censorship can we protect the Due Process rights of litigants who will come before these judges.[68] Only through government regulation can we preserve general public confidence in an impartial and openminded judiciary.[69]

Reading the dissents in isolation, without the benefit of the opinion of the Court, one would hardly know that *Republican Party of Minnesota* was an important First Amendment case. Their tone is cramped and bureaucratic, citing a variety of reports, law review articles, and

[64] *Id.* 2545 (Kennedy, J., concurring).
[65] *Id.* at 2559 (Ginsburg, J., dissenting).
[66] *Id.* at 2549 (Stevens, J. dissenting).
[67] *Id.* at 2546 (Stevens, J. dissenting).
· [68] *Id.* at 2555 (Ginsburg, J. dissenting).
[69] *Id.* at 2549 (Stevens, J. dissenting).

lower court opinions to justify balancing two interests.[70] The dissents sound more like policy memos from the American Bar Association than Supreme Court opinions on the First Amendment. The silences are telling. There is no consideration of the uneven history of political speech in this country, no reference to the historical literature, no citation to the Court's grand precedents on the First Amendment, and no recognition of the right of citizens to hear from the candidates who seek their votes. Permeating the dissents is the unstated assumption that any policy problems arising from judicial elections must, naturally, be solved by government action.

A classic example occurs in Ginsburg's dissent when she writes, in so many words, that Wersal has little to complain about because the Lawyers Board that investigates and punishes speech did not ultimately rule against him.[71] What she fails to realize, however, is that the proper question is not, what did the board rule but, rather, why is there a speech board at all?

Part IV: The Case Against the Code

That the Minnesota speech code violates the First Amendment is reason enough to abolish it. But because those who favor censoring the speech of judicial candidates insist that *Republican Party of Minnesota v. White* is not an important First Amendment case, and resort instead to a variety of policy arguments to promote censorship, it becomes necessary to respond to those arguments. They are flawed for three reasons. First, they attempt to draw an impossible line between the kind of speech that does and does not indicate how a judge might decide a case. The announce clause turns regulators into linguistic gymnasts whose hopeless task is to hypothesize whether this turn of a phrase or that "really" means more than it actually says in words. Second, they celebrate a mythical creature

---

[70] *See* De Muniz, *Politicizing State Judicial Elections: A Threat to Judicial Independence*, 38 WILLIAMETTE L. REV. 367 (2002); O'Neil, *The Canons in the Courts: Recent First Amendment Rulings*, 35 IND. L. REV. 701 (2002); Shepard, *Campaign Speech: Restraint and Liberty in Judicial Ethics*, 9 GEO. J. LEGAL ETHICS 1059 (1996); P. McFadden, ELECTING JUSTICE: THE LAW AND ETHICS OF JUDICIAL ELECTION CAMPAIGNS 86 (1990).

[71] Republican Party of Minn. v. White, 122 S. Ct. 2528, 2554 (2002) (Ginsburg, J., dissenting) ("Wersal has thus never been sanctioned under the Announce Clause for any campaign statement he made. On the facts before us, in sum, the Announce Clause has hardly stifled the robust communication of ideas and views from judicial candidate to voter.").

that does not exist—the judge with no views. Third, they suffer from a fatal case of paternalism. The announce clause harms the very people, the voters, that it claims to protect.

A: Linguistic Jujitsu: Announcements, Pledges, and Points in Between

Enforcement of the announce clause is unworkable because it is impossible to determine which speech should be suppressed. At exactly what point does a general statement become too specific, and thus forbidden? The dissents propose inconsistent and ambiguous rules that would make it impossible for a candidate to know when his political speech crossed the boundary between permissible and impermissible. Justice Ginsburg believes that the announce clause, properly interpreted, still gives candidates wide latitude to declare views on disputed legal and political issues; it merely bars them, she says, from discussing issues, and revealing how they might decide them, in disputes that are likely to come before them on the bench.[72] Of course that is no narrowing at all. Judge Richard Posner has explained how *any* controversial issue can wind up in court. "There is almost no legal or political issue that is unlikely to come before a judge of an American court, state or federal, of general jurisdiction."[73] Thus, it is impossible to divide issues into those that will or won't come before a judge. Trying to do so is a futile exercise.

In dissent, Justices Ginsburg and Stevens state, separately, that they would apply two different, inconsistent standards to a candidate's speech. According to Ginsburg, "[w]hat candidates may not do . . . is . . . declare how they would decide an issue."[74] Stevens proposes a much stricter standard and would regulate *any* statements that "obscure the appearance of openmindedness."[75] Indeed, he insists that "the judicial reputation for impartiality and openmindedness is compromised by" any statement that "emphasizes the candidate's personal predilections rather than his qualifications for judicial office."[76]

[72] *Id.* at 2553 (Ginsburg, J., dissenting).

[73] Buckley v. Ill. Judicial Inquiry Board, 997 F. 2d 224, 229 (7th Cir. 1993).

[74] Republican Party of Minn. v. White 122 S. Ct. 2528, 2553 (2002) (Ginsburg, J., dissenting).

[75] *Id.* (Stevens, J. dissenting).

[76] *Id.*

Stevens and Ginsburg highlight their confusion and inconsistency by discussing the example of a candidate who campaigns on his prior judicial record. According to Stevens, "Expressions that stress a candidate's unbroken record of affirming convictions for rape, for example, imply a bias in favor of a particular litigant (the prosecutor) and against a class of litigants (defendants in rape cases)."[77] Not so, says Ginsburg. Citing the record is fine. "[P]lace[d] beyond the scope of the Announce Clause [is] a wide range of comments that may be highly informative to voters . . . [S]uch comments may include statements of historical fact ('As a prosecutor, I obtained 15 drunk driving convictions')."[78] Ginsburg provides other examples of permissible statements: "'Judges should use *sparingly* their discretion to grant lenient sentences to drunk drivers'" and "'Drunk drivers are a threat to the safety of every driver.'"[79] Stevens would likely ban such statements because they reveal a "predilection" for ruling against a class of litigants, drunk drivers. In contrast, Ginsburg would ban only the outright statement that she says "essentially" commits the candidate to a position: "'I think all drunk drivers should receive the maximum sentence permitted by law.'"[80]

In fact, general statements of the type that the dissenters, or at least Ginsburg, would permit can telegraph as effectively as a blatant, explicitly stated promise how a judge might decide an issue. In any of Ginsburg's hypotheticals, the message is clear: things aren't looking good for drunk drivers. Surely she would not ban a candidate from announcing "I believe in a color-blind society." Yet, how far is that statement of general principle from simply announcing "I will vote against affirmative action." Although not an explicit promise, the color-blind society comment surely reveals a tendency, a predilection, that violates the Stevens standard. What about the following statement? "The U.S. Supreme Court says that the death penalty is constitutional, and I say that the law has coddled criminals too long." How far is this announcement from pledging "Don't worry, I won't be overturning too many death sentences on appeal"?

---

[77] *Id.* at 2548 (citation omitted) (Stevens, J., dissenting).

[78] *Id.* at 2553 (Ginsburg, J., dissenting).

[79] *Id.*

[80] *Id.*

The power of language is subtle. A speaker can convey messages without using specific words. Under the Stevens criteria for impartiality and openmindedness, it is hard to see how candidates could even discuss their general views, let alone speak about rival candidates and prior cases. The ambiguous nature of language demonstrates that a candidate can use almost any kind of statement to communicate with voters about his predilections. Thus, the only way to prevent candidates from telegraphing secret messages to voters—committing the sins of partiality, non-openmindedness, or the appearance of partiality—would be to ban a spectrum of speech much broader than even the announce clause, or Justice Ginsburg, contemplated. Indeed, the only way to stop candidates from hinting at their predilections is to ban language altogether from judicial campaigns.

The most convincing proof of the impossibility of regulating the meaning of language in a political campaign is the behavior of the Court in this case. Nine justices, learned experts in law and the Constitution, after extensive briefing, oral argument, and three months of contemplation, could not agree on which type of speech crosses the line. How then can a local speech board, working under the pressure of time and the heat of a political campaign, possibly make principled distinctions? And how could candidates ever know in advance when their speech might provoke investigation and punishment? They could, of course, submit all campaign literature, prepared speeches, and television commercials to the speech board, which would then rule on the permissibility of each communication. Aside from the obvious constitutional problems, such a scheme is absurdly impractical.

B. Openmindedness: Impartiality and the Myth of the Tabula Rasa Judicial Mind

The Minnesota announce clause seeks plateaus of "independence," "impartiality," and "openmindedness" that are neither possible nor desirable. No judge is totally "neutral," approaching each case at exactly the midpoint between opposing sides or issues. Judges have preexisting theories about the federal Constitution, state constitutions, statutes, the common law, "judicial restraint," "judicial activism," and "first principles." They do not reinvent the wheel and start from scratch in each case by asking themselves questions like "What are enumerated powers?" or "What is strict scrutiny and should I apply it?" or "What is the theory of original intent and do I believe in it?" Prior to becoming candidates, many judges wrote law review articles, or gave speeches or interviews, taking positions on disputed issues. Does this mean that no author who ever adopted a position on a controversial issue can ever be a fair judge? Of course not. Does this mean that a judge who wrote an opinion in a prior case must never again be allowed to hear another case involving the identical issue because his prior opinion now taints him as impartial? Of course not. But in the alternative universe of announce clauses, isn't every judge with a prior record partial and closeminded the next time he hears a similar case?

Then-Justice Rehnquist identified the poverty and impracticality of this view long ago when a litigant attempted to force him to recuse himself in a case that involved an issue on which he opined while serving in the Department of Justice.

> Such a contention raises rather squarely the question of whether a member of this Court, who prior to his taking that office has expressed a public view as to what the law ought to be, should later sit as a judge in a case raising that particular question. . . . My impression is that none of the former Justices of this Court since 1911 have followed a practice of disqualifying themselves in cases involving points of law with respect to which they had expressed an opinion. . . .[81]

Opponents of judicial elections, advocates for the announce clause, and the dissenters in *Republican Party of Minnesota v. White* all celebrate the *beau ideal* of a judge whose predilections remain so hidden from the public that the judge does not even give the appearance of being predisposed on any issue or controversy. That view perpetuates the misconception of a judge as an empty vessel who simply looks up the law in a book and applies it to the case of the moment. Openmindedness becomes emptymindedness. Rehnquist stated the point well.

> Since most Justices come to this bench no earlier than their middle years, it would be unusual if they had not by that time formulated at least some tentative notions that would influence them in their interpretation of the sweeping clauses of the Constitution and their interaction with one another. It would be not merely unusual, but extraordinary, if they

---

[81] Laird v. Tatum, 409 U.S. 824, 830, 831, 835 (1972).

had not at least given opinions as to constitutional issues in their previous legal careers. Proof that a Justice's mind at the time he joined the Court was a complete *tabula rasa* in the area of constitutional adjudication would be evidence of lack of qualification, not lack of bias.[82]

Again, a few examples from the real world illustrate the point. It is well known that Chief Justice Rehnquist is more likely than Justice Stevens to find that a land use regulation is a taking. It is well known that Justice Scalia might be more likely than Justice Ginsburg to determine that a race-based, affirmative action program is unconstitutional. These observations are widely known among professors, lawyers, litigants, and the media. By having predilections, and by failing to conceal them, have these justices undermined the appearance of impartiality that the announce clause deems so compelling an interest? Or, by showing how an overarching theory of law and the Constitution inevitably influences the result in particular cases, have they exposed the myth of the openminded judge?

C. *Confounding Democracy: How the Announce Clause Harms Voters by "Protecting" Them*

The announce clause is paternalistic. It seeks to protect voters from potentially harmful speech that might cause them to lose faith in the judicial system. The clause is antidemocratic. It deprives voters of information about candidates during an election and it protects incumbents. The clause is cynical. It does not trust voters to elect ethical judges. If judicial elections need one thing more than anything else, it is more public interest and knowledge. Voters do not know much about candidates running for judicial office.[83] The announce clause impedes voter education and makes the market for information less efficient. Citizens cast their votes while possessing imperfect information, not because information about judges is a naturally scarce good, but because speech regulators make it artificially scarce through regulation. The announce clause increases the search costs

---

[82] *Id.* at 835.

[83] Lloyd B. Snyder, *The Constitutionality and Consequences of Restrictions on Campaign Speech by Candidates for Judicial Office*, 35 UCLA L. Rev. 207, 211 (1987) ("By prohibiting judicial candidates from speaking about disputed legal and political issues, the ABA has diminished the ability of candidates to disseminate information that would make the electorate more knowledgeable about candidates and would make elections more interesting.").

of citizens who want more information about judicial candidates. No election takes place under conditions of perfect information, of course, but unmuzzling the candidates will unleash a large amount of information for the voters' consumption. By making information about candidates artificially scarce, the announce clause helps incumbents, since they are always advantaged when information about alternatives is scarce.[84]

The regulators do not trust the citizens to sort out ethical candidates from unethical ones. The regulators also assume that voters will be seduced by the blandishments of pandering opportunists. Many voters, however, will take a long-term view and conclude that candidates who do not pander for votes will make better judges. They might reject candidates who cravenly express prejudices against litigants for reasons of race, ethnicity, religion, sex, or politics. They may reject candidates who seem to adopt positions not out of personal conviction but based on insincere political expediency. Opponents of judicial elections also assume that voters can be driven into a frenzy to oust a judge who wrote an opinion that the majority opposes. Evidence suggests that this occurs rarely.[85]

D. Freeing Political Speech

Justice Scalia's opinion for the Court, although it reached the correct result and recognized the central importance of political speech in the Court's jurisprudence, was a measured victory for the First Amendment. His aside that the speech of judicial candidates might be regulated in other contexts has no doubt inspired the regulators to go back to their drawing boards to attempt to craft

---

[84] *Id.* at 237 ("[I]t is not at all clear that the public will reject conscientious, competent judges who are willing to render decisions that do not conform to the popular political views of the day. Experience suggests that the public will not reject such judges.") (citation omitted).

[85] Republican Party of Minn. v. Kelly, 247 F.3d 854, 895, 896, 899 (8th Cir. 2001) (Beam J., dissenting). "Not surprisingly, then, in recent history prior to the 1998 election which spawned this suit, only two incumbent judges had lost elections." *Id.* at 899. As Judge Posner explains in the context of funding, equally applicable here when speech is a regulated good, "Limiting campaign expenditures may create its own distortion of the market of ideas by making it harder to challenge incumbents. To get a foothold in the market, a new product has to be advertised more heavily than existing products, which are already familiar to consumers." RICHARD POSNER, FRONTIERS OF LEGAL THEORY (2001).

language for a new clause that will circumvent the Court's opinion.[86] And, because only the announce clause was before the Court, much of Minnesota's regime for controlling the speech and association of candidates remains intact. For example, judicial candidates are still forbidden to make pledges and promises, to identify their party affiliation to the voters, to seek the endorsement of political parties, and to speak before certain groups or attend their gatherings.[87] Thus, despite the result in *Republican Party of Minnesota*, judicial candidates still possess second class First Amendment rights.

There is, however, another approach that properly recognizes the right of all candidates to enjoy equal First Amendment protection. In a brief but insightful dissent Justice Kennedy, concurring in the result reached by the Court, proposed exactly that. Kennedy's fidelity to first principles would sweep away, at least in the context of First Amendment cases involving political speech during election campaigns, the complex analytical system of balancing tests, compelling interests, narrow tailoring, strict scrutiny, intermediate scrutiny, skeptical scrutiny, and rational basis that has bedeviled constitutional law for half a century. He would replace that complexity with the following simplicity: "[C]ontent-based restrictions that do not fall within any traditional exception should be invalidated without inquiry into narrow tailoring or compelling government interests."[88] Free speech wins. It will be interesting to see if Justice Kennedy expands this approach to embrace other categories of First Amendment cases, and whether other justices join him.

[86]Republican Party of Minn. v. White, 122 S. Ct. 2528, 2539 (2002). Justice Scalia probably had in mind the canon banning "pledges" and "promises," which was not before the court. The ABA reacted swiftly. Six weeks after the Court's opinion the ABA announced "a new national campaign . . . on behalf of a fair and impartial judiciary." An ABA Commission on the 21st Century Judiciary will "conduct four public hearings across the country where judges, lawyers, bar leaders, academics, politicians and other interested citizens will address problems of increasingly politicized judicial campaigns and identify possible solutions." News Release, American Bar Association (Aug. 13, 2002).

[87]These restrictions on speech and association also conflict with the First Amendment, but it is likely that the petitioners did not raise them because they feared that the Court would be less likely to rule that they, as compared to the announce clause, suppressed freedom of speech.

[88]Republican Party of Minn. v. White, 122 S. Ct. 2528, 2544 (2002) (Kennedy, J., concurring). Kennedy named obscenity, defamation, criminal acts, and incitement to lawless action calculated or likely to bring about imminent harm as exceptions.

Justice Kennedy's solution alarmed Justice Stevens, who warned that "Kennedy would go even further and hold that no content-based restriction of a judicial candidate's speech is permitted under the First Amendment."[89] Stevens worries that candidates, freed from all restraints, might say anything. "[T]his extreme position would preclude even Minnesota's prohibition against pledges or promises by a candidate for judicial office."[90] Exactly. Stevens is right to see that Kennedy's approach would unmuzzle candidates, but he is wrong to oppose it. Judicial candidates *should* be allowed to say whatever they want, even announcing that after the election they will be open for business and soliciting bribes. They should be free to announce that they will vote to convict all African American criminal defendants, that they will side against all Muslims in contract disputes, that they will rule against all Jews in personal injury suits, that they will uphold every death sentence, and that, if it were up to them, before trial all accused rapists would be burned at the stake.

Voters are better informed if those positions are disclosed rather than kept secret. No judge exposing those beliefs would be elected. But some judges having those views, nondisclosed, might well be elected. And if that possibility highlights the potential for corruption inherent in judicial elections, then opponents of such elections should welcome this First Amendment free-for-all. If the opponents are right, then elections will become so degenerate, the candidates so depraved, the announcements, pledges, and promises so grotesque, that the public will rise up in disgust, amend their state constitutions, and abolish judicial elections.

But if they are wrong, something else will happen. Private speech and public opinion, not government regulation, will preserve the integrity of the judiciary. Numerous checks independent of the state exist to discourage unethical behavior by candidates and judges.[91] As Justice Kennedy states, "The legal profession, the legal academy,

---

[89] *Id.* at 2549 (Stevens, J., dissenting).

[90] *Id.*

[91] To name a few independent checks: Judges issue written opinions explaining their decisions. Judges are subject to appellate review. Judges must comply with a rigorous code of professional conduct. Judges can recuse themselves, or be reversed for failure to do so, if they exhibit bias toward any of the litigants.

the press, voluntary groups, political and civic leaders, and all interested citizens can use their own First Amendment freedoms to protest statements inconsistent with standards of judicial neutrality and judicial excellence."[92] In other words, democracy is its own corrective.[93]

Under this plan, the First Amendment, having driven out the regulators and been restored to its rightful place in the constitutional pantheon, will allow candidates in judicial elections to say whatever they want. The democratic process, and not government censorship, will deal with those who say what they should not. "Free elections and free speech are a powerful combination: Together they may advance our understanding of the rule of law and further a commitment to its precepts."[94] Under our Constitution, we must trust the people, and not the state, to protect themselves from unprincipled rogues.

Conclusion

This essay is not a brief arguing in favor of judicial elections. Perhaps Alexander Hamilton was correct to write in *Federalist* No. 78 that judges should be appointed, not elected. Justice Scalia was certainly right to point out the "obvious tension between the article of Minnesota's popularly approved Constitution which provides that judges shall be elected, and the Minnesota Supreme Court's announce clause which places most subjects of interest to the voters off limits."[95] But the dissenters were wrong in attempting to resolve that tension by treating the alleged consequences of judicial elections and the constitutional liberty of free speech as though they were competing policy choices. The First Amendment is not a mere policy option: It is an imperative.

---

[92] Republican Party of Minn. v. White, 122 S. Ct. 2528, 2545 (2002) (Kennedy, J., concurring).

[93] *See, e.g.* Snyder, *supra* note 83, at 235 ("Were judicial candidates afforded the right to speak freely about their beliefs on disputed legal and political matters and to make campaign pledges, the public would be able to weed out those candidates whose personal views were incompatible with the duties of judicial office.").

[94] Republican Party of Minn. v. White, 122 S. Ct. 2528, 2545 (2002) (Kennedy, J., concurring).

[95] *Id.* at 2541 (Scalia, J.).

Republican Party of Minnesota v. White is not without its larger implications. Five justices ruled in favor of the central importance of the First Amendment and the principle that political speech is at the core of democracy and must be unfettered. What, if anything, does that suggest about how those justices will rule when litigation over the Bipartisan Campaign Reform Act of 2002 reaches the Court? And if four justices are willing to accept opaque definitions of "impartiality" and its "appearance" as compelling state interests that trump the First Amendment during an election campaign, what is the prospect that they will also support campaign finance regulation, justified by the compelling state interest to prevent "corruption" and its "appearance" in other elections? Time will tell.

In the meantime, the First Amendment prevailed in *Republican Party of Minnesota*. A compulsory speech code that misused government power to prohibit candidates from announcing their views on controversial legal and political issues had undermined the principles of limited government and freedom of speech. Censorship had turned free elections into faux elections. The Supreme Court was right to stand athwart this regime and identify it for what it was—unsound in practice, undemocratic in spirit, and unconstitutional in law.

Cyberspace Cases Force Court to Reexamine Basic Assumptions of Obscenity and Child Pornography Jurisprudence

Robert Corn-Revere

Two cyberspace cases from the Supreme Court's 2001 Term forced the justices to reexamine basic constitutional assumptions underlying the obscenity and child pornography doctrines. In *Ashcroft v. Free Speech Coalition*, the Court struck down a federal ban on "virtual" child pornography in the 1996 Child Pornography Prevention Act (CPPA) as a "textbook example" of why the law permits facial challenges to overbroad statutes. It found that a prohibition of images that "appear to be a child" engaging in sexual conduct where no actual children were involved prohibited a substantial amount of protected expression and violated the First Amendment.[1] Meanwhile, in *Ashcroft v. ACLU*, the Supreme Court reversed a decision of the United States Court of Appeals for the Third Circuit to enjoin enforcement of the Child Online Protection Act (COPA), successor to the ill-fated Communications Decency Act (CDA). The Court rejected the court of appeals' reasoning that the borderless nature of the Internet rendered unconstitutional restrictions on expression deemed "harmful to minors" where legal liability is on the basis of "community standards." It remanded the case to the lower court to further explore the meaning of obscenity law in the Internet age.[2]

Both cases tackled issues that go to the heart of the Court's complicated rulings governing the regulation of sexually oriented speech. *Ashcroft v. ACLU* reopened questions at the center of the Court's more than four-decade-long struggle to establish a workable standard for

---

[1] 122 S. Ct. 1389, 1398–99 (2002).
[2] 122 S. Ct. 1700 (2002).

regulating obscenity. Although COPA applied a "variable obscenity" test for material considered "harmful to minors," that legal standard is based essentially on the same analytic factors that define obscenity for adults. Obscenity law had been relatively settled since the 1973 decision in *Miller v. California*, in which the Court reaffirmed that the "patent offensiveness" and "prurient appeal" of sexually oriented materials should be determined by reference to contemporary community standards. But the decision in *Ashcroft v. ACLU* revived the debate that raged on the Court before *Miller*, about which kind of standards—and which community—should govern obscenity determinations. It directed the court of appeals to address the legal conundrums that plagued the Supreme Court in the years before *Miller*.

Ashcroft v. Free Speech Coalition, on the other hand, reaffirmed the traditional conception of child pornography—that such material is illegal because actual children are abused in its production. Congress had sought to extend the concept of child pornography to include images of "virtual" children, thus removing the direct link to child abuse, but the Court held that such an expansion of the child pornography concept would outlaw speech that traditionally has been protected by the First Amendment. The decision immediately prompted legislative efforts to adopt a new version of the virtual child pornography ban, thus ensuring a prolonged debate over the permissible scope of the prohibition.

By touching on core issues that define the essential nature of obscenity and child pornography, these two cases breathed new life into disputes about which kind of speech may be excluded from First Amendment protection and how courts should draw the line between protected and unprotected speech. In *Ashcroft v. ACLU*, the debate will continue in the court of appeals, which must decide whether COPA survives constitutional scrutiny and under what standard. With *Ashcroft v. Free Speech Coalition*, on the other hand, the judicial debate ended with the Court's April 16, 2002, decision, at least for now. Legislation introduced immediately after the decision ensures that the constitutional arguments over child pornography will continue in Congress and, eventually, in the courts.

Protected versus Unprotected Speech

To understand these issues and their significance, it is necessary to review the development of obscenity and child pornography as categories of speech that are unprotected by the First Amendment. Despite the seemingly absolute command of the First Amendment that "Congress shall make no law ... abridging the freedom of speech, or of the press," the Supreme Court has held that the restriction of certain categories of speech does not present a constitutional problem. This is because, as Professor Alexander Meiklejohn explained, the First Amendment "does not forbid the abridgement of speech [but] it does forbid the abridging of *freedom of speech*."[3] The Court sketched the general contours of the exclusions from constitutional protection in a 1942 case in which it identified "certain well-defined and narrowly limited classes of speech" that included "the lewd and obscene, the profane, the libelous and the insulting or 'fighting' words."[4] But this categorical approach to First Amendment protection obscures a deeper complexity: Restricting unprotected speech may not present a "constitutional problem," as the Court put it, but determining what expression may be heaped into these exclusions certainly does.

The law of defamation illustrates this point. It has long been recognized that the publication of libelous statements constitutes a tort for which courts may order a remedy, but in 1964 the Supreme Court decreed, in *New York Times v. Sullivan*, that the First Amendment sharply constrains what expression may be considered defamatory. This constitutional oversight of state tort law is necessary, according to the Court, because freedom of expression needs "breathing space" to survive.[5] Consequently, it erected formidable constitutional hurdles against any recovery in a defamation action by public officials. And in the years since 1964, the Supreme Court and lower courts have developed a rich and complex body of First Amendment law that extends both substantive and procedural protections in all libel cases.

The Quest for a Workable Obscenity Test

Much of the same legal development has occurred in the other categories of "unprotected" speech, and the law governing obscenity

---

[3] ALEXANDER MEIKLEJOHN, FREE SPEECH AND ITS RELATION TO GOOD GOVERNMENT 19 (1948) (emphasis added).

[4] Chaplinsky v. New Hampshire, 315 U.S. 568, 571–572 (1942).

[5] N.Y. Times Co. v. Sullivan, 376 U.S. 254, 271–272 (1964).

is no exception. When the Supreme Court in 1957 reaffirmed the concept that obscenity is beyond the First Amendment's protection, it also ruled that the question of whether a particular work is obscene necessarily implicates constitutional law. In distinguishing protected from unprotected speech involving sexual matters, the Court noted that "sex and obscenity are not synonymous" because sex is "a great and mysterious force in human life [and] has indisputably been a subject of absorbing interest to mankind through the ages; it is one of the vital problems of human interest and public concern."[6]

Accordingly, the First Amendment presumptively protects sexually oriented expression unless a court determines that the average person, applying contemporary community standards, would find that the dominant theme of the material taken as a whole is patently offensive and appeals to the prurient interest. The Court in *Roth* noted that "[a]ll ideas having even the slightest redeeming social importance—unorthodox ideas, controversial ideas, even ideas hateful to the prevailing climate of opinion—have the full protection of the [First Amendment] guarantees."[7] It subsequently clarified that no expression could be declared obscene, and therefore placed outside the First Amendment's protective umbrella, unless it is found to be "utterly without redeeming social value."[8]

Over time, however, the analytic tools that make up the obscenity test proved to be far more slippery than the ones used to define other categories of unprotected speech. In defamation actions involving public officials or public figures, for example, the wronged party must prove that the defendant published a false statement of fact about the plaintiff that injured his reputation, *and* that it was published with reckless disregard of whether or not it was true. Although no test involving language can be applied with mathematical precision, it is much easier to determine whether a purported "fact" about a person is false and published in the face of actual doubts about its truth, than it is to evaluate whether a work is "prurient" according to community standards or that it lacks any social importance.

[6] Roth v. United States, 354 U.S. 476, 487 (1957).

[7] *Id.* at 484, 489. *See* Manual Enters., Inc. v. Day, 370 U.S. 478, 486–487 (1962).

[8] A Book Named "John Cleland's Memoirs of a Woman of Pleasure" v. Massachusetts, 383 U.S. 413, 418–419 (1966).

The Court has characterized the separation between obscenity and constitutionally protected expression about sex as a "dim and uncertain line."[9] Not surprisingly, where—and even whether—the line should be drawn has generated a great deal of disagreement. Two justices, William O. Douglas and Hugo Black, never accepted the proposition that obscenity was beyond constitutional protection.[10] Douglas wrote that the obscenity standard on the basis of an appeal to the "prurient interest" was an exercise in thought control, and he concluded that "[a]ny test that turns on what is offensive to the community's standards is too loose, too capricious, too destructive of freedom of expression to be squared with the First Amendment."[11]

Although Justices Black and Douglas represented a distinctly minority view, there was hardly consensus among those in the majority. Justice Harlan noted that the 13 obscenity cases at the Supreme Court between 1957 and 1968 produced a total of 55 separate opinions, and that the quest to find a coherent test for obscenity had only "produced a variety of views among the members of the Court unmatched in any other course of constitutional adjudication."[12] Justice Potter Stewart took the position that only "hard core pornography" could be suppressed,[13] while others concluded that material short of the hard core could be banned, so long as it was patently offensive and lacked any redeeming value.[14] Another view, advanced by Justice Harlan, was that the federal role was limited to restricting hard-core pornography, while the states had greater latitude to regulate books on the basis of "offensive" portrayals of sex.[15]

---

[9] *See* Bantam Books, Inc. v. Sullivan, 372 U.S. 58, 66 (1963).

[10] *E.g.*, Jacobellis v. Ohio, 378 U.S. 184, 196 (1964) (Black, J., and Douglas, J., concurring).

[11] *Roth*, 354 U.S. at 512 (Douglas, J., dissenting).

[12] Interstate Circuit, Inc. v. Dallas, 390 U.S. 676, 704–705 & n.1 (1968) (Harlan, J., dissenting).

[13] *E.g.*, Ginzberg v. United States, 383 U.S. 463, 497 (1966) (Stewart, J., dissenting); *Jacobellis*, 378 U.S. at 197 (Stewart, J., concurring).

[14] *Memoirs*, 383 U.S. at 418 (Brennan, J., joined by Warren, C.J., and Fortas, J.); *Jacobellis*, 378 U.S. at 193–195 (Brennan, J., joined by Goldberg, J.).

[15] *Roth*, 354 U.S. at 496–508 (Harlan, J., concurring in part and dissenting in part); *Interstate Circuit, Inc.*, 390 U.S. at 706 (Harlan, J., dissenting).

Notwithstanding the range of opinion on this doctrinal scale, the justices seemed to agree that the concept of obscenity could not be defined precisely. In describing the Court's efforts to "define what may be undefinable," Justice Stewart eschewed any attempt to come up with an intelligible formula for obscenity but added most famously (if unhelpfully) that "I know it when I see it."[16] Somewhat less pithily, Justice Black wrote that "no person, not even the most learned judge much less a layman, is capable of knowing in advance of an ultimate decision in his particular case by this Court whether certain material comes within the area of 'obscenity.'"[17] And Justice Brennan, the author of the *Roth* opinion, who later concluded that it was impossible to fashion a constitutional test for obscenity, agreed that "one cannot say with certainty that material is obscene until at least five members of this Court, applying inevitably obscure standards, have pronounced it so."[18] He wrote that the Court was "manifestly unable" to describe the obscenity concept in advance "except by reference to concepts so elusive that they fail to distinguish clearly between protected and unprotected speech."[19]

Justice Harlan, who would have accorded more latitude for the enforcement of state obscenity laws than for federal proscriptions, wrote that the Court in *Roth* erred in assuming that "'obscenity' is a peculiar genus of 'speech and press,' which is as distinct, recognizable, and classifiable as poison ivy is among other plants." Accordingly, he concluded that whether a particular book may be suppressed is not "a mere matter of classification, of 'fact,' to be entrusted to a fact-finder and insulated from constitutional judgment." Such determinations do not end with a jury verdict or trial court ruling because they involve "a question of constitutional judgment of the most sensitive and delicate kind." For that reason, Justice Harlan foresaw that "every such suppression raises an individual constitutional problem, in which a reviewing court must determine for itself whether the attacked expression is suppressable within constitutional standards."[20]

---

[16] *Jacobellis*, 378 U.S. at 197 (Stewart, J., concurring).

[17] *Ginzburg*, 383 U.S. at 480–481 (Black, J., dissenting).

[18] Paris Adult Theatre I v. Slaton, 413 U.S. 49, 92 (1973) (Brennan, J., dissenting, joined by Marshall, J., and Stewart, J.).

[19] *Id.* at 84.

[20] *Roth*, 354 U.S. at 497–498 (Harlan, J., dissenting).

Because of this need for ultimate constitutional review, a significant number of cases were presented to the Supreme Court for a final determination of obscenity, thus requiring the justices to examine the challenged material themselves. If at least five justices, applying their respective tests, decided that the material was not obscene, the conviction was reversed without opinion, typically with the unadorned statement: "The petition for a writ of certiorari is granted and the judgment of the [court below] is reversed."[21] By 1964, Chief Justice Warren complained that most of the Court's obscenity decisions since *Roth* had been issued without opinion.[22] Nevertheless, the practice became more prominent after the Court's 1967 decision in *Redrup v. New York*, in which the Court summarily reversed convictions in three consolidated cases.[23] The Court issued 31 similar reversals between 1967 and 1971, and countless other decisions denying review and upholding lower court convictions.[24]

The practice was wholly unsatisfactory for many reasons, not the least of which is that it turned the justices into censors of last resort. Justice Harlan complained that the members of the Court were tied to "the absurd business of perusing and viewing the miserable stuff that pours into the Court."[25] Justice Brennan observed that the material may have varying degrees of social importance, but complained "it is hardly a source of edification to the members of this Court who are compelled to view it before passing on its obscenity."[26] Justice Douglas, on the other hand, who never subscribed to the majority position that obscenity could be denied constitutional protection, always refused to look at the material because, he said, "I have thought the First Amendment made it unconstitutional for me to act as a censor."[27]

But the Court's practice of subjecting salacious materials to final review caused a bigger problem than just ruffling judicial sensibilities. Regardless of whether it upheld convictions by denying review

[21] *E.g.*, Keney v. New York, 388 U.S. 440 (1967) (per curiam).

[22] *Jacobellis*, 378 U.S. at 200 (Warren, C.J., dissenting).

[23] 386 U.S. 767 (1967).

[24] *Paris Adult Theatre I*, 413 U.S. at 82 n.8 (Brennan, J., dissenting) (collecting cases).

[25] *Interstate Circuit, Inc.*, 390 U.S. at 707 (Harlan, J., dissenting).

[26] *Paris Adult Theatre I*, 413 U.S. at 92–93 (Brennan, J., dissenting).

[27] *Id.* at 71 (Douglas, J., dissenting).

of lower court rulings or reversing them without opinion, the summary review process provided no guidance to lower courts. Final decisions by the Supreme Court only resolved disputes between individual litigants without providing any doctrinal guidance. Justice Brennan wrote that "the practice effectively censors protected expression by leaving lower court determinations of obscenity intact even though the status of the allegedly obscene material is entirely unsettled until final review here."[28] Accordingly, he found, "judicial attempts to follow our lead conscientiously have often ended in hopeless confusion."[29]

The obscenity puzzle was further complicated by the need to decide which community dictated "community standards" for determining the patent offensiveness of sexual expression. Beginning with the 1957 *Roth* decision, Justice Harlan argued that local standards should govern state obscenity prosecutions, while national standards should apply in federal cases. He wrote that the same book "which is freely read in one State might be classed as obscene in another," but he foresaw little danger to our system of ordered liberty "so long as there is no uniform nation-wide suppression of the book, and so long as other States are free to experiment with the same or bolder books." At the same time, Justice Harlan opposed a single national standard for obscenity, warning that "the dangers of federal censorship in this field are far greater than anything the States may do."[30]

The debate over community standards intensified as the Court began to apply the *Roth* standard in the 1960s. In *Manual Enterprises, Inc. v. Day*, the Court overturned a Post Office ruling that certain gay-themed magazines were "unmailable" under federal law. Following its own independent review of the magazines in question, the Court found that "the most that can be said of them is that they are dismally unpleasant, uncouth and tawdry," but that such qualities were not sufficient to render them obscene. With respect to the applicable community, however, Justice Harlan's plurality opinion applied a national standard of decency to the federal law because it covers "all parts of the United States whose population

---

[28] *Id.* at 93 (Brennan, J., dissenting).

[29] *Id.* at 84.

[30] *Roth*, 354 U.S. at 505–506 (Harlan, J., dissenting).

reflects many different ethnic and cultural backgrounds." The Court declined to rule on whether Congress could "prescribe a lesser geographical framework for judging this issue that would not have the intolerable consequence of denying some sections of the country access to material, there deemed acceptable, which in others might be considered offensive to prevailing community standards of decency."[31]

The issue was presented squarely two years later in *Jacobellis v. Ohio*, and a plurality again purported to reaffirm the holding of *Roth* that "the constitutional status of an allegedly obscene work must be determined on the basis of a national standard." Justice Brennan wrote that sustaining the suppression of a particular book or film in one locality "would deter its dissemination in other localities where it might be held not obscene, since sellers and exhibitors would be reluctant to risk criminal conviction in testing the variation between the two places." Noting that "[i]t is, after all, a national Constitution we are expounding," Justice Brennan pointed out that the Court "has explicitly refused to tolerate a result whereby 'the constitutional limits of free expression in the Nation would vary with state lines.'"[32]

Chief Justice Warren, however, disagreed, writing that "there is no provable 'national standard' and perhaps there should be none." Joined by Justice Clark, he noted that the Supreme Court had been unable to articulate a national standard for obscenity "and it would be unreasonable to expect local courts to divine one." The Chief Justice read *Roth* to endorse the application of local community standards, and reasoned that the Supreme Court should limit its role to determining whether lower courts had sufficient evidence before them to sustain an obscenity finding. Otherwise, he concluded, the Supreme Court would be required to review the contested materials and to sit as "Super Censor of all the obscenity purveyed throughout the Nation."[33]

After more than a decade and a half of doctrinal turmoil, the Court confronted the definitional problems involving obscenity and the community standards issue in *Miller v. California*. In upholding

---

[31] 370 U.S. 478, 488–490 (1962).

[32] *Jacobellis*, 378 U.S. at 194–195 (citation omitted).

[33] *Id.* at 200–203 (Warren, C.J., dissenting).

a conviction under state law, the Court articulated the current three-part test for obscenity: (1) whether the average person, applying contemporary community standards would find that the work, taken as a whole, appeals to the prurient interest, (2) whether the work depicts or describes, in a patently offensive way, sexual conduct specifically defined by the applicable state law, and (3) whether the work, taken as a whole, lacks serious literary, artistic, political, or scientific value."[34] Although the decision was 5–4, it was the first time since *Roth* that a majority of the Court endorsed a test for obscenity.

The *Miller* majority abandoned the requirement that a work must be shown to be "utterly without redeeming social value," but it also clarified that obscenity is limited to depictions of hard-core sexual conduct. Because of the greater agreement among the justices regarding the governing standard, the Court abandoned the "casual practice" of *Redrup v. New York* of issuing decisions without opinions in obscenity cases. It also reduced the need for judicial review of lower court decisions by classifying the "prurient interest" and "patently offensiveness" determinations as "essentially questions of fact" for juries to decide.[35]

On the issue of community standards, the Court held that the Constitution does not require a national standard, finding that "[p]eople in different States vary in their tastes and attitudes, and this diversity is not to be strangled by the absolutism of imposed uniformity." The Court upheld a conviction on the basis of community standards of the state of California, and it found there cannot be "fixed, uniform national standards of precisely what appeals to the 'prurient interest' or is 'patently offensive.'" Describing a search for a national standard as "an exercise in futility," Chief Justice Burger's opinion for the Court emphasized that "our nation is simply too big and too diverse for this Court to reasonably expect that such standards could be articulated for all 50 states in a single formulation, assuming the prerequisite consensus exists."[36] He noted that the First Amendment does not require "that the people of Maine or Mississippi accept public depiction of conduct found tolerable in Las Vegas or New York City." But he also acknowledged the converse

[34] Miller v. California, 413 U.S. 15, 24 (1973).

[35] *Id.* at 29–30.

[36] *Id.* at 20, 30–33.

proposition—that community reactions to literature in, say, rural Georgia or Tennessee, should not dictate what is acceptable in urban centers.[37]

The four-justice minority in *Miller* distilled a different lesson from the history of disputes over the meaning of obscenity. Justice Brennan, author of the *Roth* majority opinion, wrote in another case decided the same day as *Miller*, "after 16 years of experimentation and debate I am reluctantly forced to the conclusion that none of the available formulas, including the one announced today, can reduce the vagueness to a tolerable level."[38] Justice Brennan was joined by Justices Stewart and Marshall (Justice Stewart evidently no longer of the opinion that he would know obscenity when he saw it). Justice Douglas also wrote separately to highlight his long-held belief that obscenity could not be excluded from First Amendment protection. The dissenters in *Miller* questioned the notion that obscenity questions could be resolved definitively by juries applying community standards. The role of appellate courts in making independent judgments in obscenity cases could be reduced, they reasoned, only by exposing "much protected, sexually oriented expression to the vagaries of jury determinations" thus leading to an "unprecedented infringement of First Amendment rights."[39]

Despite the sharp divisions between the majority and minority opinions, the *Miller* test for obscenity ushered in a period of relative doctrinal stability. The following year, in *Hamling v. United States*, the same majority applied its new obscenity test to a prosecution in California under federal law, and found that the community standards requirement did not require the "substitution of some smaller geographical area" any more than it called on jurors to apply hypothetical and unascertainable "national standards." Rather than focusing on some "precise geographic area" as the relevant "community," the Court held that the purpose of a community standards approach was to ensure "that the material is judged neither on the basis of each juror's personal opinion, nor by its effect on a particularly sensitive or insensitive person or group."[40]

---

[37] *Id.* at 32–33 & n.13.

[38] *Paris Adult Theatre I*, 413 U.S. at 84 (Brennan, J., dissenting).

[39] *Id.* at 102.

[40] Hamling v. United States, 418 U.S. 87, 103–107 (1974).

The Court also clarified that the "serious merit" requirement of the *Miller* test was not predicated on community standards. In *Pope v. Illinois*, the Court held that the test for serious literary, artistic, political, or scientific value did not hinge on the vagaries of local tastes, but instead must be judged by reference to the hypothetical reasonable person.[41] Although all nine justices agreed (albeit in five separate opinions) that local standards should not dictate questions of merit, four took the position that the sale of obscene materials to adults could not be banned consistently with the Constitution. Once again, the key was community standards: "The question of offensiveness to community standards, whether national or local, is not one that the average juror can be expected to answer with evenhanded consistency," Justice Stevens wrote in dissent. "In the final analysis, the guilt or innocence of a criminal defendant in an obscenity trial is determined primarily by individual jurors' subjective reactions to the materials in question rather than by the predictable application of rules of law."[42]

Variable Obscenity: The "Harm to Minors" Standard

If the question of obscenity was not already sufficiently complicated, the Supreme Court added another level of complexity by creating a category of materials that could be classified as "obscene for minors" but not for adults. Under the variable obscenity standard (sometimes called "obscenity lite"), the Supreme Court has held that the government may designate some sexually oriented material as being "harmful to minors" and may limit the sale or display of such things as "girlie magazines" to children.[43] Such "variable obscenity" restrictions, however, are rather limited. The Supreme Court has held that it will not tolerate vague, open-ended restrictions on speech—not even for the benefit of minors—and that the government cannot "reduce the adult population . . . to reading only what is fit for children."[44]

---

[41] 481 U.S. 497, 500–501 (1987).

[42] *Id.* at 514 (Stevens, J., dissenting) (quoting Smith v. United States, 431 U.S. 291, 315–316 (1977) (Stevens, J., dissenting)).

[43] Ginsberg v. New York, 390 U.S. 629 (1968).

[44] Butler v. Michigan, 352 U.S. 380, 383–84 (1957). *See* Bolger v. Youngs Drug Prod. Corp., 463 U.S. 60, 73–74 (1983); Erznoznik v. Jacksonville, 422 U.S. 205 (1975); Interstate Circuit v. Dallas, 390 U.S. 676 (1968).

As this subspecies of obscenity has evolved, the Supreme Court has ruled that the three-part *Miller* factors should be used to determine what material is obscene for minors, but with a slight difference. Reviewing courts must determine whether the average person, applying contemporary community standards would find that the work, taken as a whole, appeals to the prurient interest *of minors*, and whether the work lacks serious literary, artistic, political, or scientific value *for minors*. Over the years, courts have held that to meet this standard, the material must lack serious value for "a legitimate minority of normal, older adolescents."[45] Under this approach, "if any reasonable minor, including a seventeen-year-old, would find serious value, the material is not harmful to minors."[46] Accordingly, the Supreme Court has indicated that regulation in this area is limited to "borderline obscenity" or to material considered to be "virtually obscene."[47]

However much the concept of variable obscenity might have been limited by this formulation, it necessarily added more ambiguity to the elusive concept of obscenity. A reviewing court must first resolve the question of how the average person can apply "community standards" to divine what material appeals to the prurient interest of the normal 17-year-old. The obvious rhetorical response (and probably the most accurate answer)—what doesn't?—no doubt would fail to satisfy judicial standards of precision. The question of "serious merit" for minors is at least as difficult to answer because it suggests that material that has serious literary, artistic, political, or scientific merit for adults does not necessarily have the same value for teens at the threshold of majority.

Few courts have ever addressed this issue, but one Ohio court in the mid-1970s held that the books *One Flew Over the Cuckoo's Nest* and *Manchild in the Promised Land* violated the state's "harmful to juveniles" law. It found that the books "have no literary, artistic, political or scientific value whatsoever" and "were designed by the authors to appeal to the base instincts of persons and to shock others

---

[45] Am. Booksellers Ass'n. v. Virginia, 882 F.2d 125, 127 (4th Cir. 1989).

[46] Am. Booksellers v. Webb, 919 F.2d 1493, 1504–05 (11th Cir. 1990); Davis-Kidd Booksellers, Inc. v. McWherter, 866 S.W.2d 520, 528 (Tenn. 1993).

[47] Virginia v. Am. Booksellers Ass'n., 484 U.S. 383, 390 (1988).

for the purpose of effectuating sales."[48] It is not known how the Supreme Court would evaluate the Ohio court's analysis under the current rule that "harmful to minors" material must be "virtually obscene," but Justice O'Connor's partial dissent in *Reno v. ACLU* provides some insight into at least one view. Joined by Chief Justice Rehnquist, she observed that although "discussions about prison rape or nude art . . . may have some redeeming education value for adults, they do not necessarily have any such value for minors."[49] Which material falls into this "merit gap" between expression of value for adults but unfit for minors remains a mystery.

Ashcroft v. ACLU and the Online Obscenity Puzzle

The Child Online Protection Act was the second effort by Congress to enact restrictions on Internet speech to shield children from sexually oriented expression. The first attempt, the ban on "indecent" material in the CDA, ended with a near unanimous Supreme Court decision invalidating the restriction. The Court unanimously struck down a provision of the CDA that prohibited the display of "indecent" materials online, and voted 7–2 to void a provision that banned the transmission of indecent information to a minor. It held that the Internet receives the full protection of the First Amendment, and that the CDA's prohibitions were both vague and overly broad. The Court unfavorably contrasted the CDA's indecency standard, borrowed from the FCC's restrictions on vulgar language on the radio, with the three-part test for obscenity.[50]

In response, Congress adopted COPA in 1998. In doing so, it sought to avoid the same fate for the new law by making it narrower than its predecessor. Unlike the CDA, COPA does not apply to all sexually oriented information on the Internet, but prohibits making "any communication for commercial purposes" over the World Wide Web that "is available to any minor and that includes any material that is harmful to minors." COPA covers material that "depicts, describes, or represents, in a manner patently offensive with respect to minors, an actual or simulated sexual act or sexual

---

[48] Grosser v. Woollett, 341 N.E.2d 356, 360–361, 367 (Ohio C.P. 1974).

[49] Reno v. ACLU, 521 U.S. 844, 896 (O'Connor, J., concurring in part, dissenting in part).

[50] *Id.* at 872–874.

contact, an actual or simulated normal or perverted sexual act, or a lewd exhibition of the genitals or post-pubescent female breast." Incorporating the variable obscenity standard, the Act requires a finding that the average person, applying contemporary community standards, would find that the material taken as a whole would appeal to the prurient interest or minors, and that it lacks "serious literary, artistic, political, or scientific value for minors."[51]

Despite this somewhat narrower focus compared with the CDA, Judge Lowell A. Reed of the U.S. District Court for the Eastern District of Pennsylvania issued a preliminary injunction blocking enforcement of COPA. The court found that plaintiffs were likely to succeed on the merits of their constitutional claim—that the law would burden constitutionally protected speech, that it would chill online speech in general, and that the government had failed to demonstrate that COPA is the least restrictive means of serving its purpose.[52]

On appeal, the United States Court of Appeals for the Third Circuit affirmed the decision, but did so for reasons not found in the district court order and not argued by the parties. Instead, the court of appeals focused on the futility of applying "contemporary community standards" to a global medium. The court found that "web publishers are without any means to limit access to their sites on the basis of the geographic location of particular Internet users." Accordingly, that First Amendment analysis was affected dramatically by "the unique factors that affect communication in the new and technology-laden medium of the web."[53]

The court distinguished the way obscenity law applies to other technologies, noting that publishers can choose not to mail unsolicited sexually explicit material to certain locales and phone-sex operators can refuse to accept calls from particular communities. Because the court found that "the Internet 'negates geometry'" and a Web publisher "will not even know the geographic location of visitors to its site," it reasoned that application of a First Amendment standard on the basis of community standards "essentially requires that

---

[51] 47 U.S.C. § 231(e)(6).

[52] ACLU v. Reno II, 31 F. Supp.2d 473 (E.D. Pa. 1999). *See also* ACLU v. Reno II, 1998 WL 813423 (E.D. Pa. 1998) (issuing temporary restraining order).

[53] ACLU v. Reno II, 217 F.3d 162, 174–175 (3d Cir. 2000).

every Web publisher subject to the statute [must] abide by the most restrictive and conservative state's community standards in order to avoid criminal liability."[54] It held that "this aspect of COPA, without reference to its other provisions, must lead inexorably to a holding of the likelihood of unconstitutionality of the entire COPA statute."[55] The court based its holding entirely on the likely unconstitutionality of "community standards" in the Internet context.

The court of appeals made clear that its critique of the "harmful to minors" standard applies equally to the test for obscenity. It stated that *Miller v. California* "has no applicability to the Internet and the Web, where Web publishers are currently without the ability to control the geographic scope of the recipients of their communications." It further noted that "[t]he State may not regulate at all if it turns out that even the least restrictive means of regulation is still unreasonable when its limitations on freedom of speech are balanced against the benefits gained from those limitations."[56]

The Supreme Court Weighs In

The Third Circuit's decision set the stage for a comprehensive review of the jurisprudence governing obscenity, and the Supreme Court did not shy away from this task. By a vote of 8–1, the Court reversed the court of appeals and remanded the case for further proceedings, keeping the injunction in place in the interim. Although ostensibly a very narrow ruling that affected only the Third Circuit's rationale, the Court's decision in *Ashcroft v. ACLU* opened a new chapter in the ongoing debate over obscenity. The five separate opinions recalled the doctrinal conflicts of the 1960s with some justices embracing local standards for obscenity, others endorsing national standards (as interpreted by local juries), and still others remaining undecided or choosing none of the above. It leaves to the court of appeals the unenviable task of deciding whether COPA lives or dies and fashioning a rationale that will garner majority support on a fractured Supreme Court.

Finding a majority view in *Ashcroft v. ACLU* is a daunting task. Although five justices signed onto various portions of the opinion

[54] *Id.* at 169, 175.
[55] *Id.* at 174.
[56] *Id.* at 179–180.

of the Court, the only point on which they could agree was that "COPA's reliance on community standards to identify 'material that is harmful to minors' does not *by itself* render the statute substantially overbroad for purposes of the First Amendment."[57] Beyond that one point of agreement, there was a significant division over how community standards should apply to the Internet.

Justice Thomas, joined by Justice Scalia and Chief Justice Rehnquist, took the hardest line, reasoning that jurors may draw on their personal knowledge of their own communities for which the law does not specify a particular geographic area. If, as a result, speakers on the Internet must conform to varying local standards, so be it. Those who fear draconian local enforcement can simply avoid using the Internet as a means of communication. As Justice Thomas put it, "[I]f a publisher wishes for its material to be judged only by the standards of particular communities, then it need only take the simple step of utilizing a medium that enables it to target the release of its material into those communities." In this view, unreasonable local standards are moderated by the "serious merit" criterion, which enables appellate courts to set "a national floor for socially redeeming value."[58]

Justices O'Connor and Breyer each wrote separately to express their disagreement over which community standard to apply. Although both concurred in the judgment of the Court, they argued that the Constitution requires the use of a national standard to judge speech on the Internet. Otherwise, Justice Breyer wrote, "the most puritan of communities" would have "a heckler's Internet veto affecting the rest of the nation."[59] He cited language from COPA's legislative history for support that Congress intended to employ an "adult" standard rather than a "geographic" standard for determining which material is "suitable for minors." Justice O'Connor similarly expressed some concern that the use of local community standards "will cause problems for regulation of obscenity on the Internet, for adults as well as children, in future cases." She suggested that *Miller* allowed the application of local standards but did

---

[57] 122 S. Ct. 1700, 1713 (2002) (emphasis in original).

[58] *Id.* at 1710, 1712 (citation omitted).

[59] *Id.* at 1716 (Breyer, J., concurring).

not mandate their use, and disputed the Court's earlier conclusion that a national standard is "unascertainable."[60]

Although Justices O'Connor and Breyer expressed concern about applying local community standards to Internet speech, both acknowledged that jurors inevitably would base their assessments of a national standard to some extent on their local perceptions. They found the prospect of such inherent regional variations to be constitutionally acceptable "in a system that draws jurors from a local geographic area."[61] Their two concurring opinions suggested that applying a national standard on remand might be sufficient to cure any constitutional defects in COPA.

Justice Kennedy, on the other hand, was far less positive about the law's prospects. Joined by Justices Souter and Ginsburg, he wrote that there is a very real likelihood that COPA is overbroad and cannot survive a facial challenge. He suggested that the Court should proceed cautiously in light of Congress's attempt to fashion a narrower law than the CDA, and, for that reason, the Third Circuit's community standards rationale "stated and applied at such a high level of generality" could not be sustained. Nevertheless, Justice Kennedy explained that a range of concerns may invalidate COPA's variable obscenity standard, including the variation in community standards, the question of what constitutes the work "as a whole" on the Internet, and the type and amount of speech restricted by COPA, among other factors.

Such questions, he reasoned, are interrelated and require comprehensive review by the court of appeals. Justice Kennedy stressed that such review must give special weight to the Internet's unique status, because "when Congress purports to abridge the freedom of a new medium, [courts] must be particularly attentive to its distinct attributes, for 'differences in the characteristics of new media justify . . . differences in the First Amendment standards applied to them.'" Despite "grave doubts that COPA is consistent with the First Amendment," Kennedy concluded that the Court should await a more thorough analysis by the Third Circuit.[62]

---

[60] *Id.* at 1714–15 (O'Connor, J., concurring).

[61] *Id.* at 1716 (Breyer, J., concurring); *Id.* at 1715 (O'Connor, J., concurring).

[62] *Id.* at 1718–22 (Kennedy, J., concurring) (citations omitted).

The sole dissenter was Justice Stevens, author of the Court's opinion in *Reno v. ACLU*. In his view, it is "quite wrong to allow the standards of a minority consisting of the least tolerant communities" to regulate access to the World Wide Web. In its original form, Justice Stevens noted that the community standards formulation "provided a shield for communications that are offensive only to the least tolerant members of society." Before *Roth* infused obscenity determinations with First Amendment considerations, courts judged such cases by the presumed impact of sexually oriented material on the most vulnerable members of society. After *Roth*, courts asked whether the *average* person, rather than the most sensitive, would find that material patently offensive, considering contemporary community standards. In the Internet context, however, Justice Stevens found that "community standards become a sword rather than a shield" because "[i]f a prurient appeal is offensive in a puritan village, it may be a crime to post it on the World Wide Web."[63]

Acknowledging that COPA was an improvement over the CDA, Justice Stevens nevertheless concluded that the changes were insufficient to cure the law's constitutional deficiencies. The elements of COPA's "harm to minors test" did not narrow the law sufficiently, he concluded, because the "patently offensive" and "prurient interests" elements of the standard depended on a community standard. The requirement that the material be "in some sense erotic" similarly did not narrow its scope, because "[a]rguably every depiction of nudity—partial or full—is in some sense erotic *with respect to minors*."[64] Similarly, the "serious value" prong of the test did not narrow the scope of COPA, because it requires juries to determine whether the material has serious value for minors. Accordingly, Justice Stevens concluded that the community standards analysis alone was sufficient to doom COPA.

In sum, the Court in *Ashcroft v. ACLU* not only declined to decide whether COPA violates the First Amendment, it also provided no clear guidance for how the court of appeals should answer that ultimate question. The only point of clarity was that eight justices were dissatisfied with the Third Circuit's initial attempt. On remand, the appellate court must craft a decision that will survive Supreme

[63] *Id.* at 1722–23 (Stevens, J., dissenting)

[64] *Id.* at 1725 (emphasis in original).

Court review by parsing the five separate opinions. Three justices (Thomas, Scalia, and Chief Justice Rehnquist) clearly support the law and approve using local community standards to define obscenity; one justice (Stevens) clearly opposes the law because of its reliance on local community standards; three justices (Kennedy, Souter, and Ginsburg) are deeply skeptical of the law and are wary of imposing local standards on a global medium; and the two remaining justices (Breyer and O'Connor) may support the law if it employs a national standard for variable obscenity.

The Third Circuit could look to earlier Supreme Court decisions for guidance, but will find no definitive answers there. The current divisions on the Court largely replicate the debates that took place between 1957 and 1973, the tumultuous period between the decisions in *Roth* and *Miller*. While *Miller*'s three-part obscenity test settled, at least for a time, how obscenity should be determined, *Ashcroft v. ACLU* reopened the old controversies and raised new questions of how to define and enforce a "variable obscenity" standard for a medium that does not respect geographic boundaries.

The Problem of Child Pornography

Although the Court last term left many unanswered issues regarding obscenity, it faced squarely and answered clearly some fundamental questions involving what, for most people, is a far more difficult subject—the problem of child pornography. Like obscenity, child pornography is a category of communication that is unprotected by the First Amendment. The Supreme Court has approved laws that ban the creation, distribution, or even the mere possession of material that depicts the sexual exploitation of children.[65] Unlike the judicial dispute in the obscenity cases, however, there is no disagreement about whether child pornography should be outlawed, because the focus of the law is on the child abuse committed in its production. As Justice Kennedy explained in *Ashcroft v. Free Speech Coalition*, the rationale for treating child pornography as unprotected speech is "based upon how it [is] made, not on what it communicate[s]."[66]

---

[65] Osborne v. Ohio, 495 U.S. 103 (1990); Ferber v. New York, 458 U.S. 747 (1982).
[66] 122 S. Ct. 1389, 1401 (2002).

Because the purposes to be served by the laws are distinct, the respective tests for obscenity and child pornography are quite different. In *Ferber v. New York*, the Supreme Court noted that in child pornography cases the usual test for obscenity is "adjusted" in several respects. First, if the material depicts a minor engaged in sexual conduct there is no requirement that it appeal to the prurient interest of the average person. Second, the material need not be considered as a whole. Third, the "serious merit" or a work cannot save it to the extent it contains child pornography.[67] As the Court noted, "[i]t is irrelevant to the child [who has been abused] whether or not the material . . . has a literary, artistic, political or social value." It added that "[t]he value of permitting live performances and photographic reproductions of children engaged in lewd sexual conduct is exceedingly modest, if not de minimis."[68]

This stricter standard of liability has been upheld because of the government's interest in protecting children from actual sexual abuse. At the same time, however, the Supreme Court has stressed that the First Amendment limits the range of conduct that can be prohibited. In *Ferber*, the Court stated that the government's interest was limited to prohibiting "sexual conduct by children below a specified age," and it noted that "descriptions or other depictions . . . which do not involve live performance or photographic or other visual reproduction of live performances, retain First Amendment protection." It suggested that a person could avoid the reach of child pornography laws by using "a person over the statutory age who perhaps looked younger," or by depicting a "[s]imulation outside of the prohibition."[69]

Congress Targets High-Tech Kiddy Porn

As in the case of obscenity, technological advances prompted changes in the law prohibiting child pornography. In 1996 Congress passed the Child Pornography Prevention Act of 1996 (CPPA) to restrict "high-tech kiddie porn" by prohibiting the possession, sale, receipt, or distribution of computer-generated images that "appear to depict minors engaging in sexually explicit conduct." The law

---

[67] *Ferber*, 458 U.S. at 764–765.
[68] *Id.* at 761–762 (citation omitted).
[69] *Id.* at 763–765.

also targeted "pandering," defined as advertising, promoting, or distributing any sexually oriented image "in such a manner that conveys the impression" it depicts a minor engaging in sexually explicit conduct.[70] A separate section of the law prohibited the creation of child pornography using "morphed" images of actual children. Even before the passage of these amendments, federal law prohibited the distribution of actual child pornography by computer, and a number of individuals had been convicted for their online activities.[71]

Unlike the Supreme Court's rationale in *Ferber* that child pornography laws exist to protect children who are exploited in the production of sexually explicit materials, the CPPA was predicated on the assumption that computer-generated child pornography could be used as "a tool of incitement for pedophiles and child molesters, and a tool of seduction for child victims" even if it does not involve the use of children in its production. The Senate Report on the legislation described computer-generated images "which appear to depict minors engaging in sexually explicit conduct" as being "just as dangerous to the well-being of our children as material produced using actual children."[72]

By expanding federal child pornography law to prohibit images that do not depict actual humans, the CPPA created significant tensions with the Supreme Court's jurisprudence in this area. The new focus on depictions of "virtual children" having sex severed the direct link between the law and child abuse and strained the constitutional boundaries articulated in *Ferber*. Accordingly, Congress sought to reduce the constitutional friction by indicating in the legislative history (but not in the law's text) that the CPPA did not prohibit nonobscene images of adults engaging in sexually explicit conduct "even where a depicted individual may appear to be a minor."[73] This attempt to keep faith with *Ferber*, however, undermined the CPPA's internal logic. If minors may be seduced

---

[70] 18 U.S.C. §§ 2256(8)(B), 2256(8)(D).

[71] *E.g.*, United States v. Kimbrough, 69 F.3d 723 (5th Cir. 1995) *cert. denied.*, 517 U.S. 1157 (1996); United States v. Can., 921 F. Supp. 362 (E.D. La. 1996); United States v. Maxwell, 42 M.J. 568 (A.F. 1995).

[72] S. REP. 104–358, 19 (1996).

[73] *Id.* at 21.

using computer-generated images that appear to be minors, they certainly could be seduced through the use of constitutionally protected materials depicting youthful looking adults. The question posed by the CPPA was whether the courts would accept the government's argument that the indirect link between sexual abuse and computer-generated images of virtual children could support the law.

Reaffirming First Principles: *Ashcroft v. Free Speech Coalition*

The Court in *Ashcroft v. Free Speech Coalition* directly addressed this question and rejected the government's attempt to extend the concept of child pornography to include images of imaginary children. Justice Kennedy's majority opinion explained that CPPA's prohibition of virtual child pornography exceeded the logic of *Ferber*, which identified the state's interest as "protecting the children exploited by the production process."[74] The litigants in the case did not challenge the CPPA provisions targeting "morphed" images of actual children, and the Court did not address that issue. With respect to the other CPPA restrictions, however, it was unwilling to expand the categories of unprotected speech to include "virtual" child pornography, and it held that the law violated the First Amendment.

In contrast to actual child pornography, the Court pointed out that CPPA prohibits speech "that records no crime and creates no victims by its production." It rejected the government's claim that computer-generated images are "intrinsically related" to child abuse, finding that the causal link is "contingent and indirect." The First Amendment distinguishes between speech and conduct, and it sharply limits the government's ability to regulate speech on the basis of its "bad tendency" to encourage misconduct. Consequently, the Court found that the CPPA could not be justified by arguments that virtual child porn promotes the bad thoughts of pedophiles. Justice Kennedy stressed that "First Amendment freedoms are most in danger when the government seeks to control thought or to justify its laws for that impermissible end."[75]

---

[74] 122 S. Ct. 1389, 1396, 1401 (2002).
[75] *Id.* at 1403.

Nor could the law rest on the argument that pedophiles might use virtual pornography to lure and seduce children. The majority pointed out that "many things, innocent in themselves . . . such as cartoons, video games, and candy . . . might be used for immoral purposes, yet we would not expect those to be prohibited because they might be misused."[76] Again, conduct is the key. If an adult supplies a minor with obscene materials or solicits a child to engage in sex, that behavior can be punished without imposing any restrictions on speech. The Court cited its precedents relating to incitement to highlight the principle that the government cannot suppress speech "because it increases the chance an unlawful act will be committed 'at some indefinite future time.'"[77]

The majority opinion also emphasized the significant First Amendment impact of the CPPA. Its discussion outlined the distinctions between obscenity and child pornography, pointing out that the latter category does not require the government to show that the material to be prohibited, when taken as a whole, appeals to the prurient interest or is patently offensive. Nor must a prosecutor demonstrate that the material lacks serious literary, artistic, political, or scientific value. Images that satisfy the requirements of the CPPA can be proscribed, regardless of the way in which they are presented, including possibly "a picture in a psychology manual, as well as a movie depicting the horrors of sexual abuse." Because child pornography enables the criminalization of speech without regard to its merit, Justice Kennedy pointed out that well-regarded depictions of teenage sexuality could be banned, including performances of *Romeo and Juliet*, or contemporary films such as *Traffic* or *American Beauty*.[78]

The Court's holding does not impair the government's ability to prohibit obscene depictions of child pornography—virtual or real—so long as the material falls within the three-part *Miller* test. The majority suggested that "[p]ictures of young children engaged in certain acts might be obscene where similar depictions of adults, or perhaps even older adolescents, would not," although it also noted that images of "what appear to be 17-year-olds engaging in sexually

---

[76] *Id.* at 1402.
[77] *Id.* at 1403 (quoting Hess v. Indiana, 414 U.S. 105, 108 (1973) (per curiam)).
[78] *Id.* at 1400.

explicit activity do not in every case contravene community standards."[79]

The *Free Speech Coalition* decision generated four opinions, but provided far more clarity than the decision in *Ashcroft v. ACLU*. Four justices (Stevens, Souter, Ginsburg, and Breyer) joined Justice Kennedy's majority opinion, providing a clear rule on the limits of the child pornography doctrine. Justice Thomas issued an opinion concurring in the result, but indicating that he might withdraw support for the ultimate finding if the government in a future case could demonstrate technical advances in virtual imaging that hamper its ability to prosecute actual child pornography.[80] Justice O'Connor concurred in part and dissented in part, disagreeing with the majority's rejection of a ban on computer-generated child pornography. She agreed that the possible application of CPPA restrictions to images produced using youthful-looking adults was overly broad and that the ban on pandering material that "conveys the impression" it is child pornography was invalid, but took the position that the government could prohibit virtual child pornography to the extent it is "virtually indistinguishable" from the real thing. Justice O'Connor shared Justice Thomas's view that advances in computer technology could thwart enforcement efforts, and suggested that a narrowing construction to the law would assuage concerns that a ban on virtual child pornography might be too vague or selectively applied.[81]

Only Chief Justice Rehnquist, joined by Justice Scalia, dissented outright. The opinion did not address directly the majority's central premise that *Ferber*'s child pornography standard derives from the need to stop actual child abuse, but defended the CPPA with the argument that the law was carefully crafted to target only hardcore depictions of child sexuality. The dissenters suggested that the majority should have deferred to congressional findings regarding advances in technology and should not have granted a facial challenge without first attempting to interpret the law more narrowly. The Chief Justice (in a paragraph not joined by Justice Scalia) noted that CPPA's legislative history indicated that Congress did not

---

[79] *Id.* at 1396, 1400.

[80] *Id.* at 1406–07 (Thomas, J., concurring).

[81] *Id.* at 1407–11 (O'Connor, J., concurring in part and dissenting in part).

intend to apply the law to depictions produced with young-looking actors, and, in any event, the danger of overly broad enforcement was remote. The dissent discounted the risk to contemporary films identified by the majority, noting that if the CPPA could be applied "to reach the sort of material the Court says it does, then films such as *'Traffic'* and *'American Beauty'* would not have been made the way they were."[82]

Where Do We Go from Here?

Whatever else may be said of the Court's decisions in these two cases, it is clear that they are not the final word on the thorny issues of obscenity and child pornography. The decision in *Ashcroft v. ACLU* remanded the case to the Third Circuit, thus perpetuating the debate that the Supreme Court did not resolve. *Ashcroft v. Free Speech Coalition* effectively answered the legal question before the Court, but provoked a political reaction that inevitably will test the resilience of the majority's reasoning.

Virtual Child Pornography: The Sequel

The ink was scarcely dry on the *Free Speech Coalition* opinion when Attorney General John Ashcroft announced the introduction of new legislation to replace the CPPA. Two weeks after the Court's decision, the attorney general unveiled H.R. 4623, the Child Obscenity and Pornography Prevention Act of 2002. The bill, crafted by the Justice Department to respond to the Supreme Court, was introduced in the House of Representatives by Rep. Lamar Smith and 69 cosponsors. It quickly passed the House and was referred to the Senate.

Part of H.R. 4623 simply puts into statutory form Justice Kennedy's observation that most images of young children engaged in sex acts could be considered obscene under the *Miller* test. Although it sets forth a detailed definition of the term "prepubescent child" and lists the sex acts for which depictions are proscribed, the legislation would add little—if anything—to existing obscenity law. Although it raises the question of whether the government may ban mere possession of virtual child pornography, in most circumstances materials covered by the proposed obscenity ban fall under the current federal obscenity statute.

---

[82] *Id.* at 1412 (Rehnquist, C.J., dissenting).

Otherwise, the provisions of H.R. 4623 seeking to restore the general prohibition of virtual child pornography, and to reimpose restrictions against pandering child pornography, represent a direct challenge to the majority opinion in *Free Speech Coalition*. The legislation seeks to prohibit depictions of children engaged in sexually explicit conduct, including computer-generated images that are "indistinguishable" from actual minors. It defines such imagery to be "virtually indistinguishable" from reality "in that the depiction is such that an ordinary person viewing the depiction would conclude that the depiction is that of an actual minor engaged in sexually explicit conduct." It excludes noncomputer-generated images from the definition of virtual child pornography, including drawings, cartoons, sculptures, or paintings depicting minors or adults.[83]

Although this proposed rewrite of the standard for virtual child pornography is narrower than the CPPA's prohibition on sexual imagery that "appears to be" of a child, it is far from certain that it would make a difference to a reviewing court if H.R. 4623 (or something like it) is enacted. The Court in *Free Speech Coalition* rejected the government's argument that the CPPA was valid because the material prohibited by it is "virtually indistinguishable" from actual child pornography, and that such images are "part of the same market and are often exchanged." The majority explained that the child pornography doctrine is concerned with the "production of the work, not its content."[84] Thus, any attempt to ban child pornography on the basis of purely imaginary images of children faces an uphill battle.

Thus, while H.R. 4623 is faithful to the arguments presented in Chief Justice Rehnquist's dissenting opinion and Justice O'Connor's partial dissent, it cannot be reconciled with the *Free Speech Coalition* majority. What is missing from the proposed law is any recognition that the Court struck down CPPA's ban on virtual child pornography precisely because it is virtual and not real. As Justice Kennedy put it, a prohibition of virtual child pornography "prohibits speech that records no crime and creates no victims by its production." Such a law ignores the First Amendment's "vital distinctions between words and deeds, between ideas and conduct."[85]

[83] H.R. 4623, 107th Cong., §§ 3, 5, (June 26, 2002).
[84] 122 S. Ct. at 1401, 1404.
[85] *Id.* at 1402, 1404.

Redefining Obscenity

Assuming Congress adopts a new ban on virtual child pornography, reviewing courts will face a relatively straightforward task of measuring the new law's constitutionality by the principles articulated in *Free Speech Coalition*. This job may be affected somewhat by changes in computer imaging technology, but such complications pale compared with the puzzle the Third Circuit must unravel in *Ashcroft v. ACLU*. That court has been tasked with resolving the disputes over the meaning of obscenity that fractured the Warren and Burger Courts, and to apply its findings to a borderless medium of communications.

It is possible that the court of appeals will try to tackle this assignment without reopening the argument over community standards. After all, the district court was able to enjoin COPA without getting into that issue by focusing instead on the overbreadth of the law, its chilling effect on protected expression, and its failure to employ the least restrictive means of protecting children. The litigants similarly avoided the community standards issue and did not brief it their first time before the Third Circuit, largely because they were unwilling to raise questions they could not answer. But despite the appeal of changing the focus of the inquiry away from the more difficult questions, that option probably is unavailable on remand since the Third Circuit teed up the community standards issue and the Supreme Court framed the renewed debate in the same terms.

For six of the nine justices in *Ashcroft v. ACLU*, the community standards question was central to their analyses. Justice Stevens wrote that the issue alone was sufficient to invalidate COPA, while Justices Breyer and O'Connor suggested that the law could be upheld only if the Court applied a national standard for variable obscenity. Justice Kennedy, joined by Justices Souter and Ginsburg, agreed that the court of appeals was correct to focus on the national variation in community standards, but wanted the court to reexamine that issue in light of other First Amendment concerns, such as COPA's overbreadth.

Even if a majority of the Court were not focused on the community standards issue, the prospects of success for a renewed argument based primarily on overbreadth are uncertain. Most members of the Court seemed skeptical of claims that COPA would restrict significant amounts of protected speech. The plurality headed by

Justice Thomas outlined language in COPA that "substantially limit[s] the material covered by the statute," and noted that the "serious value" requirement would permit appellate courts to set a national floor for any material at risk.[86] Justice O'Connor wrote that the record on appeal failed to show substantial overbreadth and that COPA applied to a "narrow category of speech."[87] She indicated that the serious merit requirement limited significantly the range of material covered by the law, a point Justice Breyer made during oral argument. He challenged ACLU's counsel to give him a single example of a work that would have serious value for a 21-year-old but not for a 17-year-old, adding, "I can't think of an example."

But to recognize that the community standards issue will be a necessary (although nonexclusive) part of the ongoing debate over COPA is a long way from being able to predict how the issue may be resolved. It probably is safe to suggest that Justice Thomas's *caveat netizen* approach, in which those who fear applying local notions of patent offensiveness should simply stay off the Web, will not gain added traction among the six justices who expressed concern about local standards. However, it is impossible to say whether a majority might opt for a national variable obscenity standard and what that might mean for the future of COPA.

One of the enduring questions of the Warren and Burger Court obscenity cases, left wide open by the Court in *Ashcroft v. ACLU*, is how a national standard could be applied. The Court in *Miller* described national standards as "unascertainable" and an "exercise in futility" that would subject conservative communities to racier material than they otherwise would permit while simultaneously restricting expression in more permissive locales. Justice O'Connor took issue with this conclusion, suggesting that the Internet has facilitated a national dialogue that has made potential jurors more aware of the views of other adults throughout the United States.[88] Others on the Court expressed doubt about this assumption. As Justice Scalia asked at oral argument, "Can a North Carolina jury decide what is obscene in Los Angeles or Las Vegas?" "What does a person raised all his life in North Carolina know about Las Vegas?"

[86] 122 S. Ct. at 1710.

[87] *Id.* at 1714 (O'Connor, J., concurring in part and concurring in the judgment).

[88] *Id.* at 1714–15.

But these questions sidestep a critical issue that the Court eventually must face—whether a final obscenity determination is a factual matter for juries to decide. Justice Brennan, among others, maintained that reviewing courts have an obligation to independently review challenged materials to ensure that constitutional protections are enforced. This position contributed to the recurring practice in the 1960s of requiring the justices to personally review allegedly obscene publications. Chief Justice Warren disagreed, arguing that no national standard was possible, and that juries could determine "patent offensiveness" and "prurient appeal" under local standards as matters of fact. Justice Harlan, squarely in the middle, argued that national standards should govern federal prosecutions, but that local obscenity standards, and the findings of state courts, should not be second-guessed by federal judges.

In light of this history, the current proposals invoking a national variable obscenity standard for COPA merely raise the same questions previously debated by members of the Court but do not resolve them. Although Justices O'Connor and Breyer implicitly reject Justice Brennan's position that reviewing courts must resolve obscenity questions as a matter of constitutional law, they would require local juries to determine and apply a "uniform" national standard. In doing so, Justice Breyer acknowledged that regional variations inherent in the jury system would still exist, while Justice O'Connor noted that jurors asked to construe a national standard "will inevitably base their assessments to some extent on their experience of their local communities."[89] Given these understandings, it is far from obvious that local variations in enforcement on the basis of the tacit application of local standards masked by jury determinations would be less significant than differences attributable to overtly applied (and more easily reviewable) local community standards. Although Justices Breyer and O'Connor echo former Chief Justice Warren's call to rely on juries, they ignore his warning that it would be unreasonable to expect local juries to be able to divine a national standard.

If the Court ultimately tried to adopt a national standard for "harmful to minors" material on the Internet, the result would likely

---

[89] *Id.* at 1716 (Breyer, J., concurring in part and concurring in the judgment); *Id.* at 1715 (O'Connor, J., concurring in part and concurring in the judgment).

create a legal fiction in which the standard was national as a matter of law but local in practice. The alternative would be to revive the Court's function as the final arbiter of the legal status of contested materials, a role it is unlikely to embrace. Neither option settles the long-standing disputes in the obscenity debate, and Justice Breyer addressed the issue by pointing to legislative history defining the relevant community nongeographically to encompass "the Nation's adult community taken as a whole" and asking jurors to apply the "reasonably constant" understanding of what material is unsuitable for minors.[90]

Justice Breyer's concept of a national "adult community" begs the important questions of whether any kind of national adult consensus exists for expression that is "inappropriate for minors" and how this consensus may be determined. More important, it undermines the central assumption of both the Supreme Court and the Third Circuit that any ruling on the constitutionality of COPA's variable obscenity test applies equally to the *Miller* standard for adult obscenity. By focusing the inquiry on what the "adult community" considers to be "unsuitable," Justice Breyer accentuated the differences between obscenity under *Miller* and variable obscenity under COPA. This distinction may provide a touchstone for resolving the case on remand without the need to rewrite the law of obscenity, and it highlights an important point about community standards.

As the five majority justices in *Ashcroft v. ACLU* recognized, the concept of contemporary community standards articulated in *Roth* and reaffirmed in *Miller* was intended to replace a 19th century English standard that based obscenity on its presumed impact on the most sensitive or vulnerable members of society. When the Supreme Court infused obscenity law with First Amendment concerns, it used the community standards notion "to assure that the material is judged neither on the basis of each juror's personal opinion, nor by its effect on a particularly sensitive or insensitive person or group."[91] Despite the continuing disputes over the composition of the community, the guiding principle was clear that speech was not to be punished on the basis of a jury's perceptions of how certain speech may affect members of a vulnerable population.

---

[90] *Id.* at 1715–16 (Breyer, J., concurring in part and concurring in the judgment).

[91] *Id.* at 1707–08 (quoting Hamling v. United States, 418 U.S. 87, 107 (1974)).

But the assumptions underlying variable obscenity, with its emphasis on "harm to minors" are just the opposite. Although the doctrine has been dressed up with the trappings of the three-part *Miller* test and its references to community standards, it essentially asks whether the expression at issue appeals to the prurient interest and lacks serious value *for minors*. Indeed, under Justice Breyer's analysis of the issue, references to "community standards" are largely superfluous and simply confuse the issue. All that really matters under this conception of a national standard is what most adults think is bad for kids, and whether it has enough merit to outweigh the bad.

How such a thing might be determined is anybody's guess. But by reducing the question to its essence, the constitutional issues surrounding COPA become clearer. The law seeks to impose restrictions on Internet speech on the basis of an evaluation of the likely impact of that speech on the vulnerable population of minors. Such an evaluation is difficult to reconcile with the original concept of community standards regardless of whether its implementation comes through local or national standards. And because the notion of community standards no longer provides a discernable limiting principle in a "harm to minors" analysis, the restrictions in COPA begin to resemble quite closely the CDA's ban on "indecent" Internet speech. Indeed, the FCC's indecency standard, rejected by the Court as hopelessly vague when applied to the Internet, applies in just this way: the Commissioners penalize indecent speech on the basis of their notions of a national standard for what is patently offensive for minors.

Although the *Ashcroft* plurality cited cases such as *Hamling v. United States* and *Sable Communications of California, Inc. v. FCC* to support the proposition that local community standards may be used to enforce federal obscenity laws, the same conclusion does not follow for regulating nonobscene speech such as the material covered by COPA. In *Sable*, for example, the Court upheld applying community standards to determine the obscenity of phone-sex services, but it invalidated restrictions on "indecent" dial-a-porn services as a violation of the First Amendment.[92] Similarly, the Court in *Hamling* approved federal restrictions on sending obscene material

---

[92] 492 U.S. 115 (1989).

through the mails without requiring that community standards be on the basis of a precise geographic area. At the same time, however, the Court imposed a narrowing construction of the federal statute to make clear that it applied only to obscenity as defined in *Miller*, and not to material considered "lewd, lascivious, indecent, filthy or vile" as set forth in the law.[93] In sum, there are no precedents that provide clear guidance on how a national "harm to minors" law should be applied.

The Third Circuit must now determine whether COPA limits too much constitutionally protected speech for both minors and adults, and whether less restrictive alternatives forestall the need for such a law. The court is likely to focus on the importance of community standards, if only because of the litigation history and in response to the Supreme Court's various views on the issue. If the court accepts Justice Breyer's "adult community" concept, it must explain how to reconcile a community standards approach with a law that, by its nature, seeks to protect the vulnerable population of minors. If, on the other hand, the court defines the community geographically, it must explain how to determine a national standard, a feat that so far has eluded the Supreme Court. It seems unlikely that the court of appeals will attempt to apply local standards to the Web because a majority of the justices rejected that approach and because it is utterly inconsistent with the panel's initial decision.

The court must also find a way to determine what sexually oriented material lacks serious literary, artistic, political, and scientific merit for minors. This inquiry will determine whether COPA restricts as much speech as the CDA's "indecency" standard, or whether its reach is more limited, akin to adult obscenity under *Miller*. Justice Breyer's suggestion at oral argument that everything that has serious merit for a 21-year-old is equally meritorious for older teenagers would merge the obscenity and variable obscenity doctrines. However, Justice O'Connor's claim in *Reno v. ACLU* that nude art or discussions of prison rape may lack merit for minors implies that variable obscenity is much like the discredited indecency standard. This "merit gap" between the unconstitutional regulation of indecency and the valid regulation of obscenity is what COPA is all about. Yet no one has up to this point offered a satisfactory way

[93] *Hamling*, 418 U.S. at 114.

of determining how much speech falls into this gap, or how it may be regulated without unduly restricting speech that is fully protected for adults.

Conclusion

New technology has prompted the Supreme Court to reexamine some of the basic assumptions of its First Amendment jurisprudence. In *Reno v. ACLU*, the Court held that the Internet deserves the strongest protections of the First Amendment. It was the first time that the Court has extended full constitutional immunity to a new communications medium without first applying a reduced level of protection. The Court is now exploring the limits of that conclusion, and in *Ashcroft v. ACLU* and *Ashcroft v. Free Speech Coalition* it examined the interplay of Internet and computer technology with its established doctrines of obscenity and child pornography. By viewing these issues through the lens of new technology, the Court reopened old disputes about the nature of protected and unprotected speech. These controversies are far from settled, and will continue in both the legislative and judicial arenas.

School Choice: Sunshine Replaces the Cloud

Clint Bolick

As its 2001 term concluded, the Supreme Court handed long-suffering parents and children a major victory: *Zelman v. Simmons-Harris*[1] is the Court's most important education decision in almost 50 years—since *Brown v. Board of Education.*[2] By a vote of 5 to 4, the Court made a historic pronouncement: The school choice program before it does not violate the Establishment Clause of the First Amendment and is, therefore, constitutional. The decision opens an array of policy options to address the urgent crisis of urban education. Of equal importance, it provides strong jurisprudential support for the right of parents to direct and control their children's education.

The response to the decision from opponents of school choice[3] was swift and vigorous. The National Education Association and People for the American Way pronounced the opinion a disaster for public education. Barry Lynn of Americans United for Separation of Church and State characterized the decision as a "wrecking ball" for the First Amendment's prohibition of religious establishment.[4] The Court's dissenters agreed, predicting all manner of religious strife.

---

[1] 122 S. Ct. 2460; No. 00-1751, slip op. (U.S. June 27, 2002).

[2] 347 U.S. 483 (1954).

[3] "School choice" can have a variety of meanings. It is used here to encompass publicly supported private school options, whether through vouchers, tax credits for tuition, or scholarships. I support deregulated public "charter" schools but believe that choice is not meaningful (or optimal in its competitive effects) if it is confined to the public sector. For a broader discussion of the arguments for school choice, see CLINT BOLICK, TRANSFORMATION: THE PROMISE AND POLITICS OF EMPOWERMENT 43–53 (1998).

[4] *Quoted* in David G. Savage, *School Vouchers Win Backing of High Court*, L.A. TIMES, June 28, 2002, at A1.

In reality, the decision marks no significant jurisprudential innovation for, as the Court observed, it fits neatly within "an unbroken line of decisions rejecting challenges to similar programs."[5] But its real-world impact is potentially titanic. The case is not really about religion at all: it is about the distribution of power over education. That is why the main challengers were not separation-of-church-and-state enthusiasts but teachers' unions that otherwise could not care less about religious establishment. In the end, the Court recognized that the "primary effect" of the Cleveland scholarship program was not to advance religion but to expand educational opportunities. Accordingly, the Court concluded that allowing parents to direct a portion of public education funds to the schools of their choice, public or private, does not constitute religious establishment. What is far more surprising than the outcome of this case is that four justices could dissent.[6]

The Omnipresent Cloud

For as long as school choice has appeared on the policy horizon, constitutional questions have dogged it. Every school choice program adopted before 2000—whether vouchers or tax credits—was promptly subjected to legal challenge. The teachers' unions deployed federal Establishment Clause (or, as they call it, "separation of church and state")[7] claims as well as state analogs. Moreover, as we pointed out in our petition for writ of *certiorari* in the U.S. Supreme Court, constitutional objections repeatedly have been raised against school choice proposals. So it was imperative for school choice proponents to remove that major obstacle to reform. Dating from the enactment of the first urban school choice program in Milwaukee in 1990, the task took a dozen years.

---

[5] *Zelman*, slip op. at 21.

[6] Illustrating the wide academic consensus that school choice is constitutional was an *amicus curiae* brief prepared by Professor Jesse Choper, former dean of the law school of the University of California at Berkeley, on behalf of three dozen law professors reflecting a broad philosophical spectrum. In addition to the professors signing the brief, prominent liberal academics taking a similar view included Laurence Tribe, Douglas Laycock, Jeffrey Rosen, Samuel Estreicher, Akhil Amar, and Walter Dellinger, acting U.S. Solicitor General in the Clinton administration.

[7] The First Amendment provides in relevant part that "Congress shall make no law respecting an establishment of religion, or prohibiting the free exercise thereof."

Before and during that time, the Supreme Court considered a number of cases dealing with various types of programs in which aid found its way into religious institutions. Two seemingly irreconcilable sets of precedents emerged. The first, reflecting a long period in which the Court's jurisprudence demanded a rigorous separation of church and state and evidenced a hostility toward religion, culminated in *Committee for Public Education v. Nyquist*,[8] a 1973 decision striking down a package of religious school aid programs. The second, emanating from the view that the religion clauses of the First Amendment require governmental "neutrality" toward religion, produced six consecutive decisions sustaining direct and indirect aid programs.[9] The apparently disparate frameworks resulted in divergent decisions among lower courts over school choice. Courts that found *Nyquist* controlling invariably found school choice programs unconstitutional; courts that found the subsequent cases controlling upheld school choice programs.

In fact, the two sets of precedents are harmonious. In *Nyquist*, the state provided loans, tax deductions, and other support exclusively for private schools and students who patronized them. The program was aimed at bailing out religious schools that were closing, and whose students were returning to public schools at considerable taxpayer expense. Applying the three-part Establishment Clause framework first set forth in *Lemon v. Kurtzman*,[10] the Court concluded that the program's "primary effect" was to advance religion. The reasons for the Court's decision were understandable. Though acknowledging the strong secular purpose of providing educational opportunities outside of the public sector, the Court found that the aid was skewed entirely in favor of private schools. And among private schools, religious schools heavily predominated. Because the program was not "neutral"—for example, beneficiaries were defined in terms of the (private and overwhelmingly religious)

---

[8] 413 U.S. 756 (1973).

[9] Mitchell v. Helms, 530 U.S. 793 (2000); Agostini v. Felton, 521 U.S. 203 (1997); Rosenberger v. Rector & Visitors of Univ. of Va., 515 U.S. 819 (1995); Zobrest v. Catalina Foothills Sch. Dist., 509 U.S. 1 (1993); Witters v. Wash. Dep't of Serv for the Blind, 474 U.S. 481 (1986); Mueller v. Allen, 463 U.S. 388 (1983).

[10] 403 U.S. 602 (1973). In assessing aid programs, the Court examined whether the program (1) has a secular purpose, (2) has a primary effect that neither advances nor inhibits religion, and (3) excessively entangles the state and religion.

schools they attended—the Court held that the aid scheme was impermissible. Given that the program's aim was to help religious schools and their patrons, the decision was not surprising.

Had *Nyquist* been more categorical in its repudiation of school choice—adopting the separationists' position that a single dollar of public funds may not constitutionally cross the threshold of a religious school—it would have destroyed any chance for school choice programs. Fortunately, the Court created an escape valve. It probably did so because the door to such aid already had been opened through enormously popular programs like the G.I. Bill and Pell Grants. So in a footnote, the Court planted the seeds of an exception— one that eventually became the general rule to which *Nyquist* became the exception. Specifically, the Court held open the question of "whether the significantly religious character of the statute's beneficiaries might differentiate the present cases from a case involving some form of public assistance (for example, scholarships) made available generally without regard to the sectarian-nonsectarian, or public-nonpublic nature of the institution benefited."[11]

The Court returned to that question for the first time a decade later in *Mueller*. There the Court examined a Minnesota tax deduction for educational expenses. Because public school parents incur few expenses, the vast majority of tax deductions—allegedly 96 percent—were claimed by private school parents. The facts seemed eerily like those presented in *Nyquist*. But by a 5–4 vote, the Court upheld the deductions in a decision authored by then-Associate Justice William Rehnquist and, notably, joined by Justice Powell, who had authored *Nyquist*. The Court distinguished *Nyquist* on two main grounds. First, all of the money that flowed to religious schools through tax deductions did so as a result of independent choices made by families. Second, the program was neutral on its face, extending benefits to public and private school parents alike.

The Court rejected the invitation to determine the program's primary effect by applying some sort of mathematical formula regarding the percentage of the program's beneficiaries that attend religious schools. "We would be loath to adopt a rule grounding the constitutionality of a facially neutral law on annual reports reciting the extent to which various classes of private citizens claimed benefits under

---

[11] *Nyquist*, 413 U.S. at 782 n.38.

the law," the Court declared.[12] Departing from a rule of facial neutrality, the Court emphasized, would render the constitutional inquiry hopelessly subjective. "Such an approach would scarcely provide the certainty that this field stands in need of," the Court explained, "nor can we perceive principled standards by which such statistical evidence might be evaluated."[13] The Court concluded that "[t]he historic purposes of the [Establishment] Clause simply do not encompass the sort of attenuated financial benefit, ultimately controlled by the private choices of individual parents, that eventually flows to parochial schools from the neutrally available tax benefit at issue in this case."[14]

Jurisprudentially, the battle over school choice was over once *Mueller* was decided—a fact that the dissenters in *Zelman* nearly two decades later explicitly would acknowledge. *Mueller* provided the framework that would henceforth consistently apply, holding that aid that found its way into religious schools was constitutionally permissible so long as two criteria were satisfied: (1) the aid was directed to religious institutions only as a result of the independent decisions of parents and students ("indirect aid"), and (2) religious entities were not the only option available ("neutrality"). That framework was entirely congenial to school choice programs, whether vouchers or tax credits, and school choice advocates now had a constitutional roadmap by which to craft programs.

Mueller also disposed of a troublesome argument, articulated by the Court in prior cases, that college aid programs were conceptually different from elementary and secondary school programs because children in elementary and secondary schools are more impressionable and therefore more susceptible to religious school indoctrination. Though *Mueller* did not address the question directly, it was implicitly subsumed within the concept of parental choice. In cases involving public schools, such as school prayer cases, a doctrine of relative impressionability seems appropriate. But in indirect aid cases, children are hearing a religious message only because of their parents' choice. In essence, parental choice operates as a constitutional "circuit breaker" between church and state.

---

[12] *Mueller*, 463 U.S. at 401.
[13] *Id.*
[14] *Id.* at 400.

Mueller also would affect *Zelman* in its rejection of a mathematical formula for determining Establishment Clause violations. In Cleveland, the overwhelming majority of students receiving scholarships were attending religious schools. *Mueller* confronted that issue head-on, subsuming it within both prongs of the inquiry, facial neutrality and indirect aid, and established a firm rule basing a program's constitutionality on facial neutrality.

The Court reinforced those criteria three years later in *Witters*, which involved the use of college aid by a blind student studying for the ministry in a school of divinity. It is hard to imagine an atmosphere more pervasively sectarian than that; yet the Court upheld the use of the aid in a unanimous decision by Justice Thurgood Marshall.[15] The Court emphasized that only a few students would likely use the aid in religious schools or for religious vocations. In *Zelman*, anti-school choice advocates seized on that language to suggest that religious schools appropriately could compose only a small part of a broader aid program.

But writing separate concurring opinions in *Witters*, five justices reiterated the more expansive criteria set forth in *Mueller*. Most notably, Justice Powell articulated a clear neutrality standard, declaring that "state programs that are wholly neutral in offering educational assistance to a class defined without reference to religion do not violate" the primary effect test.[16] Justice Powell also emphasized that such programs should not be viewed in isolation. Instead the proper inquiry must encompass "the nature and consequences of the program *viewed as a whole.*"[17] That observation would prove helpful in the Cleveland case in which the Court viewed the scholarship program in the broader context of school choices available to Cleveland families.

The next case, *Zobrest*, began to blur the lines between direct and indirect aid. In that case, a school district refused on First Amendment grounds to provide an interpreter for a deaf student attending a Catholic high school. If he had chosen a public or nonsectarian

---

[15] Despite the decisive win, Witters came away emptyhanded. When the case was remanded, the use of the aid was invalidated by the Washington Supreme Court under the "Blaine Amendment" of its state constitution, discussed below.

[16] *Witters*, 474 U.S. at 490–91 (Powell, J., concurring).

[17] *Id.* at 492 (emphasis in original).

private school, the student would have been entitled to an interpreter. The district asserted, however, that an interpreter in a Catholic school would sign religious as well as secular lessons. *Zobrest* raised a crucial question: Would aid have to be segregated between religious and nonreligious instruction? If so, it surely would trigger the third part of the Establishment Clause test, excessive entanglement between the state and religion.[18] Fortunately for subsequent school choice programs, the answer was no. Again the Court assessed the issue in terms of indirectness of the aid: The fact that the child is attending a religious school and receiving religious instruction "cannot be attributed to state decisionmaking."[19]

The *Zobrest* dissenters focused on the symbolism created by a public school employee interpreting lessons in a religious school. In their view, that raised the specter of state sponsorship. Because of that special problem, *Zobrest* in some ways presented a *tougher* case than a school choice program, which has no physical indicia of state sponsorship. Indeed, perhaps unwittingly, the dissenters acknowledged as much. Justice Harry Blackmun, joined by Justice David Souter, objected to the symbolic message when a public employee is involved "in the teaching and propagation of religious doctrine." By contrast, the dissenters aptly observed, "When government dispenses public funds to individuals who employ them to finance private choices, it is difficult to argue that government is actually endorsing religion."[20] Unfortunately, Justice Souter did not share that insight nine years later in *Zelman*.

Rosenberger buttressed the neutrality principle even more. The University of Virginia excluded student-sponsored religious publications from receiving student fees on the ground that it would violate the First Amendment to include them. To the contrary, the Court ruled that it constitutes impermissible content-based speech discrimination and thereby violates the First Amendment to *exclude*

---

[18] The excessive governmental entanglement prong of the *Lemon* test addresses legitimate libertarian concerns about government regulation of private schools in school choice programs.

[19] *Zobrest*, 509 U.S. at 10.

[20] *Id.* at 22–23 (Blackmun, J., dissenting).

the religious publications. The Court applied its now-familiar Establishment Clause framework to find that financial support for religious publications, within the broader context of student activities, did not have the primary effect of advancing religion.

The criteria set forth in *Mueller* and subsequent cases seemed hospitable to school choice programs. By definition, such programs are indirect when funds flow to religious schools only if parents choose to send their children there. Neutrality is slightly more difficult to establish when suburban public schools are unwilling to participate. But if the courts look at the broader context of school choices—including open public school enrollment and charter schools as well as parochial and nonsectarian private schools—the neutrality criterion could easily be satisfied. And all of the contemporary school choice programs were designed with the Supreme Court's framework in mind.

The two most recent cases—*Agostini*, which involved providing public school teachers for remedial instruction in religious schools, and *Mitchell*, which considered computers and other materials for aid-eligible students in religious schools—also authorized neutral aid. Because the aid was provided directly to the school, however, the Court considered it relevant whether public funds "ever reach the coffers of religious schools."[21]

Justice O'Connor wrote the 5–4 majority opinion in *Agostini* and applied the two-part framework of the post-*Nyquist* cases. *Agostini* signaled a willingness on the part of the Court to overrule *Nyquist*-era precedents that seemed to require discrimination against religious schools rather than neutrality. The Court also subtly modified the definition of neutrality. In *Nyquist*'s footnote 38 and in subsequent decisions, the Court had gauged neutrality in the context of both public and private choices. But in *Agostini*, the Court found that the neutrality criterion was satisfied where "the aid is allocated on the basis of neutral, secular criteria that neither favor nor disfavor religion, and is made available to both religious and secular beneficiaries on a nondiscriminatory basis."[22] Under that standard, school choice programs qualify even if they do not explicitly include public schools within the range of options.

---

[21] *Agostini*, 521 U.S. at 228.

[22] *Id.* at 231.

In *Mitchell,* the plurality opinion for four justices, written by Justice Clarence Thomas, treated neutrality as the sole criterion in aid cases. That prompted a separate concurrence by Justices O'Connor and Breyer. Though joining in the plurality's conclusion that the aid was permissible, they differentiated between indirect ("true private choice") and direct aid programs, emphasizing again that direct aid programs may be unconstitutional if they result in public funds reaching religious school coffers. Justice O'Connor seemed merely to be reiterating the two-pronged approach—neutrality plus true private choice—that the Court had applied since *Mueller;* but her alliance with Justice Breyer, who had not previously displayed moderation on Establishment Clause issues—was worrisome. Was Justice Breyer now a possible vote in favor of school choice? Or was Justice O'Connor a possible vote against?

The Cleveland Program

It was amidst that uncertainty—a congenial constitutional standard but a closely divided Court—that the Cleveland case went up to the U.S. Supreme Court, with the future of educational freedom at stake.

The Cleveland program arose amidst a chronically mismanaged school system whose control had been seized by a federal court from local officials and transferred to the state. When the program was enacted in 1995, Cleveland students had a 1-in-14 chance of graduating on time with senior-level proficiency—and a 1-in-14 chance of being a victim of crime inside the public schools each year. The state responded in part with an array of educational options, including the Cleveland scholarship program.[23]

The Cleveland program was designed to satisfy the Court's Establishment Clause criteria. Eligible students, defined by residence and family income, could direct a portion of their state education funds as full payment of tuition at participating schools. Both private

---

[23] Milwaukee has the oldest urban school choice program for low-income students, dating to 1990. It was expanded in 1995 to include religious schools. Florida created a state-wide choice program for students in failing public schools in 1999. Arizona enacted scholarship tax credits, by which taxpayers can receive a tax credit for contributions to private scholarship funds, a program that subsequently has been emulated by Pennsylvania and Florida. All of those programs and others were implicated in the U.S. Supreme Court's deliberations over the Cleveland program.

schools in Cleveland and public schools in the surrounding suburbs were invited to participate. Private schools would receive a maximum of $2,500 per student, while suburban public schools would receive approximately $6,000. Unfortunately, although all private schools in Cleveland signed up for the program, no suburban public schools did. Moreover, the two largest nonsectarian private schools in the program converted to community (charter) school status, thereby receiving about twice as much reimbursement as they had received in the scholarship program. As a result, approximately 82 percent of the schools in the program were religious, enrolling about 96 percent of the scholarship students.

A panel of the U.S. Court of Appeals for the Sixth Circuit, by a 2–1 vote, found that those facts amounted to a violation of the Establishment Clause.[24] In assessing the program's neutrality, the court did not examine the program on its face, but instead looked at the percentage of schools in the program that were religious and the percentage of students in the program who attended religious schools. The court viewed the scholarship program in isolation, declining to consider the broader context of school choices, including publicly funded private nonsectarian community schools. The court also concluded that no true private choice existed because few of the participating schools were nonsectarian—which the court attributed to the small amount of the scholarship and the state's failure to compel suburban public schools to participate.

In taking the case to the Supreme Court, we expected one of the following outcomes: (1) the Court would issue an opinion broadly validating school choice; (2) the Court would strike down the program on the basis of some peculiar aspect of its design but provide a roadmap for future school choice programs; or (3) the Court would uphold the program, but the majority would factionalize, as in *Mitchell*, thereby depriving us of a clear rule of law. On the basis of recent precedents, we did not think the Court would broadly disavow school choice. Any of the likely scenarios would give us greater certainty; but naturally the first scenario—a clear and decisive victory—would have the greatest beneficial impact for school choice.

---

[24]Simmons-Harris v. Zelman, 234 F.3d 945 (6th Cir. 2000). Previously the Ohio Supreme Court had reached the opposite result. Simmons-Harris v. Goff, 711 N.E.2d 203 (Ohio 1999).

And that, of course, is what school choice advocates aimed to achieve.

Knowing that the state of Ohio would focus on the Establishment Clause issues, we decided to take a more expansive approach in our brief.[25] First we moved to blunt the plaintiffs' tactical advantage of defining the terms of the debate. We did that by setting forth crucial "background principles" that should inform the Court's deliberation. The case did not merely implicate religious establishment issues, we argued. It also raised important considerations of federalism, parental liberty, and equal educational opportunities, all of which are values deeply embedded in our nation's constitutional tradition, and all of which are promoted by expanding parental choice and educational options. Moreover, the First Amendment contains not only a prohibition against religious establishment but also a guarantee of the free exercise of religion. That combination translates appropriately, as the Court has recognized, into a requirement of nondiscrimination, or neutrality, toward religion. Again, we suggested, the program serves the principle of nondiscrimination, whereas the exclusion of religious schools would violate it.

We then went on to address the "primary effect" criterion in real-world terms. The Cleveland scholarship program grew out of a severe crisis in the Cleveland city public schools, whose administration had been turned over to the state by federal court order. In the previous school year, those schools had satisfied 0 out of 28 state performance criteria. The scholarship program sought to enlist the widest possible range of educational options, and to operate within a broad array of public educational choices. The program's neutrality, we urged, should be determined on its face, not on the basis of statistics, for two reasons. First, hitching a program's constitutionality to the actions of third parties, such as suburban public schools, renders the process hopelessly arbitrary. Indeed, suburban public schools could effectively "veto" the constitutionality of the program by refusing to participate. It seemed perverse that because some schools refused to throw inner-city youngsters an educational life preserver, no schools would be allowed to do so. Second, statistics change from year to year.

---

[25] I will discuss our broader litigation strategy in much greater detail in my forthcoming book, VOUCHER WARS.

Moreover, the program should be evaluated not in isolation, we argued, but in its broader context. We presented a study by education researcher Jay Greene showing that if all schools of choice in Cleveland—including magnet and community schools—were taken into account, only 16.5 percent of Cleveland schoolchildren were enrolled in religious schools. If the state had adopted all of the choice programs at one time, under a statistical standard the program unquestionably would be constitutional. Why should it matter that the state adopted different options one step at a time? We introduced evidence showing that after the litigation ceased in Milwaukee, the number of nonsectarian private schools participating in the program—and the percentage of children attending them—increased substantially. We also cited affidavits and studies demonstrating the educational effects of school choice, showing again that the program's primary effect was not to advance religion but to expand educational opportunities for children who desperately needed them.

Finally, we argued that the program marked no revolution in Establishment Clause jurisprudence. Others who were involved in the litigation were interested in reforming that area of the law, urging the Court to overrule *Nyquist*, or even *Lemon*. We always have taken a much less radical approach: Our goal is to defend school choice programs, rather than to remake Establishment Clause law. So we argued that *Nyquist* need not be overruled. To the contrary, Cleveland's school choice program presented an easier case than the programs presented in *Agostini* and *Mitchell* because the transmission of aid depended entirely on the independent decisions of parents. That characteristic attenuates any perception of state endorsement of religion, a recurrent Establishment Clause concern.

In sum, our approach and that of our allies was to depict the case as one about education, not religion. And if the program really was about education, we reasoned, then its "primary effect" could not be to advance religion.

Supreme Decision

The Court's decision vindicated the most optimistic hopes of school choice supporters. Despite the narrow 5–4 victory, the Court majority spoke with a single, decisive voice, providing precisely the clarity necessary for the school choice movement to progress. Inexplicably, Justice Breyer retreated from the framework he had set forth in *Mitchell*, but Justice O'Connor remained true. Writing for the majority,[26] Chief Justice Rehnquist moderated his position in *Mitchell*, accommodating Justice O'Connor by retaining the "true private choice" criterion that the *Mitchell* plurality sought to jettison.

Justices O'Connor, Kennedy, Scalia, and Thomas fully joined Rehnquist's majority opinion. The chief justice began by recounting the grievous educational conditions giving rise to the Cleveland scholarship program. Against that backdrop, the Court observed, the scholarship program was adopted as "part of a broader undertaking by the State to enhance the educational options of Cleveland's schoolchildren."[27] The Court examined other educational options, including magnet and community schools as well as the higher dollar amount they commanded.

Rehnquist observed that "our decisions have drawn a consistent distinction between government programs that provide aid directly to religious schools . . . and programs of true private choice, in which government aid reaches religious schools only as a result of the genuine and independent choices of private individuals."[28] Whereas the Court's recent cases had expanded the permissible realm of direct aid, "our jurisprudence with respect to true private choice programs has remained consistent and unbroken."[29] Recounting that jurisprudence, Chief Justice Rehnquist declared that "where a government aid program is neutral with respect to religion, and provides assistance to a broad class of citizens who, in turn, direct government aid to religious schools wholly as a result of their own genuine and independent private choice, the program is not readily subject to challenge under the Establishment Clause."[30]

The Court was convinced that the program was both neutral and "a program of true private choice," as part of "a general and multifaceted undertaking by the State of Ohio to provide educational opportunities to the children of a failed school district."[31] Continuing,

[26] It was fitting that the chief justice wrote the majority opinion, for he also authored the *Mueller* decision in 1983, which inaugurated the modern era of Establishment Clause jurisprudence.

[27] *Zelman*, No. 00-1751, slip op. at 5.

[28] *Id.* at 7.

[29] *Id.*

[30] *Id.* at 10.

[31] *Id.* at 11.

the Court noted that the program "confers educational assistance directly to a broad class of individuals defined without reference to religion."[32] Moreover, "[t]he program permits the participation of *all* schools within the district, religious or nonreligious. Adjacent public schools also may participate and have a financial incentive to do so."[33] By contrast, the program did not provide a financial incentive for parents to choose religious schools. To the contrary, it creates "financial *dis*incentives for religious schools."[34] Parents receiving scholarships have to co-pay a part of their tuition ($250), whereas parents choosing traditional, magnet, or community schools pay nothing. Emphasizing that "such features of the program are not necessary to its constitutionality," they "clearly dispel" any notion that the program is skewed toward religion.[35]

Citing the Greene study, the Court viewed the program in the broader context of school choices, and rejected the statistical snapshot as a touchstone of constitutionality. "The Establishment Clause question is whether Ohio is coercing parents into sending their children to religious schools, and that question must be answered by evaluating *all* options Ohio provides Cleveland schoolchildren, only one of which is to obtain a private scholarship and then choose a religious school."[36] Beyond that, the Court emphasized, "The constitutionality of a neutral educational aid program simply does not turn on whether and why, in a particular area, at a particular time, most private schools are run by religious organizations, or most recipients choose to use the aid at a religious school."[37]

Finally, the Court considered *Nyquist*, finding no reason to overrule it because it did not compel the Court to strike down the Cleveland program. After all, *Nyquist* involved programs that were designed unmistakably to aid religious schools, and the Court expressly had left open the question—answered subsequently in *Mueller* and other cases—of the constitutionality of a genuinely neutral aid program. Hence, the Court's ruling changed jurisprudence not at all.

---

[32] *Id.* (citations omitted).

[33] *Id.* (emphasis in original).

[34] *Id.* at 12 (emphasis in original).

[35] *Id.*

[36] *Id.* at 14 (emphasis in original).

[37] *Id.* at 17.

In closing, the Court underscored the moderation of its decision:

> In sum, the Ohio program is entirely neutral with respect
> to religion. It provides benefits directly to a wide spectrum
> of individuals, defined only by financial need and residence
> in a particular school district. It permits such individuals to
> exercise genuine choice among options public and private,
> secular and religious. The program is therefore a program
> of true private choice. In keeping with an unbroken line of
> decisions rejecting challenges to similar programs, we hold
> that the program does not offend the Establishment Clause.[38]

Justice O'Connor wrote separately to emphasize two points: that
the decision does not mark "a dramatic break from the past," and
that the inquiry regarding "true private choice" should "consider
all reasonable educational alternatives to religious schools that are
available to parents."[39] In the overall context of school choices in
Cleveland, Justice O'Connor emphasized, religious schools played
a small role. Moreover, government policies in general, including tax
exemptions for religious institutions, already bestow a substantial
financial benefit. That context, she explained, "places in broader
perspective the alarmist claims about implications of the Cleveland
program" sounded by the dissenters.[40]

Justice Thomas's concurring opinion was especially poignant,
remarking that "[t]oday many of our inner-city public schools deny
emancipation to urban minority students," who "have been forced
into a system that continually fails them."[41] He observed, "While
the romanticized ideal of universal public education resonates with
the cognoscenti who oppose vouchers, poor urban families just want
the best education for their children, who will certainly need it to
function in our high-tech and advanced society."[42] The Cleveland
scholarship program, he concluded, "does not force any individual
to submit to religious indoctrination or education. It simply gives
parents a greater choice as to where and in what manner to educate

---

[38] *Id.* at 21.

[39] *Id.* at 1–2 (O'Connor, J., concurring).

[40] *Id.* at 7.

[41] *Id.* at 1–2 (Thomas, J., concurring).

[42] *Id.* at 8.

their children. This is a choice that those with greater means have routinely exercised."[43]

Justice Thomas also raised the question about whether the Establishment Clause should be construed to limit state action. By its terms, the First Amendment is addressed to Congress. Most of the provisions of the Bill of Rights have been "incorporated" to apply to the states through the 14th Amendment. But as Thomas observed, "When rights are incorporated against the States through the Fourteenth Amendment they should advance, not constrain, individual liberty."[44] He concluded with this warning: "Converting the Fourteenth Amendment from a guarantee of opportunity to an obstacle against education reform distorts our constitutional values and disserves those in the greatest need."[45]

Dissenting Justices Stevens, Souter, and Breyer rejected the Establishment Clause framework that the Court has applied for the past two decades. Stevens raised concerns about "religious strife," invoking the specter of "the Balkans, Northern Ireland, and the Middle East"[46]—concerns echoed by Souter's claims of "divisiveness"[47] and Breyer's warnings of "religiously based conflict"[48]—all notwithstanding that, as the majority pointed out, "the program has ignited no 'divisiveness' or 'strife' other than this litigation."[49] Nor, as the majority observed, do the dissenters propose any rule of law by which the Court could discern when a program is too religiously divisive to sustain.

The government already dispenses billions of dollars through the G.I. Bill, Pell Grants, student loans, and other programs that can be used for religious education. Yet Americans are not at each other's throats in religious conflict. Strife is minimized because benefits are used in a nondiscriminatory fashion and directed by individual choice. That actually promotes a value that liberals are supposed to support: diversity. No one views a Pell Grant used at Georgetown

[43] *Id.* at 6.
[44] *Id.* at 4.
[45] *Id.* at 9.
[46] *Id.* at 3 (Stevens, J., dissenting).
[47] *Id.* at 34 (Souter, J., dissenting).
[48] *Id.* at 13 (Breyer, J., dissenting).
[49] *Id.* at 20–21, n.7. (Rehnquist, C.J.)

or Yeshiva University as primarily advancing religion, because of the plethora of available options. Nor have the Cleveland, Milwaukee, or Florida school choice programs created religious strife because they correctly are perceived as educational programs.

The main dissenting opinion, written by Souter and signed by Stevens, Ginsburg, and Breyer, castigated the Court's jurisprudence beginning with *Mueller*. It also concluded that no true private choice exists in Cleveland. Instead parents are presented with a Hobson's choice[50] between bad public schools and much better religious schools—a choice without a realistic alternative. It seems odd that the proposed solution would be to eliminate the only positive choice. Souter concedes that in his view there is nothing the state permissibly can do to make religious options available. "The majority notes that I argue both that the Ohio program is unconstitutional because the voucher amount is too low to create real private choice and that any greater expenditure would be unconstitutional as well," he observes. "The majority is dead right about this."[51] For the dissenters, the only constitutionally permissible option is for the state to consign students to government schools, no matter how defective.

The dissenters warn that "the amount of federal aid that may go to religious education after today's decision is startling: according to one estimate,[52] the cost of a national voucher program would be $73 billion, 25% more than the current national public-education budget."[53] That estimate is grossly misleading. Private school education in the lower grades can actually save the government money. Consider that $2,250 in public funds, supplemented by $250 from each student, covers full private school tuition in the Cleveland program. Moreover, Establishment Clause jurisprudence never has turned on the amount of money spent—in the view of rigid separationists, one dollar is too much—but rather on the absence of government coercion. The dissenters would return us to an era in which the U.S. Supreme Court grafted onto the Constitution a requirement of discrimination against religion.

[50] *Id.* at 24 (Souter, J., dissenting).

[51] *Id.* at 23.

[52] The "projection" is from the anti-school choice People for the American Way, whose studies are copiously cited by the dissenters, although they are not part of the case record.

[53] *Zelman,* slip op. at 27 n.20 (Souter, J., dissenting).

Finally, the four dissenters take up the role of lobbyists, beseeching the "political branches [to] save us from the consequences of the majority's decision," and expressing the "hope that a future Court will reconsider today's dramatic departure from basic Establishment Clause principle."[54]

Justice Breyer presented a separate dissent, joined by Stevens and Souter (but curiously, not by Ginsburg). He wrote separately "because I believe that the Establishment Clause concern for protecting the Nation's social fabric from religious conflict poses an overriding obstacle to the implementation of this well-intentioned school voucher program."[55] For Breyer, school choice programs not only must comply with the express intent of the First Amendment—to prohibit laws "respecting an establishment of religion"—but also must avoid promoting "religiously based social conflict."[56] In that regard, it doesn't seem to matter that the Cleveland program, in its sixth year of existence, has not created religious conflict. Neither does it seem to matter that the aim of the program is educational. Instead, Breyer views the program against the backdrop of religious strife. He notes that in the United States, "[m]ajor religions include, among others, Protestants, Catholics, Jews, Muslims, Buddhists, Hindus, and Sikhs. . . . And several of these major religions contain different subsidiary sects with different religious beliefs."[57] Does that suggest we can all get along only if each group is denied the opportunity to direct government benefits as it sees fit? Even worse, must non-Catholic families be denied an opportunity to send their children to inner-city Catholic schools?

Justice Breyer concedes that the "consequence" of existing aid programs that include religious options "has not been great turmoil."[58] Nor is there evidence that the Cleveland program—or any other school choice program—has caused religious strife. But a voucher program, in Justice Breyer's view, "risks creating a form of religiously based conflict potentially harmful to the Nation's social

---

[54] *Id.* at 34. Justice Souter took the additional dramatic step of reading his dissent from the bench.

[55] *Id.* at 1 (Breyer, J., dissenting).

[56] *Id.* at 7.

[57] *Id.*

[58] *Id.* at 10.

fabric.''[59] Note the hypothetical language: it does not *do* it, it only *risks* it, and what it risks is not invariable harm but *potential* harm. On that double hypothesis, the dissenters would substitute their abstract concerns for the state of Ohio's urgent effort to deliver educational opportunities to the children of Cleveland.

One wonders whether, in 5 years or 10, when the dire prognostications of religious strife remain unfulfilled, the dissenters would reconsider. Likewise, one wonders why the dissenters focused on an argument that the plaintiffs made only in passing. While the plaintiffs tried mainly to shoehorn the Cleveland program into the *Nyquist* construct, they expended relatively little effort in raising religious strife concerns. For their part, the dissenters implicitly acknowledged that the past 20 years of jurisprudence firmly sanction school choice programs. Yet, they substituted the subjective fears of individual justices for the clear command of governmental neutrality embodied in the First Amendment's religion clauses. Fortunately, that view did not prevail, but it is genuinely alarming that it attracted four votes.

The Road Ahead

Notwithstanding the dissenters' rhetoric, the majority opinion is the law of the land, and it dissipates the cloud over school choice programs. All recent voucher programs and proposals readily satisfy the applicable criteria. So do scholarship and tuition tax credit programs.[60] It now seems entirely permissible for the government to adopt a program in which *all* education funding is channeled through students—to public and private schools alike. The decision could help usher in an era of child-centered public education reform whereby the state is a *funder* of education even if not a *provider*— focusing less on *where* children are being educated and more on *whether* children are being educated.

The immediate beneficiaries of the *Zelman* decision are families in school choice programs who have lived in constant fear that their children would be pried out of the only good schools they have ever

---

[59] *Id.* at 13.

[60] Indeed, because *Mueller* is so closely on point, tax credit programs have fared more easily in litigation so far. In three cases defending tax credits, we have not lost a single round in any court.

attended. The anti–school choice lobby is deprived of its federal constitutional argument. In Florida, where litigation challenging the state's opportunity scholarship program is ongoing, the federal constitutional cause of action has evaporated. The federal constitutional objection had not only presented a legal obstacle but a legislative one as well. School choice opponents surely will continue to resist any effort to dismantle the public school monopoly, but no longer will they be able to credibly assert that such efforts are unconstitutional.

The litigation focus will shift to state constitutions. Forty-seven states have religious establishment provisions that are more explicit than the First Amendment. About three dozen are "Blaine Amendments," tracing back to the late 19th century when anti-Catholic activists succeeded in adding restrictive language to state constitutions in an effort to preserve Protestant hegemony over public schools and taxpayer funding.[61] Most of the provisions prohibit "aid" or "support" of private or religious schools. Some states, such as Wisconsin and Arizona, have construed their provisions in harmony with the First Amendment, finding that school choice programs do not aid or support private schools but instead aid and support students.[62] But at least a dozen states have interpreted their constitutions as forbidding aid to students in religious schools.

The *Zelman* decision allows the school choice movement, for the first time in 12 years, to shift from defense to offense in the courts. Rather than fighting the Blaine Amendment issue state by state, we plan to file test cases that will invoke the neutrality principle to strike down all state constitutional provisions that discriminate against religious options. Moreover, school choice advocates now have ultimate legal authority for this proposition: Instead of remedies calling merely for more money, educational deprivations can be remedied through vouchers.

Remarkably, it took 12 years of intense litigation to establish the baseline principle that parents can decide how to direct the spending devoted to their children's education. It will take much more work

---

[61] *See, e.g.*, Joseph P. Viteritti, *Blaine's Wake: School Choice, the First Amendment, and State Constitutional Law*, 21 HARV. J. L. & PUB. POL'Y 657 (1998).

[62] Kotterman v. Killian, 972 P.2d 606 (Ariz.), *cert. denied*, 528 U.S. 921 (1999); Jackson v. Benson, 578 N.W.2d 602 (Wis.), *cert. denied*, 525 U.S. 997 (1998).

to establish even more ambitious principles of educational freedom, but the task is an essential one. To paraphrase Winston Churchill, this triumph marks only the end of the beginning.

For now, advocates of educational freedom have much to celebrate. In common cause with economically disadvantaged families, we have prevailed in our first big test in the U.S. Supreme Court. The special interest groups dedicated to the status quo are momentarily vanquished. The empire will strike back, to be sure; but this decision shows that they can be beaten, that David can indeed slay Goliath.

When the unions first challenged the Cleveland scholarship program in 1997, they characterized the parents as "inconsequential conduits" for the transmission of aid to religious schools. The unions merely revealed their arrogance and cynicism. Yes, the parents *were* inconsequential, but they no longer are. In fact, in Cleveland and Milwaukee and other pockets in America, the parents are finally, and forever, in charge.

That's exactly what threatens the education establishment. Let's hope it proves contagious.

An Eerie Efficiency

Timothy Lynch

I. Introduction

More and more prosecutors are adopting so-called "fast track" plea bargaining programs. Although such programs vary from jurisdiction to jurisdiction, the basic idea is this: If the person who has been accused of a crime will agree to forgo his right to a trial and an appeal, the government will agree to impose a lighter prison sentence. Should the person who has been accused of a crime decline the government's offer and invoke his constitutional right to trial by jury, the government promises to impose a harsher prison sentence if the person is convicted. More recently, some prosecutors have been trying to further economize their time and resources by having criminal defendants waive their right to receive exculpatory information from the government before entering into binding plea agreements. Such plea bargain arrangements have come under fire from criminal defense attorneys and civil libertarians who have condemned such deals as "adhesive, unconscionable, and unconstitutional."[1]

This article scrutinizes the constitutionality of fast track plea bargaining programs, summarizes the Supreme Court's unanimous ruling in *United States v. Ruiz,*[2] critiques the Court's treatment of the subject by placing the constitutional controversy in the broader context of plea bargaining in general, and concludes that fast track plea bargaining agreements violate the Constitution because plea bargaining violates the Constitution.

---

[1] Larry Kupers and John T. Philipsborn, *Mephistophelian Deals: The Newest in Standard Plea Agreements,* CHAMPION, Aug. 1999.

[2] 70 U.S.L.W. 4677 (June 24, 2002).

II. The *Ruiz* Case: The Supreme Court Signs Off on Fast Track Deals

The United States Attorney's Office for the Southern District of California adopted a "fast track" plea bargaining program to minimize the expenditure of government resources and expedite the processing of routine cases. Thus, when Angela Ruiz was arrested on charges of importing marijuana from Mexico into the United States, the federal prosecutor offered Ruiz a typical fast track plea bargain. The essence of the proposed "deal" was this: If Ruiz would agree to plead guilty to the charge and waive (a) her right to a trial by jury, (b) her right to file an appeal, (c) her right to file pretrial motions, and (d) her right to receive exculpatory and impeachment evidence, the prosecutor would agree to recommend a lighter prison sentence to the sentencing judge. The propriety of that arrangement would subsequently form the basis of Ruiz's legal appeal.

By way of background, plea bargaining has been widely practiced for many years, but prosecutors have only recently begun to incorporate additional waivers relating to the receipt of exculpatory and impeachment information into their "standard" plea bargaining contracts.[3] The prosecutorial duty to disclose exculpatory and impeachment evidence arose from a line of Supreme Court rulings, beginning with *Brady v. Maryland*, which held that the government violates the constitutional guarantee of "due process of law" whenever it withholds material exculpatory information from the accused and his attorney.[4] The fast track plea bargaining contracts are based on the idea that the accused can waive his *Brady* right to receive such information by virtue of his acceptance of the government's plea bargaining offer.

Ruiz objected to the "*Brady* waiver" portion of the proposed plea agreement, but the government would not yield on that point. From the government's perspective, negotiating the central features of the "standard" plea agreement on a case-by-case basis would defeat the principal purpose of the fast track program. Thus, when Ruiz balked on the inclusion of the *Brady* waiver, the prosecution broke off the discussion and withdrew its offer.

---

[3] *See* David E. Rovella, *Federal Plea Bargains Draw Fire*, NAT. L.J., Jan. 17, 2000.

[4] *See* Brady v. Maryland, 373 U.S. 83 (1963); Giglio v. United States, 405 U.S. 150 (1972).

Ruiz nevertheless chose to forgo a trial and entered a guilty plea to the charges of marijuana importation. Even though Ruiz had no plea bargain, her legal team sought leniency from the sentencing court because she had substantially complied with all of the other fast track eligibility requirements. The prosecution nonetheless formally opposed Ruiz's motion for leniency. The sentencing judge ultimately denied the motion for leniency because the government provided no fast track recommendation and because no plea agreement required the prosecutor to do otherwise.

On appeal, Ruiz argued that the right to receive undisclosed *Brady* evidence cannot be waived with plea agreements. According to Ruiz, the sentencing court mistakenly concluded that there was nothing untoward in the government's handling of her case and thus mistakenly concluded that it had no legal discretion to remedy the unconstitutional conduct of the prosecutor by exercising leniency under the federal sentencing guidelines. The essence of Ruiz's argument was that the prosecution withheld a fast track sentencing recommendation because Ruiz refused to waive her unwaivable *Brady* rights. In other words, it is unconstitutional for the government to condition the benefits of a plea bargain on the waiver of such rights.

The U.S. Court of Appeals for the Ninth Circuit began its analysis by noting that for a guilty plea to meet the due process requirement, it must be intelligent, knowing, and voluntary.[5] Prior circuit precedent held that guilty pleas could not be deemed intelligent and voluntary if they were entered into "without knowledge of material information withheld by the prosecution."[6] That conclusion was, in turn, driven by the court's observation that a defendant's decision whether or not to plead guilty "is often heavily influenced by his appraisal of the prosecution's case."[7]

The Court of Appeals saw no reason to draw a distinction between its criterion for valid guilty pleas and valid plea agreements. To comport with due process, the accused must intelligently and voluntarily forgo his constitutional rights.[8] The court further noted that

[5] United States v. Ruiz, 241 F.3d 1157, 1164 (2001).

[6] *Id.* at 1164.

[7] *Id.*

[8] The Court also declined to draw a distinction between the prosecutorial duty to disclose exculpatory evidence and its duty to disclose impeachment evidence. The Justice Department argued that even if the court found a constitutional objection with waivers of exculpatory evidence, that issue should be addressed in another case. The only evidence withheld from Ruiz involved impeachment evidence. *Id.* at 1165.

in situations in which there is not going to be a trial, *Brady* evidence is only valuable to the accused if it is disclosed before the acceptance of the plea agreement. Thus, the court rejected the government's contention that the disclosure of exculpatory evidence was only necessary in the event of a trial. The court declared *Brady* waivers to be invalid, vacated Ruiz's sentence, and remanded the case to the district court for resentencing. The appellate court instructed the district judge to hold an evidentiary hearing to determine whether or not the prosecution withheld its fast track recommendation for the reasons alleged by Ruiz. Because the Ninth Circuit ruling undermined a key aspect of the fast track plea bargaining program, the prosecution appealed the case to the Supreme Court, which agreed to review the case.

The Supreme Court overturned the Ninth Circuit decision with a unanimous ruling that was authored by Justice Stephen Breyer. The Court's conclusion that the Constitution does not require pre-guilty plea disclosure of impeachment information rested on three arguments:

First, the Court agreed with the government's argument that although disclosure of impeachment information is necessary to ensure a fair trial, it is not necessary to ensure the "voluntary" nature of a guilty plea.[9] Although the Court acknowledged that more information in the possession of the accused will likely improve the wisdom of his decision, it noted that the prosecutor has never been legally required to share all useful information with the defense.[10]

Second, the Court could not find "significant support" for the Ninth Circuit's ruling in case law.[11] Instead, Justice Breyer found that the case law hewed to the proposition that so long as the accused understood the general nature of the rights he was waiving, it mattered not if he suffered from "various forms of misapprehension," concerning such matters as the actual strength of the government's case, or ignorance concerning viable legal defenses.[12]

Third, and most disturbing, the Court said its due process analysis had to weigh the constitutional benefit that would redound to the

---

[9] *Ruiz*, 70 U.S.L.W. 4677, 4679 (June 24, 2002).

[10] *Id.*

[11] *Id.* at 4679–4680.

[12] *Id.* at 4680.

accused against the "adverse impact" on the "Government's interests."[13] In the words of Justice Breyer, "a constitutional obligation to provide impeachment information during plea bargaining, prior to entry of a guilty plea, could seriously interfere with the Government's interest in securing those guilty pleas that are factually justified, desired by defendants, and help to secure the efficient administration of justice."[14]

Fast track plea bargaining programs indisputably help to secure a more efficient system of caseload disposition. What is disputable, however, is whether the fast track programs can truly be reconciled with the constitutional rights of the accused. To show that the Supreme Court did indeed reach an erroneous conclusion in *Ruiz*, it will be necessary to broaden the discussion and to critically examine prior Supreme Court precedents that have fostered a jurisprudence that is now far removed from the system of criminal justice contemplated by the text of the Constitution.

III. The Rise and Fall of Adversarial Trials

Because any person who is accused of violating the criminal law can lose his liberty, and perhaps his life, depending on the offense and the prescribed penalty, the Framers of the Constitution took pains to put explicit limits on the awesome powers of government. Here are a few of the safeguards that are explicitly guaranteed by the Bill of Rights:

- The accused has the right to be informed of the charges.
- The accused cannot be compelled to incriminate himself.
- The accused has a right to a speedy and public trial.
- The accused has a right to an impartial jury trial in the state and district where the offense allegedly took place.
- The accused has the right to cross-examine the state's witnesses and has the right to call witnesses on his own behalf.
- The accused has the right to the assistance of counsel.

Justice Hugo Black once noted that, in America, the defendant "has an absolute, unqualified right to compel the State to investigate its own case, find its own witnesses, prove its own facts, and convince

[13] *Id.*
[14] *Id.*

175

the jury through its own resources. Throughout the process the defendant has a fundamental right to remain silent, in effect challenging the State at every point to: 'Prove it!' "[15] By limiting the powers of the police and prosecutors, the Bill of Rights safeguards freedom.

Given the Fifth Amendment's prohibition of compelled self-incrimination and the Sixth Amendment's guarantee of impartial juries, one would think that the administration of criminal justice in America would be marked by adversarial trials—and yet the opposite is true. Less than 10 percent of the criminal cases brought by the federal government each year are actually tried before juries with all of the accompanying procedural safeguards noted earlier.[16] More than 90 percent of the criminal cases in America are never tried, much less proven, to juries.[17] The overwhelming majority of individuals who are accused of crime forgo their constitutional rights and plead guilty. The rarity of jury trials is not the result of criminals who come into court to relieve a guilty conscience or to save the taxpayers the costs of a trial. Nor is it simply a matter of happenstance. The truth is that government officials have deliberately engineered the system to "assure that the jury trial system established by the Constitution is seldom utilized."[18] And plea bargaining is the primary technique used by the government to bypass the institutional safeguards in trials.

Plea bargaining consists of an agreement (formal or informal) between the defendant and the prosecutor. The prosecutor typically agrees to a reduced prison sentence in return for the defendant's waiver of his constitutional right against self-incrimination and his right to trial. As one critic has written, "the leniency is payment to a defendant to induce him or her not to go to trial. The guilty plea or no contest plea is the quid pro quo for the concession; there is no other reason."[19] Plea bargaining unquestionably alleviates the workload of judges, prosecutors, and defense lawyers, but the key question is this: Is it proper for a government that is constitutionally

---

[15] Williams v. Florida, 399 U.S. 78, 112 (1970) (Black, J., dissenting).

[16] Corinna Barrett Lain, *Accuracy Where It Matters: Brady v. Maryland in the Plea Bargaining Context*, 80 WASH. U. L.Q. 1 (2002).

[17] *Id.*

[18] Note, *The Unconstitutionality of Plea Bargaining*, 83 HARV. L. REV. 1387, 1389 (1970).

[19] Ralph Adam Fine, *Plea Bargaining: An Unnecessary Evil*, in CRIMINAL JUSTICE? THE LEGAL SYSTEM V. INDIVIDUAL RESPONSIBILITY 85 (Robert James Bidinotto ed., 1994).

required to respect the right to trial by jury to use its charging and sentencing powers to pressure an individual to waive that right?

IV. Can Plea Bargaining Be Justified?

There is no doubt about the fact that government officials deliberately use their power to pressure people who have been accused of crime, and who are presumed innocent, to confess their guilt and to waive their right to a formal trial. We know this to be true because prosecutors freely admit that this is what they do.

Paul Hayes, for example, was indicted for attempting to pass a forged check in the amount of $88.30, an offense that was punishable by a prison term of 2 to 10 years.[20] The prosecutor offered to recommend a sentence of 5 years if Hayes would waive his right to trial and plead guilty to the charge. The prosecutor also made it clear to Hayes that if he did not plead guilty and "save the court the inconvenience and necessity of a trial," that the state would seek a new indictment from a grand jury under Kentucky's "Habitual Criminal Act."[21] Under the provisions of that statute, Hayes would face a mandatory sentence of life imprisonment because of his prior criminal record. Despite the enormous pressure exerted upon him by the state, Hayes insisted on his right to jury trial. He was subsequently convicted and then sentenced to life imprisonment.

On appeal, Hayes argued that the prosecutor violated the Constitution by threatening to punish him for simply invoking his right to a trial. In response, the government freely admitted that the only reason a new indictment was filed against Hayes was to deter him from exercising his right to a trial. Because the indictment was supported by the evidence, the government maintained that the prosecutor had done nothing improper. The case ultimately reached the Supreme Court for a resolution. In a landmark 5–4 ruling, *Bordenkircher v. Hayes*, the Court approved the prosecutor's handling of the case and upheld the draconian sentence of life imprisonment. Because the *Hayes* case is considered to be the watershed precedent for plea bargaining, it deserves careful attention.

The *Hayes* ruling acknowledged that it would be "patently unconstitutional" for any agent of the government "to pursue a course of

---

[20] Bordenkircher v. Hayes, 434 U.S. 357 (1978).

[21] *Id.* at 358.

action whose objective is to penalize a person's reliance on his legal rights."[22] The Court, however, declined to overturn Hayes's sentence because he could have completely avoided the risk of life imprisonment by admitting his guilt and accepting a prison term of 5 years. At bottom, the constitutional rationale for plea bargaining comes down to the following contention: There is "no element of punishment or retaliation so long as the accused is free to accept or reject the prosecution's offer."[23] On first blush, the proposition seems plausible because criminal defendants have always been allowed to waive their right to a trial and because the executive and legislative branches have always had discretion with respect to their charging and sentencing policies. But a closer inspection will show that the constitutional rationale underlying plea bargaining cannot withstand scrutiny.[24]

First, it is important to note that the existence of some element of choice has never been thought to justify otherwise wrongful conduct. As the Supreme Court itself observed in another context, "It always is for the interest of a party under duress to choose the lesser of two evils. But the fact that a choice was made according to interest does not exclude duress. It is the characteristic of duress properly so called."[25]

The courts have employed similar reasoning in tort disputes between private parties. For example, a woman brought a false imprisonment action against a male acquaintance after he allegedly forced her to travel with him in his automobile when it was her desire to travel by train.[26] According to the complaint, the man boarded the train, seized the woman's purse, and then disembarked and proceeded to his car. The woman then left the train to retrieve her purse. While arguing with the man in the parking lot, the train

---

[22] *Id.* at 363–364.

[23] *Id.* at 364.

[24] This article rejects the idea that the label attached to time spent in jail resolves the constitutional question. To paraphrase Professor Elizabeth Lear, whether one calls it "retaliation," "punishment," or "denial of leniency," a longer prison sentence remains a serious restriction on a person's actual freedom. This article is concerned with jail time that is directly attributable to the invocation of a person's constitutional rights. *See* Elizabeth Lear, *Is Conviction Irrelevant?* 40 UCLA L. REV. 1179, 1185 (1993).

[25] Union Pac. R.R. Co. v. Pub. Serv. Comm'n, 248 U.S. 67, 70 (1918).

[26] Griffin v. Clark, 42 P.2d 297 (1935).

left the station. Reluctantly, the woman got into the vehicle to travel to her destination. The man maintained that the false imprisonment claim lacked merit because he exercised no physical force against the woman and because she was at liberty to remain on the train or to go her own way. The court rejected that defense and ruled that the false imprisonment theory had merit because the woman did not wish to leave the train and she did not wish to depart without her purse. The man unlawfully interfered with the woman's liberty to be where she wished to be. The fact that the man had given the woman some choices that she could "accept or reject" did not alter the fact that the man was a tortfeasor.[27]

Second, the Supreme Court has repeatedly invalidated certain governmental actions that were purposely designed to coerce individuals and organizations into surrendering their constitutional rights. In *Marshall v. Barlow's Inc.*, the Court ruled that a businessman was within his rights when he refused to allow an OSHA inspector into his establishment without a search warrant.[28] The Secretary of Labor filed a legal brief arguing that when people make the decision to go into business they essentially "consent" to governmental inspections of their property.[29] Even though the owner of the premises could have avoided such inspections by shutting down his business, the Court recognized that the OSHA regulations penalized commercial property owners for exercising their right under the Fourth Amendment to insist that government inspectors obtain search warrants before demanding access to the premises.[30]

In *Nollan v. California Coastal Commission*, the Court ruled that the State of California could not grant a development permit subject to the condition that the landowners allow the public an easement across a portion of their property.[31] Even though the landowners had the option of "accepting or rejecting" the Coastal Commission's

---

[27] *Id.* See also Ashland Dry Goods v. Wages, 195 S.W.2d 312 (1946); Nat'l Bond & Inv. Co. v. Whithorn, 123 S.W.2d 263 (1938).

[28] Marshall v. Barlow's Inc., 436 U.S. 307 (1978).

[29] In response, the Court observed that only "the most fictional sense of voluntary consent" could be discerned from the "single fact that one conducts business affecting interstate commerce." *Id.*, at 314.

[30] *Id.* at 325. *See also* Miller v. United States, 230 F. 2d 486 (1956); District of Columbia v. Little, 178 F.2d 13 (1949).

[31] Nollan v. Cal. Coastal Comm'n, 483 U.S. 825 (1987).

deal, the Court recognized that the permit condition, in the circumstances of that case, amounted to an "out-and-out plan of extortion."[32]

Similarly, in *Miami Herald Publishing Co. v. Tornillo*, the Supreme Court invalidated a so-called "right of reply" statute.[33] The Florida legislature made it a crime for a newspaper to criticize a politician and then to deny that politician a "right to equal space" in the paper to defend himself against such criticism. Even though Florida newspapers remained free to say whatever they wished, the Court recognized that the statute exacted a "penalty" for the simple exercise of free speech about political affairs.[34]

Finally, the ad hoc nature of the *Hayes* plea bargaining precedent becomes apparent when one extends its logic to other rights involving criminal procedure. The Court has never proffered a satisfactory explanation with respect to why the government should not be able to use its sentencing powers to leverage the waiver of constitutional rights pertaining to the trial itself. Can a federal prosecutor enter into "negotiations" with criminal defendants with respect to the exercise of his trial rights? For example, when a person is accused of a crime, he has the option of hiring an experienced attorney to prepare a legal defense on his behalf or representing himself without the aid of counsel.[35] Can a prosecutor induce a defendant into waiving his right to the assistance of counsel with a recommendation for leniency in the event of a conviction? Such prosecutorial tactics are presently unheard of. And yet, under the rationale of the *Hayes* case, it is not obvious why such tactics should be constitutionally barred. After all, under *Hayes*, there is no element of punishment or retaliation so long as the accused is free to accept or reject the prosecutor's offer.

Plea bargaining rests on the constitutional fiction that our government does not retaliate against individuals who wish to exercise their constitutional right to trial by jury. Although the fictional nature

---

[32] *Id.* at 837.

[33] Miami Herald Pub. Co. v. Tornillo, 418 U.S. 241 (1974).

[34] *Id.* at 256. *See also* Mahoney v. Babbitt, 105 F.3d 1452 (1997), where government officials attempted to give a citizen the following "choice": He could carry a sign along the inaugural parade route that complimented the president, but would be arrested for carrying a sign that was critical of the president!

[35] *See* Faretta v. California, 422 U.S. 806 (1975).

of that proposition has been apparent to many for some time now, what is new is that more and more people are reaching the conclusion that that fiction is intolerable.[36] Chief Judge William G. Young of the Federal District Court in Massachusetts, for example, recently filed an opinion that was refreshingly candid about what is happening in the modern criminal justice system:

> Evidence of sentencing disparity visited on those who exercise their Sixth Amendment right to trial by jury is today stark, brutal, and incontrovertible. . . . Today, under the Sentencing Guidelines regime with its vast shift of power to the Executive, that disparity has widened to an incredible 500%. As a practical matter this means, as between two similarly situated defendants, that if the one who pleads and cooperates gets a four-year sentence, then the guideline sentence for the one who exercises his right to trial by jury and is convicted will be twenty years. Not surprisingly, such a disparity imposes an extraordinary burden on the free exercise of the right to an adjudication of guilt by one's peers. Criminal trial rates in the United States and in this District are plummeting due to the simple fact that today we punish people—punish them severely—simply for going to trial. It is the sheerest sophistry to pretend otherwise.[37]

Like a lovely old home that is steadily sliding into disrepair because of neglectful owners, the American criminal justice system has been undergoing a steady regression—so much so that it would no longer be recognizible to the Framers of the Constitution.

V. A Proper Analysis of *Ruiz* and Fast Track Bargains

If plea bargaining amounts to an unconstitutional burden on the rights of the accused, how should the Supreme Court have decided the *Ruiz* case? The short answer is that the Court should have affirmed, not reversed, the ruling of the Ninth Circuit Court of Appeals.

The constitutional analysis of the Court of Appeals was fundamentally sound. No one can dispute the idea that a criminal defendant can forgo his or her right to trial. Because of the potentially dire

---

[36] Fine, *supra* note 19.; Stephen J. Shulhofer, *Plea Bargaining as Disaster*, 101 YALE L.J. 1979 (1992).

[37] Berthoff v. United States, 140 F. Supp. 2d 50, 67–69 (2001).

implications of such a move, however, the courts take the time, quite properly, to ensure that the accused is acting voluntarily and intelligently. A conscientious trial court should assure itself that the person who is waiving his constitutional rights is not pleading guilty to a crime that he did not commit and that he is not being railroaded into a prison cell.

The Court of Appeals was much more sensitive to the fact that the courtroom is the crucial way station between freedom and incarceration. And that is true not only with respect to the person who goes to trial but equally so with the person who has decided, for whatever reason, to enter a guilty plea. Whereas the Supreme Court stressed that the disclosure of exculpatory and impeachment evidence was important "trial-related rights," the Court of Appeals recognized that such information was no less important to the person who comes before the trial court and claims that he is prepared to "knowingly" forgo his constitutional rights. The question that comes to the fore in the latter situation is this: With fast track *Brady* waivers in place, how can any person *knowingly* waive his right to trial when he is unaware of material exculpatory and impeachment evidence held by the prosecution?

Further, whereas the Supreme Court seemed to be preoccupied with the "Government's interest" in avoiding "burdensome" trial-related preparation and disclosure responsibilities (e.g., its constitutionally mandated duties), the Court of Appeals locus of attention was where it belonged, namely, on how this newfangled procedure would affect the rights of the individual. That is, in the absence of exculpatory and impeachment information, the appeals court was deeply concerned that poor and unsophisticated, but innocent, individuals accused of crimes might make the dreadful mistake of pleading guilty.

A concrete example can perhaps illuminate how these constitutional principles can affect the lives of people. On the evening of September 28, 1987, Jose Antonio Rivera was murdered.[38] Rivera was chased through a New York City park by a group of teens with whom he had been feuding. Rivera was stabbed and hit repeatedly with sticks. Jose Morales, age 17, and another youth were arrested

---

[38] *See* Jim Dwyer, *Testimony of Priest and Lawyer Frees Man Jailed for '87 Murder*, N.Y. Times, July 26, 2001.

in connection with the incident. Morales maintained his innocence, but he did not deny that he was in the park. The only witness to the crime was Rivera's girlfriend—and she was prepared to identify Morales as one of the culprits.

The prosecutor offered Morales a plea bargain. If he waived his right to trial and confessed to the crime of "reckless endangerment," the prosecutor would recommend a prison sentence of 2 years. However, if Morales insisted on his innocence and invoked his right to a jury trial, the prosecutor would charge him with second degree murder and seek a 15–20 year sentence.

It is easy for some people to breezily proclaim that they would never plead guilty to a crime if they were truly innocent, but when one is confronted with the choice of 2 years in jail or quite possibly 20 years' imprisonment, the decision is not so easy. Now consider Morales' dilemma in light of a potentially important piece of impeachment information. The sole witness to the crime, Rivera's girlfriend, had been drinking that evening. Under *all* of the circumstances, the prosecution had a fairly weak case against Morales. The crime occurred at night, the park was crowded with young people running around, and the one eye witness was very likely impaired from liquor consumption.

If Morales went to trial, the prosecutor would have a legal duty to disclose the impeachment information to the defense. Under the fast track plea bargaining program, however, the prosecutor would have no duty to disclose that his only witness was drunk. Instead, because he presumably believed Morales was a thug, the prosecutor would likely try to bluff Morales into a plea bargain with a statement like, "You had better take a deal because I've got an eye witness who is prepared to identify you as the killer."[39] The point here is to show how the disclosure or nondisclosure of impeachment information, working in combination with plea bargaining pressures, can affect the decision of the accused regarding whether to go to trial.

Returning to the *Ruiz* case, the Court of Appeals was certainly on the mark when it noted that for a guilty plea to be valid, it must be both intelligent and voluntary. And because a defendant's decision

---

[39] This article does not claim that such a bluff was actually made in the Morales case. Rather, the point is to show how *Brady* waivers might have impacted the case of an innocent man who was targeted for prosecution. The only way that one can minimize future miscarriages of justice is to learn from experience.

is heavily influenced by his appraisal of the prosecution's case, the disclosure of exculpatory and impeachment evidence is necessary to ensure that the waiver is not only voluntary, but knowing and intelligent. As the court correctly noted, "a defendant's abstract awareness of his rights under *Brady* is a pale substitute for the receipt of concrete *Brady* material that, for example, may include evidence that the arresting officer was twice convicted of perjury or that another suspect confessed to the crime. Without disclosure of the *Brady* evidence itself, the plea agreement and the *Brady* waiver contained therein cannot be intelligent and voluntary."[40]

Of course, the Court of Appeals was bound by precedent and was not at liberty to challenge the constitutionality of plea bargaining per se. And because that fundamental issue was not properly before the Supreme Court, a proper disposition of the case would have been to affirm the Ninth Circuit's holding invalidating the *Brady* waiver contracts, vacate Angela Ruiz's sentence, and remand the case to the district court for resentencing. However, instead of expressing satisfaction with the federal government's "heavy reliance upon plea bargaining," as Justice Breyer did in his majority opinion, the Supreme Court should have expressed alarm about the rarity of jury trials in America and invited a more broad-based challenge to plea bargaining and to the precedents that undergird that odious practice.[41]

---

[40] *Ruiz*, 241 F. 3d at 1165. The Court of Appeals was also keenly sensitive to the potentially perverse incentives created by the *Brady* waivers. The court observed that "prosecutors could be tempted to deliberately withhold exculpatory information as part of an attempt to elicit guilty pleas." *Id.* at 1164. The Supreme Court, on the other hand, seemed to naively regard such an abuse of power as remotely possible, at best. *But see* Michelle Mittelstadt, *Federal Marshals Secure Waco Evidence From FBI Headquarters*, ASSOCIATED PRESS, Sept. 2, 1999; Bill Moushey, *Hiding the Facts*, PITTS-BURGH POST-GAZETTE, Nov. 24, 1998. *See also* Richard A. Rosen, *Disciplinary Sanctions Against Prosecutors for Brady Violations: A Paper Tiger*, 65 N.C. L. REV. 693 (1987).

[41] There is, of course, an extensive literature on the merits and demerits of plea bargaining. Although policy related arguments are beyond the scope of this article, one understandable concern that is invariably raised is that the system would "grind to a halt" if the practice were ever abandoned. The short answer to that claim is that it misstates the issue. The invocation of the constitutional right to jury trial should not be scapegoated because government officials have created an overly expansive criminal code and have concomitantly declined to devote sufficient resources to the criminal justice system so that the constitutionally mandated procedures can be complied with. As Justice Antonin Scalia observed in another context, "Formal requirements are [too] often scorned when they stand in the way of expediency." Neder v. United States, 527 U.S. 1, 40 (1999) (Scalia, J., dissenting).

VI. Conclusion

Thomas Jefferson famously observed that "the natural progress of things is for liberty to yield and government to gain ground."[42] The American experience with plea bargaining is yet another confirmation of that truth. The Supreme Court unleashed a runaway train when it sanctioned plea bargaining in *Bordenkircher v. Hayes* in 1978. Despite a steady media diet of titillating criminal trials in recent years, there is an increasing recognition that jury trials are now a rarity in America—and that something, somewhere, is seriously amiss.[43] That "something" is plea bargaining.

The *Brady* waiver controversy tells us that the government is no longer content with the surrender of the right to trial and the right to an appeal. In *Ruiz*, the government demanded that defendants surrender their right to receive exculpatory information before signing binding plea agreements. It is a safe bet that the government will be making further demands down the road—undoubtedly under the banner of securing "a more efficient administration of justice." Some prosecutors have already boldly conditioned the release of prisoners who have been exonerated by DNA evidence on the written promise that the innocent man will not bring a lawsuit against the government for prosecutorial misconduct or otherwise wrongful imprisonment.[44] With such pernicious tactics condoned by the courts, it is not inconceivable to anticipate more plea bargaining "waivers" in the future. Perhaps the government will attempt to get people to waive their right to sue the state about the prison conditions, however awful such conditions may eventually turn out to be. Such a waiver will be defended on the ground that the person remains free to "accept or reject" the prosecutor's offer—and that such waivers

---

[42] Letter from Thomas Jefferson to Edward Carrington (May 27, 1788).

[43] *See* Craig Horowitz, *The Defense Rests—Permanently*, N.Y. MAG., Mar. 8, 2002; William Glaberson, *Juries, Their Powers Under Siege, Find Their Role Is Being Eroded*, N.Y. TIMES, March 2, 2001. See also Ring v. Arizona, 70 U.S.L.W. 4666, 4674 (June 24, 2002) (Scalia and Thomas, JJ., concurring) ("The right of trial by jury is in perilous decline.")

[44] *See* Richard Willing, *Exonerated Prisoners Are Rarely Paid For Lost Time*, USA TODAY, June 18, 2002; Michael Klein, *With Murder Case Dismissed, S. Phila. Man Finally Is Freed*, PHILADELPHIA INQUIRER, Feb. 12, 2002. *See also* the Public Broadcasting Service (PBS) documentary, *Frontline: The Case for Innocence* (PBS television broadcast, Jan. 2000) (The Case of Clyde Charles).

will help to preserve scarce governmental resources related to trial preparation.[45]

As with so many other areas of constitutional law, the Court must stop tinkering around the edges of the issue and return to first principles. The Framers of the Constitution were aware of more "efficient" trial procedures when they wrote the Bill of Rights, but chose not to adopt them. The Framers believed that the Bill of Rights, and the freedom that it secured, was well worth any loss in efficiency that resulted. If that vision is to endure, the Supreme Court must come to its defense.

---

[45] *See* Hudson v. Palmer, 468 U.S. 517, 533–534 (1984); Newton v. Rumery, 480 U.S. 386 (1987).

Redefining a "Crime" as a Sentencing Factor to Circumvent the Right to Jury Trial: *Harris v. United States*

Stephen P. Halbrook

The right to trial by jury is under grave threat today. From time immemorial, whether a person is guilty of a crime has been decided by one's peers in the community. Under the United States Constitution, an accused person must be indicted by a grand jury and convicted by a petit jury of the charges beyond a reasonable doubt. However, forces are at work attempting to transfer these jury powers to the courts. By the linguistic artifice of redefining the term "crime" as a "sentencing factor," courts are usurping the jury's traditional fact-finding role and are dispensing with the standard of proof beyond a reasonable doubt. The following essay tells the story of how this menace to traditional American liberties is being carried out.

William Joseph Harris sold a small amount of marijuana out of his North Carolina pawnshop to undercover federal agents. As was his custom, he wore a pistol in a holster, at one point showing it to his new-found "friends." He was arrested for, charged with, and convicted of a minor pot offense and of carrying or using a firearm during and in relation to a drug trafficking offense, which is punishable with a minimum of 5 years imprisonment. After the trial was over, he was brought in for sentencing. Under the law, if the firearm was "brandished," the minimum prison time is seven years, but Harris was not charged with or convicted of this offense. Nonetheless, the sentencing judge found that the firearm was brandished and imposed the 7-year mandatory sentence.

The Constitution provides for several guarantees when a person is charged with a federal crime: an indictment by a grand jury must inform one of the nature of the charges, the person is entitled to a trial by jury, and the proof must be beyond a reasonable doubt.

187

However, if the existence of an act committed by a person is considered a "sentencing factor" and not the element of a "crime," courts have held that these constitutional guarantees do not exist. The person must be convicted of some crime, but the sentencing factors that increase prison time need only be decided by a judge on the basis of a mere preponderance of the evidence, that is, the scales need be tipped only slightly in one direction for the fact to be found and the higher sentence imposed. In *Harris v. United States*, decided on June 24, 2002, the United States Supreme Court held that Mr. Harris had no right to be informed in the indictment that he would be accused of brandishing a firearm, no right for a jury to decide whether he committed that act, and no right that the allegation be proven beyond a reasonable doubt.[1] The court held that brandishing was a sentencing factor, not part of the definition of a crime.

Harris is a 5–4 opinion, one significant part of which was joined in only by four justices. Justice Kennedy authored the opinion of the Court with respect to Parts I, II, and IV, in which Chief Justice Rehnquist and Justices O'Connor, Scalia, and Breyer joined. Breyer did not join in Part III, making that part a plurality opinion only. O'Connor filed a concurring opinion while Breyer filed an opinion concurring in part and concurring in the judgment. Justice Thomas filed a dissenting opinion in which Justices Stevens, Souter, and Ginsburg joined. Justice Kennedy began the opinion by noting that "Legislatures define crimes in terms of the facts that are their essential elements, and constitutional guarantees attach to these facts."[2] Specifically, the Fifth Amendment provides that "no person shall be held to answer for a capital, or otherwise infamous crime, unless on a presentment or indictment of a Grand Jury," all elements of which must be alleged. The Sixth Amendment guarantees that "in all criminal prosecutions, the accused shall enjoy the right to trial by an impartial jury," before which the government must prove each element beyond a reasonable doubt. None of these safeguards is required for judicial fact-finding that results in a sentence within the range provided by statute.[3]

---

[1] *Harris v. United States*, 122 S. Ct. 2406 (2002), U.S. LEXIS 4652 (2002).

[2] *Id.* at *9.

[3] *Id.* at *10 (citing *In re Winship*, 397 U.S. 358, 364 (1970)).

However, without constitutional safeguards, "legislatures could evade the indictment, jury, and proof requirements by labeling almost every relevant fact a sentencing factor."[4] The Court held in *Apprendi v. New Jersey* (2000) that, other than a prior conviction, any fact that increases the penalty for a crime beyond the prescribed statutory maximum must be proven to the jury beyond a reasonable doubt.[5] However, *McMillan v. Pennsylvania* (1986) upheld a statute providing for an increased minimum sentence where the court at sentencing, found on the basis of a preponderance of the evidence, that the defendant visibly possessed a firearm in the course of another crime.[6] The Court in *Harris* held that the rule in *McMillan* is consistent with *Apprendi*, that is, that the jury must determine facts that increase the maximum sentence, but not facts that increase a minimum sentence.

Before examining how the Court reached this result, the facts and statute involved in *Harris* warrant explanation. 18 U.S.C. § 924(c)(1)(A)(i) punishes with a minimum of five years imprisonment any person who, during and in relation to a federal crime of violence or drug trafficking, "uses or carries a firearm, or who, in furtherance of any such crime, possesses a firearm." Section 924(c)(1)(A) continues:

> (ii) if the firearm is brandished, be sentenced to a term of imprisonment of not less than 7 years; and
> (iii) if the firearm is discharged, be sentenced to a term of imprisonment of not less than 10 years.

The only fact recited by the Court was that "Harris sold illegal narcotics out of his pawnshop with an unconcealed semiautomatic pistol at his side."[7] However, § 924(c)(4) defines "brandish" as "to display all or part of the firearm, or otherwise make the presence of the firearm known to another person, in order to intimidate that person." These elements are not described in the Court's one-sentence factual description, but more factual detail is set forth in the dissenting opinion by Justice Thomas. As Thomas pointed out, the

[4] *Id.* at *10–11.

[5] *Id.* at *11 (citing Apprendi v. New Jersey, 530 U.S. 466, 490 (2000)).

[6] *Id.* (citing McMillan v. Pennsylvania, 477 U.S. 79 (1986)).

[7] *Id.* at *11.

district court conceded that whether Harris brandished a firearm was a "close question" because "the only thing that happened here is [that] he had [a gun] during the drug transaction."[8] Harris routinely wore the handgun at the pawnshop, not just when "he was selling small amounts of marijuana to his friends."[9] The pot distribution charge here was so minor that the presentence report recommended only zero to six months incarceration.

Still more information is contained in the Fourth Circuit opinion, which the Supreme Court affirmed. During two sales of small quantities of marijuana to undercover agents at his pawnshop, Harris carried a handgun in an unconcealed hip holster and, at one point, removed the handgun and stated that it "was an outlawed firearm because it had a high-capacity magazine," and that his homemade bullets could pierce an officer's armored jacket.[10] The Fourth Circuit rejected Harris's arguments that this was insufficient evidence of brandishing or of carrying the handgun "in relation to" a drug trafficking offense,[11] but did not explain why his actions were carried out with the intent to intimidate the undercover marijuana buyers.

The two statements attributed to Harris appear to have been idle boasting, perhaps embellished by the "narcs." High-capacity magazines do not make a firearm "outlawed"—a prohibition exists on magazines manufactured after 1994 that hold more than 10 cartridges,[12] but Harris undoubtedly possessed a legal magazine made before that date because they are in plentiful supply. It is unclear what "homemade" bullets Harris could have made that would be armor piercing,[13] and in any event no prohibition exists on mere possession of armor-piercing ammunition.

In any event, Harris was not indicted for brandishing and the jury did not consider the issue. According to the Supreme Court opinion, the government assumed that "brandishing is a sentencing factor to be considered by the judge after the trial."[14] Quite likely, the

---

[8]*Id.* at *51.

[9]*Id.*

[10]United States v. Harris, 243 F.3d 806, 807 (4th Cir. 2001).

[11]*Id.* at 812 n.7.

[12]18 U.S.C. §§ 921(a)(31), 922(w).

[13]*See* 18 U.S.C. § 921(a)(17)(A) (definition of armor-piercing ammunition).

[14]2002 U.S. LEXIS 4652 at *12.

government did not believe that it could prove to a jury beyond a reasonable doubt that Harris committed the act of brandishing as defined in § 924(c)(4), but pinned its hopes on the judge making that finding at sentencing on the basis of the mere preponderance-of-evidence standard. The government also had a strong interest in establishing in the courts its position about this statute, and others, undercutting the right to jury trial in favor of mere sentencing factors. Not unexpectedly, the presentence report recommended that Harris be sentenced to seven years for brandishing, the district court obliged, and the Fourth Circuit affirmed.[15]

The Majority Opinion

In the opinion for the Court, with which four other justices agreed, Justice Kennedy began by arguing that the "structure" of the prohibition suggests that brandishing is a sentencing factor. He states: "Federal laws usually list all offense elements 'in a single sentence' and separate the sentencing factors 'into subsections.'"[16] Yet even a cursory look at the federal criminal code disproves that this is "usually" the case. Indeed, the Gun Control Act itself lists most offenses in one section—§ 922—and all penalties (along with more offenses) in a separate section—§ 924. In *Castillo v. United States* (2000), the Court held 9–0 that § 924(c) includes aggravated offenses, including the use of a machine gun in a federal crime of violence, which are not mere sentencing factors.[17] Ironically, the Court now cites *Castillo* as supportive of interpreting everything in § 924(c) other than the "basic" offense as sentencing factors.

Harris contends that the "basic" crime of § 924(c) is carrying or using a firearm during and in relation to a federal crime of violence or drug trafficking, after which the word "shall" prefaces the five-year sentence specified in subparagraph (i). As for brandishing and discharge found in (ii) and (iii), the Court states, "Subsections (ii) and (iii), in turn, increase the minimum penalty if certain facts are present, and those subsections do not repeat the elements from the

---

[15] 243 F.3d at 812. Accord, United States v. Barton, 257 F.3d 433, 443 (5th Cir. 2001); United States v. Carlson, 217 F.3d 986, 989 (8th Cir. 2000); United States v. Pounds, 230 F.3d 1317, 1319 (11th Cir. 2000).

[16] *Harris*, 2002 U.S. LEXIS 4652 at *15 (citing Castillo v. United States, 530 U.S. 120, 125 (2000)).

[17] *See id.*

principal paragraph."[18] Yet the elements from the principal paragraph number 112 words, which would be needlessly tedious to repeat in making brandishing an aggravated form of using a firearm. Why not just say, as the statute does in 19 words, "if the firearm is brandished, be sentenced to a term of imprisonment of not less than 7 years"?

But *Harris* concedes, as it found about the carjacking statute in *Jones v. United States* (1999), that numbered subsections that "look" like sentencing factors may still be elements of an offense.[19] The structure of the statute in *Jones* was identical to that in *Harris*—a basic offense, followed by "shall," numbered subparagraphs beginning with the penalties for the basic offense, and thereafter descriptions of aggravated offenses with stiffer penalties. The structure of the statute in *Castillo* was identical except that it had no numbered subparagraphs. *Harris* seeks to distinguish amended § 924(c) as follows:

> The critical textual clues in this case, however, reinforce the single-offense interpretation implied by the statute's structure. Tradition and past congressional practice, for example, were perhaps the most important guideposts in *Jones*. The fact at issue there—serious bodily injury—is an element in numerous federal statutes, including two on which the carjacking statute was modeled; and the *Jones* Court doubted that Congress would have made this fact a sentencing factor in one isolated instance. In contrast, there is no similar federal tradition of treating brandishing and discharging as offense elements.[20]

There was no such "federal tradition" because brandishing and discharge are traditional state and local crimes, and they were made federal crimes in the context of the recent surge to over-federalize criminal conduct. As the Court notes, "The term 'brandished' does not appear in any federal offense-defining provision save 18 U.S.C. § 924(c)(1)(A), and did not appear there until 1998, when the statute was amended to take its current form."[21] Of course, going back to

[18] *Id.* at *15.

[19] *Id.* at *16 (quoting *Jones v. United States*, 526 U.S. 227, 232 (1999)).

[20] *Id.* at *16–17.

[21] *Id.* at *17.

the dawn of the federal criminal code and forward, no "federal tradition" existed for each newly enacted federal crime. But that fact does not transform elements of an offense into sentencing factors. Moreover, the Court's reasoning implies that criminal statutes with identical structures may have wholly different meanings on the basis of facts not evident from the faces of the statutes, that is, what year the prohibition was first enacted and how many similar federal statutes exist.

The Court continues: "The numbered subsections were added then [in 1998], describing, as sentencing factors often do, 'special features of the manner in which' the statute's 'basic crime' could be carried out."[22] Serious bodily injury was the manner in which the carjacking was carried out in *Jones*, yet it was an element nonetheless. Aggravated offenses always build on lesser-included offenses and describe special features that make the crime worse.

Harris further distinguished *Jones*, where "the Court accorded great significance to the 'steeply higher penalties' authorized by the carjacking statute's three subsections, which enhanced the defendant's maximum sentence from 15 years, to 25 years, to life— enhancements the Court doubted Congress would have made contingent upon judicial factfinding."[23] However, § 924(c)(1)(A) "does not authorize the judge to impose 'steeply higher penalties'—or higher penalties at all—once the facts in question are found. Since the subsections alter only the minimum, the judge may impose a sentence well in excess of seven years, whether or not the defendant brandished the firearm."[24] Yet this glosses over the fact that, even though § 924(c) authorizes a life sentence in every case, the court is required to impose mandatory minimum sentences of five, seven, and ten years, respectively, depending on how aggravated the act was committed.

Moreover, *Harris* further referred to *Castillo*,[25] in which dramatically increased mandatory minimum sentences for firearm use jumped from 5 to 10 to 30 years, depending on the type of firearm. With the 1998 amendments, § 924(c)(1)(B) continues to provide for

---

[22] *Id.*

[23] *Id.* at *18 (citing *Jones*, 526 U.S. at 233).

[24] *Id.* at *18–19.

[25] *Id.* at *18 (citing *Castillo*, 530 U.S. at 131).

the same 5-, 10-, and 30-year minimum sentences if the firearms are of certain specified types. For a subsequent conviction, subpart (C) requires a 25-year minimum sentence, and life imprisonment if the firearm is of certain types. Does this mean that brandishing and discharge in (A) are sentencing factors, but that the identically structured language concerning firearm types in (B) and (C) are elements because they have dramatically harsher mandatory minimums than the basic offense of carrying or using in (A)?

The Court next turns to the issue of constitutional avoidance, under which "when a statute is susceptible of two constructions, by one of which grave and doubtful constitutional questions arise and by the other of which such questions are avoided, our duty is to adopt the latter."[26] *Jones* applied that principle to interpret the carjacking statute as providing offense elements and not sentencing factors, to avoid resolving the issue of whether "any fact (other than prior conviction) that increases the maximum penalty for a crime must be charged in an indictment, submitted to a jury, and proven beyond a reasonable doubt."[27] *Harris* found the avoidance principle inapplicable, in that judicial fact-finding resulting in mandatory minimums had been approved in *McMillan*.[28]

The Court continued: "And if we stretched the text to avoid the question of *McMillan*'s continuing vitality, the canon would embrace a dynamic view of statutory interpretation, under which the text might mean one thing when enacted yet another if the prevailing view of the Constitution later changed."[29] One of the opinion's own precepts has the same potential: When a subject is first enacted into the federal criminal code, its presence is not a "federal tradition," so it is a sentencing factor. Does it become an element over time if the subject gains a repetitive presence in the code and becomes a "federal tradition?"

In any event, *Harris* concludes that "as a matter of statutory interpretation, § 924(c)(1)(A) defines a single offense. The statute regards brandishing and discharging as sentencing factors to be found by

---

[26] *Id.* at *19 (quoting United States *ex rel.* Attorney General v. Delaware & Hudson Co., 213 U.S. 366, 408 (1909)).

[27] *Id.* at *20 (citing *Jones*, 526 U.S. at 243, n.6).

[28] *Id.* (citing *McMillan*, 477 U.S. 79).

[29] *Id.* at *21–22.

the judge, not offense elements to be found by the jury." Besides creating incongruent aspects of the statute, this conclusion leaves one wondering why Congress did not state this in the statute itself had it so intended.

Justice Kennedy's Plurality Opinion

In Part III of the opinion, *Harris* turns to whether, as construed, the statute is unconstitutional. Only four justices agreed with this part of the opinion (Justice Breyer did not), and thus its value as a precedent is questionable. The gist of Part III is as follows:

> *McMillan* and *Apprendi* are consistent because there is a fundamental distinction between the factual findings that were at issue in those two cases. *Apprendi* said that any fact extending the defendant's sentence beyond the maximum authorized by the jury's verdict would have been considered an element of an aggravated crime—and thus the domain of the jury—by those who framed the Bill of Rights. The same cannot be said of a fact increasing the mandatory minimum (but not extending the sentence beyond the statutory maximum), for the jury's verdict has authorized the judge to impose the minimum with or without the finding. As *McMillan* recognized, a statute may reserve this type of factual finding for the judge without violating the Constitution.[30]

The opinion concedes that "Congress may not manipulate the definition of a crime in a way that relieves the Government of its constitutional obligations to charge each element in the indictment, submit each element to the jury, and prove each element beyond a reasonable doubt,"[31] and that "certain types of facts, though labeled sentencing factors by the legislature, were nevertheless 'traditional elements' to which these constitutional safeguards were intended to apply."[32] However, as long as they are sentencing within the prescribed range, judges may determine facts that give rise to a special stigma and to a special punishment. "There is no reason to believe that those who framed the Fifth and Sixth Amendments

---

[30] *Id.* at *23.

[31] *Id.* at *24 (citing *Jones*, 526 U.S. at 240–241); Mullaney v. Wilbur, 421 U.S. 684, 699 (1975).

[32] *Id.* at *24 (citing *Patterson v. New York*), 432 U.S. 197, 211 n.12 (1977).

would have thought of them as the elements of the crime."[33] However, the opinion includes not a single reference to the intent of the Framers as they expressed themselves on such issues.

The plurality opinion makes exceptions to the right to jury trial on the basis of distinctions never articulated by the Framers. It first recalls the rule in *Apprendi* that any fact that increases the penalty for a crime beyond the prescribed statutory maximum "must be submitted to a jury, and proved beyond a reasonable doubt."[34] The opinion then continues: "Those facts, *Apprendi* held, were what the Framers had in mind when they spoke of 'crimes' and 'criminal prosecutions' in the Fifth and Sixth Amendments: A crime was not alleged, and a criminal prosecution not complete, unless the indictment and the jury verdict included all the facts to which the legislature had attached the maximum punishment."[35] But this merely begs the question of what a "crime" is and simply states the constitutional procedures required to charge and convict a person of a crime. By contrast, *Harris* continues, facts giving rise to mandatory minimum sentences are not elements of a "crime" and thus are not subject to the requirements of indictment, jury trial, and proof beyond a reasonable doubt. The latter is the case even regarding facts that increase a mandatory minimum sentence. Once again, this does not explain why facts giving rise to the minimum sentence are not elements of a crime, but is simply an unsupported assertion that establishing these facts does not require the usual constitutional safeguards.

Harris argued that factual findings that increase a mandatory minimum may have far more impact on a defendant than factual findings that may increase the maximum sentence. This is because the judge must sentence the defendant to a mandatory minimum if the factual predicates exist, but may impose a sentence far below the maximum. This is well illustrated by § 924(c), which imposes mandatory minimums for each level of aggravation—5 years for carrying, 7 for brandishing, 10 for discharge, 30 for a machine gun, life for a machine gun with a prior conviction—but imposes no maximum sentences.

---

[33] *Id.* at *28.

[34] *Id.* at *33 (quoting *Apprendi*, 530 U.S. at 490).

[35] *Id.* at *33.

Because each penalty is worded "not less than," the maximum sentence for each offense is life imprisonment. But the standard punishment for each offense is the mandatory minimum.

The Court does not address this distinction between what the sentencing judge may do and what he or she must do, and what great impact it may have on the defendant. Instead of addressing the Framers' policy reasons for requiring that the trial of all crimes be by jury, the opinion merely restates its rule, newly minted in this very case in the year 2002, that

> If the grand jury has alleged, and the trial jury has found, all the facts necessary to impose the maximum, the barriers between government and defendant fall. The judge may select any sentence within the range, on the basis of facts not alleged in the indictment or proved to the jury—even if those facts are specified by the legislature, and even if they persuade the judge to choose a much higher sentence than he or she otherwise would have imposed.[36]

For the Framers, a "crime" was bad conduct for which a legislature prescribes punishment. The grand jury described the bad conduct in the indictment, the defendant was informed of the nature and cause of the accusation, and the petit jury found beyond a reasonable doubt whether the defendant committed the acts that constituted the crime. The facts having been found, the sentencing court imposes the punishment. By contrast, for the plurality in *Harris*, a court may attribute to the legislature setting up a scheme in which one instance of bad conduct is considered the "crime" for which constitutional protections apply. All other instances of bad conduct defined by the legislature in the same section are considered exempt from the term "crime" so that constitutional protections do not apply.

The above concludes the plurality's analysis in Part III. Part IV of the opinion simply holds: "Basing a 2-year increase in the defendant's minimum sentence on a judicial finding of brandishing does not evade the requirements of the Fifth and Sixth Amendments."[37] What if the increase is 25 years, or even life? The Court's analysis does not provide an answer to that question, but it is sure to arise in the provisions of § 924(c) regarding firearm types and subsequent

[36] *Id.* at *39.
[37] *Id.* at *42.

offenses, for which factual findings cause the sentences to zoom up to 30 years and even life. What is the cutoff point in years for when an increase in the minimum sentence does evade the requirements of the Constitution? Even *McMillan* conceded that the increase in sentence must not be so disproportionate that it becomes "a tail which wags the dog of the substantive offense."[38] But the Constitution makes no such distinctions—for every "crime," the indictment, jury trial, and proof-beyond-a-reasonable-doubt procedures apply.

The Concurring Opinions

Justice O'Connor filed a curt concurring opinion noting that *Jones* was the basis of Harris's statutory argument that brandishing should be interpreted as an offense element, and *Apprendi* was the basis of her constitutional argument that brandishing must be alleged in the indictment and found by the jury. O'Connor persisted in her dissenting views in those cases that they were wrongly decided.

Justice Breyer, who had also dissented in *Jones* and *Apprendi*, wrote a concurring opinion in *Harris* but did not join in Part III. He conceded—contrary to Justice Kennedy's opinion—that the issue in this case could not logically be distinguished from *Apprendi*, but that he disagreed with the holding in that case that facts that increase the maximum sentence must be proven to the jury. Breyer's concurrence makes the curious policy argument that it is against the interest of defendants to treat essential facts as elements requiring proof to the jury. He wrote:

> Applying *Apprendi* in this case would not, however, lead Congress to abolish, or to modify, mandatory minimum sentencing statutes. Rather, it would simply require the prosecutor to charge, and the jury to find beyond a reasonable doubt, the existence of the "factor," say, the amount of unlawful drugs, that triggers the mandatory minimum. In many cases, a defendant, claiming innocence and arguing, say, mistaken identity, will find it impossible simultaneously to argue to the jury that the prosecutor has overstated the drug amount. How, the jury might ask, could this "innocent" defendant know anything about that matter?[39]

[38] McMillan v. Pennsylvania, 477 U.S. 79, 88 (1986).
[39] *Harris*, U.S. LEXIS 4652, at *47–48.

Yet defense lawyers have always tried cases by requiring the prosecution to prove every element of the offense beyond a reasonable doubt. Demonstrating a reasonable doubt that the defendant possessed the drugs is hardly incompatible with showing also that the weight of the drugs has not been proven. All elements of the alleged crime portray the defendant in a bad light before the jury, but this is hardly reason to deprive a defendant of the right to have a jury determine every element of the crime. Justice Breyer seems to suggest that it is in the interest of persons charged with crimes to deprive them of requiring proof to the jury beyond a reasonable doubt, and it is in their interest to have a sentencing judge find the required facts by a preponderance of evidence, which is likely to be on the basis of assertions in the prosecution-packed presentence report.

In this very case it is doubtful that a jury would have found, beyond a reasonable doubt, that Harris brandished a firearm in relation to drug trafficking. He did not point it at anyone, and his oral statements constituted bragging, not an intent to intimidate. Breyer does not address how his theory would apply under the facts of this case. For him, the bottom line is that *Apprendi* should not be extended to the mandatory minimum sentencing context: "Doing so would diminish further Congress' otherwise broad constitutional authority to define crimes through the specification of elements, to shape criminal sentences through the specification of sentencing factors, and to limit judicial discretion in applying those factors in particular cases."[40] In short, to "define crimes" means that the legislature may decide which crimes require constitutional protections, and which crimes do not by decreeing that such crimes are not crimes at all but are sentencing factors.

The Dissenting Opinion by Justice Thomas

Justice Thomas, joined by Justices Stevens, Souter, and Ginsburg, dissented in *Harris*. Thomas argued that *McMillan* should be overruled on the basis of *Apprendi*. Regarding the Court's attempt to sever the jury role on the basis of minimum and maximum sentences,

---

[40] *Id.* at *48–49.

Thomas wrote, "Such fine distinctions with regard to vital constitutional liberties cannot withstand close scrutiny."[41] Because the indictment and jury guarantees are effective whenever a person is charged with a crime, "this case thus turns on the seemingly simple question of what constitutes a 'crime.'"[42] An expansive definition is required:

> If the legislature defines some core crime and then provides for increasing the punishment of that crime upon a finding of some aggravating fact—of whatever sort, including the fact of a prior conviction—the core crime and the aggravating fact together constitute an aggravated crime, just as much as grand larceny is an aggravated form of petit larceny. The aggravating fact is an element of the aggravated crime. Similarly, if the legislature, rather than creating grades of crimes, has provided for setting the punishment of a crime on the basis of some fact that fact is also an element. One need only look to the kind, degree, or range of punishment to which the prosecution is by law entitled for a given set of facts. Each fact for that entitlement is an element.[43]

Because a finding of brandishing increases the mandatory penalty, "as a constitutional matter brandishing must be deemed an element of an aggravated offense."[44] Imposing a special stigma and special punishment means that the conduct in question is a "crime" to which the constitutional guarantees apply. "Whether one raises the floor or raises the ceiling it is impossible to dispute that the defendant is exposed to greater punishment than is otherwise prescribed."[45] Justice Thomas concluded that "there are no logical grounds for treating facts triggering mandatory minimums any differently than facts that increase the statutory maximum."[46]

On the basis of the oral argument in *Harris*, Justice Thomas wrote, "The United States concedes that it can charge facts upon which a mandatory minimum sentence is based in the indictment and prove them to a jury."[47] That would have been a no-brainer in this case in

[41] *Id.* at *53.

[42] *Id.* at *54.

[43] *Id.* at *54–55 (quoting *Apprendi*, 530 U.S. at 501 (concurring opinion)).

[44] *Id.* at *56.

[45] *Id.* at *62.

[46] *Id.*

[47] *Id.* at *65.

that Harris could have been indicted for brandishing, although the facts suggest that a jury may not have convicted him. Thomas concluded that "it is imperative that the Court maintain absolute fidelity to the protections of the individual afforded by the notice, trial by jury, and beyond-a-reasonable-doubt requirements."[48] Justice Thomas's arguments did not win the day in this case, but will influence the continuing tug of war between juries and judges.

Given the actual holding in *Harris*, whether a firearm is brandished or discharged during and in relation to a federal crime of violence or drug trafficking will be decided by the court at sentencing. The issue will be whether the requirements of § 924(c)(4) are shown by a preponderance of evidence, that is, that the firearm was displayed or made known to intimidate another person. The effects of *Harris* on the rest of § 924(c), particularly the firearm types, is uncertain. Although *Harris* held that facts giving rise to increased mandatory minimum sentences are not subject to the indictment and jury guarantees, given the recent 5–4 precedents going both ways on these guarantees explained below, one may expect continued uncertainty in this area of the law.

Ring v. Arizona: The Jury and the Death Penalty

The same day that *Harris* was decided, the Court also announced the decision in *Ring v. Arizona*,[49] which held that, in death penalty cases, the jury must make the factual determinations that authorize imposition of the death sentence. This was a logical application of *Apprendi*, given its holding that fact-findings that increase the maximum sentence must be found by the jury. It seems ironic that the Court would render a decision curtailing the right to jury trial and the same day render another decision expanding that right. A brief analysis of *Ring* is in order.

In Arizona, a jury could find one guilty of first-degree murder, but the judge determined whether aggravating factors defined by law existed so as to warrant the death penalty. The Court previously held that these were sentencing factors that could be found without the Sixth Amendment jury guarantee.[50] *Ring* overruled that previous

---

[48] *Id.* at *65–66.
[49] Ring v. Arizona, 2002 U.S. LEXIS 4651 (2002).
[50] Walton v. Arizona, 497 U.S. 639 (1990).

decision in light of *Apprendi*, commenting, "Capital defendants, no less than noncapital defendants, are entitled to a jury determination of any fact on which the legislature conditions an increase in their maximum punishment."[51]

The evidence heard by the jury against Timothy Ring did not prove beyond a reasonable doubt that he was a major participant in the armed robbery or that he actually murdered the victim. The evidence connected him to the proceeds but not to the crime scene. At the sentencing hearing, however, the judge heard evidence from an accomplice that Ring personally murdered the victim, an aggravating circumstance that authorized the judge to impose the death penalty.

These kinds of facts, held *Ring*, must be decided by the jury. "By the time the Bill of Rights was adopted, the jury's right to make these determinations was unquestioned."[52] And the Court quoted one of its venerable precedents that stated, "The guarantees of jury trial in the Federal and State Constitutions reflect a profound judgment about the way in which law should be enforced and justice administered. If the defendant preferred the common-sense judgment of a jury to the more tutored but perhaps less sympathetic reaction of the single judge, he was to have it."[53] This reasoning is absent from the Court's opinion in *Harris*.

The array of votes by the justices in *Ring* sharply contrasts with that in *Harris*. Justice Ginsburg delivered the opinion of the *Ring* Court, in which Justices Stevens, Scalia, Kennedy, Souter, and Thomas joined. Scalia filed a concurring opinion in which Thomas joined, and Kennedy also filed a concurrence just to say that *Apprendi* was wrongly decided, but that he would grudgingly go along with it now that it was precedent. But Justice Breyer filed an opinion concurring only in the judgment, rejecting the Court's analysis because it was on the basis of the right to jury trial and *Apprendi*, preferring instead to hold that imposition of the death penalty without jury decision-making was cruel and unusual punishment under the Eighth Amendment. Not surprisingly, Justice O'Connor filed a

[51] *Ring*, 2002 U.S. LEXIS 4651 at *12.

[52] *Id.* at *29 (quoting Walton v. Arizona, 497 U.S. 639, 710–11 (1990) (Stevens, J., dissenting)).

[53] *Id.* at *44–45 (quoting Duncan v. Louisiana, 391 U.S. 145, 155 (1968)).

dissenting opinion in which Chief Justice Rehnquist joined, arguing that *Apprendi* should be overruled and that the death penalty imposed in this case should be upheld.

Justice Scalia's concurring opinion is particularly noteworthy, given his deafening silence and vote with the majority in *Harris* after running with the jury torch in other critical cases. Scalia wrote in *Ring*: "I believe that the fundamental meaning of the jury-trial guarantee of the Sixth Amendment is that all facts essential to imposition of the level of punishment that the defendant receives—whether the statute calls them elements of the offense, sentencing factors, or Mary Jane—must be found by the jury beyond a reasonable doubt."[54] Scalia wrote that he observed "the accelerating propensity of both state and federal legislatures to adopt 'sentencing factors' determined by judges that increase punishment beyond what is authorized by the jury's verdict," not to mention a near-majority of the Justices who were willing to uphold such schemes, that

> cause me to believe that our people's traditional belief in the right of trial by jury is in perilous decline. That decline is bound to be confirmed, and indeed accelerated, by the repeated spectacle of a man's going to his death because a judge found that an aggravating factor existed. We cannot preserve our veneration for the protection of the jury in criminal cases if we render ourselves callous to the need for that protection by regularly imposing the death penalty without it.[55]

Justice Scalia could not resist taking a jab against Justice Breyer for continuing to reject the jury role as exposited in *Apprendi*, noting also that jury fact-finding has nothing to do with the Eighth Amendment. Scalia concluded, "There is really no way in which Justice Breyer can travel with the happy band that reaches today's result unless he says yes to *Apprendi*. Concisely put, Justice Breyer is on the wrong flight; he should either get off before the doors close, or buy a ticket to *Apprendi*-land."[56] That criticism was well deserved, but so too is criticism warranted for Scalia's vote in *Harris* which,

[54] *Id.* at *47.
[55] *Id.* at *49–50.
[56] *Id.* at *51.

to use his above language, "cannot preserve our veneration for the protection of the jury in criminal cases."[57]

Why *Harris* Was Wrongly Decided:
The Constitutional Text

Harris was wrongly decided. The opinion contains no meaningful analysis of the Constitution's requirements for criminal prosecutions and fails to acknowledge the objective meaning of the concepts provided in the constitutional text.

The right to trial by jury was guaranteed in the original text of the Constitution before the amendments known as the Bill of Rights were ratified. Article III, § 2, of the Constitution provides that "The Trial of all Crimes, except in Cases of Impeachment; shall be by Jury; and such Trial shall be held in the State where the said Crimes shall have been committed; but when not committed within any State, the Trial shall be at such Place or Places as the Congress may by Law have directed." If the trial of "all crimes" must be by jury, the term "crime" may not be manipulated to remove the jury from this function. A crime is something that has been "committed," that is, an act that a person has carried out. No constitutional authorization exists for a law that punishes a person for an act he has "committed" to declare that such act is not a "crime" but is a mere "sentencing factor" that may be removed from trial by jury.

The Fifth Amendment imposes the following further procedural guarantees for persons accused of bad acts:

> No person shall be held to answer for a capital, or otherwise infamous crime, unless on a presentment or indictment of a Grand Jury, except in cases arising in the land or naval forces, or in the Militia, when in actual service in time of War or public danger; nor shall any person be subject for the same offence to be twice put in jeopardy of life or limb, nor shall be compelled in any criminal case to be a witness against himself, nor be deprived of life, liberty, or property, without due process of law.

If a person may not be held "to answer" for such "crime" other than by indictment by the grand jury, it is difficult to understand how a person may be required "to answer" for bad acts that are

---

[57] *Id.* at *50.

not alleged in an indictment brought by a grand jury. The double jeopardy prohibition uses the synonym "offense" for "crime," again suggesting that a crime is a bad act (something offensive) for which a person may be punished. The prohibition on compelled self-incrimination refers to "any criminal case," again linking the trial of a "crime" to the entire judicial proceeding. Finally, no person may be punished—"deprived of life, liberty, or property"—"without due process of law." Due process includes the procedures of indictment by grand jury and trial of the charges by the petit jury.

The Sixth Amendment provides that

> In all criminal prosecutions, the accused shall enjoy the right to a speedy and public trial, by an impartial jury of the State and district wherein the crime shall have been committed; which district shall have been previously ascertained by law, and to be informed of the nature and cause of the accusation; to be confronted with the witnesses against him; to have compulsory process for obtaining witnesses in his favor, and to have the assistance of counsel for his defence.

The guarantee applies to "all criminal prosecutions," which does not end until the final judgment. The subject is "the accused," and a person is being "accused" of bad acts when allegations of those bad acts are made at any time during the criminal proceeding, including at sentencing. These bad acts are "committed" in a certain location and are again called a "crime." The trial must be by an "impartial jury," not what the Framers frequently saw as partial judges. The accused must "be informed of the nature and cause of the accusation," which means an allegation that a person did an act for which he may be punished. Significant facts alleged at sentencing are "accusations" requiring prior notice and jury determination. The accused may confront "the witnesses against him," which can only mean in a public trial; by contrast, judicial fact-finding at sentencing routinely relies on anonymous witnesses and no confrontation.

The above provisions would mean little if the procedural guarantees could be circumvented simply by linguistic evasion. A person who is "accused" of having "committed" acts warranting punishment, who is being "held to answer" for those acts, and against whom "witnesses" are making "accusations" is by this vocabulary a person who is alleged to have committed a "crime." And that person is entitled to the guarantees of indictment by a grand jury and trial by an impartial jury.

Harris eschews any analysis of the meaning of the preceding fundamental terms. It simplistically declares that a "crime" is any fact-finding about wrongdoing for which the legislature allows a jury trial, and a "sentencing factor" is any fact-finding about wrongdoing that the legislature declares shall be reserved to the judge. This cannot be true to the constitutional text and the intent of the Framers.

The Text and Structure of § 924(c) Establish that Brandishing Is an Offense Element

Criminal statutes should be presumed to have been intended not to violate the paramount constitutional values of indictment, notice, jury trial, and proof beyond a reasonable doubt. This is easily accomplished here simply by considering the text and structure of § 924(c).

"The language of the statute [is] the starting place in our inquiry."[58] As amended in 1998,[59] § 924(c)(1)(A) provides in pertinent part that

> [A]ny person who, during and in relation to any crime of violence or drug trafficking crime for which the person may be prosecuted in a court of the United States, uses or carries a firearm, or who, in furtherance of any such crime, possesses a firearm, shall, in addition to the punishment provided for such crime of violence or drug trafficking crime—
> (i) be sentenced to a term of imprisonment of not less than 5 years;
> (ii) if the firearm is brandished, be sentenced to a term of imprisonment of not less than 7 years; and
> (iii) if the firearm is discharged, be sentenced to a term of imprisonment of not less than 10 years.

Subpart (B) provides for 10- and 30-year minimum sentences if the firearms are of certain specified types. For a subsequent conviction, subpart (C) requires a 25-year minimum sentence, and life imprisonment if the firearm is of certain types. Subpart (D) prohibits probation for a person so convicted.

The fact that Congress defined brandishing, carefully wording both the mens rea and acts required, demonstrates that brandishing is an aggravated crime. Section 924(c)(4) provides that

---

[58] Staples v. United States, 511 U.S. 600, 605 (1994).

[59] Pub. L. No. 105-386, 112 Stat. 3469 (1998).

> For purposes of this subsection, the term "brandish" means,
> with respect to a firearm, to display all or part of the firearm,
> or otherwise make the presence of the firearm known to
> another person, in order to intimidate that person, regardless
> of whether the firearm is directly visible to that person.

This is the type of definition typically given as a jury instruction, along with the admonition that each and every element must be proven beyond a reasonable doubt. A definition is unnecessary if brandishing is a mere sentencing factor—the judge simply considers the particular facts without being bound by whether each and every one of the preceding elements are present.

The text and structure of § 924(c)(1) make clear that brandishing is an offense. As in *Castillo v. United States* (2000), "the first part of the opening sentence clearly and indisputably establishes the elements of the basic federal offense of using or carrying a gun during and in relation to a crime of violence."[60] Further, "Congress placed the element 'uses or carries a firearm' and the word 'machine gun' in a single sentence,"[61] just as here terms such as "use" and "brandish" are in the same sentence and are separated by mere semicolons. The carjacking statute in *Jones* had numbered subsections making them "look" like sentencing factors, but that "look" was superficial.[62]

Defining the basic and aggravated crimes and stating the corresponding penalties is clear and concise draftsmanship. First the basic offense is defined and penalized (totaling 125 words). The two "if" clauses introducing the brandishing and discharge offenses define aggravated crimes and punish them (totaling 19 and 18 words, respectively). By using "if" instead of repeating all of the elements of the basic offense, economy of words is achieved over tedious repetition. Similarly, the term "if" is used to introduce subpart (B), which defines aggravated offenses involving specified firearm types, once again being concise rather than repeating all of the basic offense elements. No rule of statutory drafting requires senseless reiteration of the same elements over and over.

---

[60] Castillo v. United States, 530 U.S. 120, 124 (2000).

[61] *Id.* at 124–25.

[62] *Id.* (quoting Jones v. United States, 526 U.S. 227, 232–33 (1999)).

Both the basic and the aggravated offenses alike are in the present tense: "uses or carries," "possesses," "if the firearm is brandished," "if the firearm is discharged," "if the firearm is a short-barreled rifle" or other specified type. The present tense ties together each element in a moment in time to complete the offense. A sentencing factor may very likely be in the past tense because the judge is looking at a past event.

The following further aspects of prior § 924(c) described in *Castillo* continue to apply to the amended version here:

> The next three sentences of § 924(c)(1) refer directly to sentencing: the first to recidivism, the second to concurrent sentences, the third to parole. These structural features strongly suggest that the basic job of the entire first sentence is the definition of crimes and the role of the remaining three is the description of factors (such as recidivism) that ordinarily pertain only to sentencing.[63]

Similarly, with amended § 924(c)(1), subpart (C) concerns recidivism[64] and subpart (D) concerns the same probation and concurrent-sentence prohibitions as before.

Section 924(c)(1)(D)(i) provides that "a court shall not place on probation any person *convicted* of a violation of this subsection." Thus, one must be "convicted" of (not just sentenced for) the acts described in "this subsection." As the Court held elsewhere, "In the context of § 924(c)(1), we think it unambiguous that 'conviction' refers to the finding of guilt by a judge or jury that necessarily precedes the entry of a final judgment of conviction."[65]

---

[63] *Castillo*, 530 U.S. at 125.

[64] *Harris* did not concern whether subpart (C)'s reference to "a second or subsequent conviction" is an element or a sentencing factor. Elsewhere, the Gun Control Act treats a prior felony conviction as an element. 18 U.S.C. § 922(g) (felon in possession of firearm); *see* Old Chief v. United States, 519 U.S. 172, 174 (1997). One or more prior convictions were also elements in 18 U.S.C. App. § 1202(a) (repealed 1986). *See* United States v. Batchelder, 442 U.S. 114, 119 (1979).

[65] Deal v. United States, 508 U.S. 129, 132 (1993). Similarly, *Garrett v. United States*, 471 U.S. 773 (1985), construed 21 U.S.C. § 848(a), which provides enhanced penalties for recidivists engaged in a continuing criminal enterprise. The Court held that

> At this point there is no reference to other statutory offenses, and
> a separate penalty is set out, rather than a multiplier of the penalty

The fact that § 924 is entitled "Penalties" provides no guidance, for as *Castillo* notes, "at least some portion of § 924, including § 924(c) itself, creates, not penalty enhancements, but entirely new crimes."[66] Complete offenses abound throughout § 924, some with structures identical to § 924(c).[67]

Section 924(j) is the most dramatic example of Congress's practice of setting forth offense elements in § 924 with a structure identical to that of § 924(c):

> A person who, in the course of a violation of subsection (c), causes the death of a person through the use of a firearm, shall
>
> (1) if the killing is a murder (as defined in section 1111), be punished by death or by imprisonment for any term of years or for life; and
>
> (2) if the killing is manslaughter (as defined in section 1112), be punished as provided in that section.

To construe murder and manslaughter as mere sentencing factors would be a radical departure from due process and the right to a jury trial. The courts have held that the reference to murder in § 924(j) is an offense element.[68] Yet under the *Harris* Court's interpretation

---

established for some other offense. This same paragraph then incor-porates its own recidivist provision, providing for twice the penalty for repeat violators of this section. Significantly the language expressly refers to "one or more prior convictions . . . under this section." Next, subparagraph (2) . . . also refers to any person "who is convicted under paragraph (1) of engaging in a continuing criminal enterprise," again suggesting that § 848 is a distinct offense for which one is separately convicted.

Garrett, 471 U.S. at 780. Further, § 849 (now repealed) has "starkly contrasting lan-guage that plainly is not intended to create a separate offense": the court sits without a jury to consider prior offenses and determines status as a dangerous special drug offender by a preponderance of evidence. *Id.* at 782.

[66] *Castillo*, 530 U.S. at 125.

[67] *E.g.*, § 924(a)(6)(B) (a nonjuvenile "who knowingly violates section 922(x)," which prohibits transfer of a handgun to a juvenile, "(i) shall be . . . imprisoned not more than 1 year," "and (ii) if the person sold" the handgun "knowing . . . that the juvenile intended to" use the handgun to commit a violent crime, "shall be . . . imprisoned not more than 10 years. . . ." *See* Bryan v. United States, 524 U.S. 184, 188 (1998) (construing elements of "willfully" and "knowingly" in § 924(a)).

[68] United States v. Pearson, 203 F.3d 1243, 1269–70 (10th Cir. 2000) (jury must find murder in course of § 924(c) violation); United States v. Harris, 66 F. Supp. 2d 1017, 1033 (N.D. Iowa 1999) (distinguishing *Jones*, 526 U.S. 227, in that indictment "specifi-cally alleges murder").

only convict a defendant of causing a death through the use of a firearm in the course of a § 924(c) violation, and the court may find at sentencing that the death was murder and impose the death penalty.

Amended § 924(c) is structurally identical both to the prior version construed in *Castillo* and to the federal carjacking statute, 18 U.S.C. § 2119, construed in *Jones*. The following compares the texts of these two statutes:

18 U.S.C. § 2119	18 U.S.C. § 924(c)(1)(A)
Whoever, possessing a firearm as defined in section 921 of this title, takes a motor vehicle from the person or presence of another by force and violence or by intimidation, or attempts to do so, *shall*	any person who, during and in relation to any crime of violence or drug trafficking crime . . ., uses or carries a firearm, or who, in furtherance of any such crime, possesses a firearm, *shall*—
(1) be fined under this title or imprisoned not more than 15 years, or both,	(i) be sentenced to a term of imprisonment of not less than 5 years;
(2) *if* serious bodily injury results, be fined under this title or imprisoned not more than 25 years, or both, and	(ii) *if* the firearm is brandished, be sentenced to a term of imprisonment of not less than 7 years; and
(3) *if* death results, be fined under this title or imprisoned for any number of years up to life, or both.	(iii) *if* the firearm is discharged, be sentenced to a term of imprisonment of not less than 10 years. (Italics added.)

In short, whoever commits act A "shall" be sentenced to X, and "if" he commits aggravating act B, "shall" be sentenced to Y. Both *Jones* and *Castillo* held that act B in statutes with this structure is an element of the offense. Other statutes with the same structure must be interpreted the same as a matter of consistent construction and due process. The result cannot vary depending on, as *Harris* held, whether the federal enactment covers new rather than old ground. The criminal law would be a cruel joke if statutes with identical structures may or may not create offense elements depending on obscure circumstances not contained on the face of the statutes. The fundamental rights to notice and due process preclude the linguistic anarchy inherent in construing statutes with identical structures to mean one thing here and the opposite elsewhere. Accordingly, the Court should have decided that the text and structure of § 924(c) make clear that brandishing is an offense element.

Brandishing Is a Traditional Crime Subject to Trial by Jury

Brandishing is as typical a crime in Anglo-American history as one could imagine. All of the reasons underlying the right to jury trial support treatment of brandishing as an element of the offense and not as a sentencing factor.

Section 924(c)(4) defines brandishing as a specific-intent crime, requiring that a person display or make a firearm known to another "in order to intimidate that person." Statutes ordinarily entrust the determination of a defendant's intent to the jury.[69]

As noted in *Castillo*, courts have not "typically or traditionally used firearm types (such as 'shotgun' or 'machine gun') as sentencing factors, at least not in respect to an underlying 'use or carry' crime."[70] "Statutory drafting occurs against a backdrop of traditional treatment of certain categories of important facts."[71] "Congress is unlikely to intend any radical departures from past practice without making a point of saying so."[72]

It was an indictable offense at common law to go armed with the intent of committing crimes of violence.[73] Brandishing and discharge

---

[69] *See* Mullaney v. Wilbur, 421 U.S. 684, 703 (1975) ("although intent is typically considered a fact peculiarly within the knowledge of the defendant, this does not . . . justify shifting the burden to him").

[70] *Castillo*, 530 U.S. at 126.

[71] *Id.* (quoting *Jones*, 526 U.S. at 234).

[72] *Jones Id.* at 234.

[73] "If any man "Ride[s] Armed covertly or secret with Men of Arms against any other to Slay him, or Rob him, or Take him, or Retain him till he hath made Fine and Ransom . . ." it . . . shall be judged Felony or trespass, according to the Laws of the Land of old time used. . . ." EDWARD COKE, THE THIRD PART OF THE INSTITUTES OF THE LAWS OF ENGLAND 160 (6th ed. 1680). Carrying arms "malo animo" (with an evil mind) was a crime. Rex v. Knight, Comb. 38, 90 Eng. Rep. 330 (K. B. 1686).

of firearms were included within this offense.[74] Such common-law offenses were recognized in the early American Republic.[75]

Brandishing and inappropriate discharge of firearms, while labeled differently, are crimes in the laws of every state.[76] Many state statutes prohibit brandishing or pointing *per se*,[77] some define assault-type offenses to encompass those terms,[78] and others simply punish acts of brandishing under general assault statutes.[79] Brandishing may be an aggravation of another violent crime.[80] Brandishing is an element to be found by the jury.[81]

[74] An affray was committed "where a man arms himself with dangerous and unusual weapons, in such a manner as will naturally cause a terror to the people, which is said to have been always an offence at common law...." 2 William Hawkins, Pleas of the Crown 488 (8th ed., London 1824). *See* Rex v. Meade, 29 L.T.R. 540, 541 (1903) (offense charged was "under the common law," if the defendant was "firing a revolver in a public place, with the result that the public were frightened or terrorized").

[75] State v. Huntley, 25 N.C. (3 Ired.) 284 (1843) (defendant exhibited "dangerous and unusual weapons" and declared intent to kill); Cf. Simpson v. State, 13 Tenn. (5 Yer.) 356, 358–60 (1833) (indictment for affray insufficient unless it alleges fighting in a public place).

[76] *See* State Firearms Laws, in Stephen P. Halbrook, Firearms Law Deskbook: Federal and State Criminal Practice App. A, 2002.

[77] *E.g.*, Va. Code Ann. § 18.2-282.A (2001) ("It shall be unlawful for any person to point, hold or brandish any firearm . . . in such manner as to reasonably induce fear in the mind of another"). *See also* Conn. Gen. Stat. § 53-206c(c) (2001); Ind. Code Ann. § 35-47-4-3 (2001); Mich. Comp. Laws § 750.234e(1) (2001); NY Penal Law § 265.35.3 (2001); Vt. Stat. Ann. tit. 13 § 4011 (2001); Idaho Code § 18-3304 (2000); Minn. Stat. § 609.66 Subd. 1(a) (2000); S.C. Code Ann. § 16-23-420(B) (2000); 13; Wis. Stat. § 941.20(1) (2000).

[78] *E.g.*, Iowa Code § 708.1 (2001) ("A person commits an assault when, without justification, the person does any of the following: . . . 3. Intentionally points any firearm toward another"). *See* Mich. Comp. Laws § 750.329 (2001); Mont. Code Ann., § 45-5-213(1) (2001); N.J. Stat. Ann. § 2C:12-1.b(4) (2001); W. Va. Code § 61-7-11 (2001); Wyo. Stat. Ann. § 6-2-504(b) (2001); Minn. Stat. § 609.713 Subd. 3(a) (2000).

[79] *E.g.*, Brown v. State, 305 S.E.2d 386, 387 (1983) ("he deliberately got the gun and brandished it at his wife in order to scare her, thus committing an aggravated assault").

[80] *E.g.*, Ohio Rev. Code Ann. § 2911.01 (Anderson 2001) ("Aggravated robbery. (A) No person, in attempting or committing a theft offense, . . . shall do any of the following: (1) Have a deadly weapon on or about the offender's person or under the offender's control and either display the weapon, brandish it, indicate that the offender possesses it, or use it.").

[81] *E.g.*, Kelsoe v. Commonwealth, 226 Va. 197, 308 S.E.2d 104 (1983) ("There are two elements of the offense: (1) pointing or brandishing a firearm, and (2) doing so in such a manner as to reasonably induce fear in the mind of a victim."). *See* Nantz v. State, 740 N.E.2d 1276, 1283 (Ind. App. 2001); State v. Tate, 377 N.E.2d 778 (1978).

Just as the difference between use of a pistol and of a machine gun "is great, both in degree and kind," and "numerous gun crimes make substantive distinctions between" such weapons,[82] brandishing and discharge are aggravated crimes compared with less serious but unlawful use and carrying of firearms. The difference between these activities "is both substantive and substantial—a conclusion that supports a 'separate crime' interpretation."[83]

Harris argued that brandishing was not a crime, but only a sentencing factor, because there was no tradition in federal statutes of treating brandishing as a crime. Yet this could be said about every new federal crime when first enacted in the long march since 1789 of the creation of a federal criminal code. The only federal crimes explicitly authorized by the Constitution, which appear in Article I, § 8, concern such matters as counterfeiting and piracy on the high seas. Powers such as the establishing of post offices may be the subject of criminal legislation under the Necessary and Proper Clause.[84] "It is clear, that Congress cannot punish felonies generally."[85]

But it is a double stretch of the Constitution to argue that each new offense created by Congress to appear tough on what have long been state crimes is not triable by jury but is only a sentencing factor. This just happens to be the first time Congress made brandishing an element of a crime. Parallel with brandishing, § 924(c) also makes discharge a crime, and discharge may be found as an element of numerous federal crimes.

In addition to traditional treatment as a crime, *Castillo* postulates the parallel traditional preference for fact-finding by the jury. To reword *Castillo* so that it applies here, "to ask a jury, rather than a judge, to decide whether a defendant [brandished a firearm] would rarely complicate a trial or risk unfairness."[86] "As a practical matter, in determining whether a defendant used or carried a 'firearm,' the jury ordinarily will be asked to assess the particular weapon at issue as well as the circumstances under which it was allegedly used."[87] These circumstances include brandishing.

---

[82] *Castillo*, 530 U.S. at 126–27.

[83] *Id.* at 127.

[84] McCulloch v. Maryland, 17 U.S. (4 Wheat.) 316, 416–17 (1819).

[85] Cohens v. Virginia, 19 U.S. (6 Wheat.) 264, 428 (1821).

[86] *Castillo*, 530 U.S. at 126–27.

[87] *Id.* at 127–28.

Inherent in the jury function of determining "uses or carries" is the finding of *how* a firearm was used.[88] It would be illogical to conclude that Congress intended that the jury must determine whether a firearm was used, but not whether this use included brandishing or discharge.

Whether the firearm was brandished or discharged may also bear on the jury's determination of whether it was used or carried "during and in relation to" a predicate offense. Transforming brandishing or discharge into a sentencing factor "might unnecessarily produce a conflict between the judge and the jury," particularly when "the sentencing judge applies a lower standard of proof" and "additional years in prison are at stake."[89] In sum, brandishing is a traditional crime that is subject to determination by the jury, not the sentencing judge.

The Rules of Lenity and Constitutional Doubt

To the extent that any uncertainty exists, § 924(c) should have been interpreted according to the rules of lenity and of constitutional doubt. Both require that brandishing be treated as an element to be found by the jury.

To reword *Castillo*, "the length and severity of an added mandatory sentence that turns on the presence or absence of [brandishing or discharge] weighs in favor of treating such offense-related words as referring to an element."[90] Here, the 5-year sentence increases to 7 years for brandishing and 10 years for discharge. If uncertainty exists, "we would assume a preference for traditional jury determination of so important a factual matter."[91] The "rule of lenity requires that 'ambiguous criminal statutes be construed in favor of the accused.'"[92] Like the more dangerous firearms in *Castillo*, brandishing "refer[s] to an element of a separate, aggravated crime."[93]

As the Court held in construing earlier versions of § 924(c), "This policy of lenity means that the Court will not interpret a federal

---

[88] *See* Bailey v. United States, 516 U.S. 137, 148 (1995) (resolving "what evidence is required to permit a jury to find that a firearm had been used at all").

[89] *Castillo*, 530 U.S. at 128.

[90] *Id.* at 131.

[91] *Id.*

[92] *Id.* (quoting Staples v. United States, 511 U.S. 600, 619 n.17)(1994).

[93] *Id.*

criminal statute so as to increase the penalty that it places on an individual when such an interpretation can be on the basis of no more than a guess as to what Congress intended."[94] The test is whether Congress has "plainly and unmistakably" enacted the harsher alternative,[95] which it obviously did not do here.[96]

Moreover, the rule of constitutional doubt requires that brandishing and discharge be considered as elements of the offense. A "crime" cannot be construed as a sentencing factor so as to undercut the requirements that "the trial of all crimes shall be by jury,"[97] or that "[i]n all criminal prosecutions, the accused shall enjoy a right to a speedy and public trial, by an impartial jury, and to be informed of the nature and cause of the accusation."[98] Blackstone explained the policy behind the right to jury trial as follows:

> But in settling and adjusting a question of fact, when entrusted to any single magistrate, partiality and injustice have an ample field to range in. This therefore preserves in the hands of the people that share which they ought to have in the administration of public justice.[99]

Blackstone further wrote that trial by jury is secure only "so long as this palladium remains sacred and inviolate, not only from all open attacks, but also from all secret machinations, which may sap and undermine it; by introducing new and arbitrary methods of

---

[94] Simpson v. United States, 435 U.S. 6, 15 (1978); *accord*, Busic v. United States, 446 U.S. 398, 405–06 (1980).

[95] *United States v. Bass*, 404 U.S. 336, 348–49 (1971).

[96] *Bass* explained why "doubts are resolved in favor of the defendant" as follows: First, a fair warning should be given to the world in language that the common world will understand, of what the law intends to do if a certain line is passed. . . . Second, because of the seriousness of criminal penalties, and because criminal punishment usually represents the moral condemnation of the community, legislatures and not courts should define criminal activity.
Id. at 347–48 (citations and quotation marks omitted).

[97] U.S. CONST., art. III, § 2, ¶ 3.

[98] *Id.* amend. VI.

[99] 3 BLACKSTONE, COMMENTARIES, *380.

trial."[100] Indeed, Blackstone even held that "the jury may, if they think proper, take upon themselves to determine at their own hazard, the complicated question of fact and law."[101]

John Adams quoted this passage in 1771, when the colonists were asserting the power of juries to decide not just the facts, but also the law.[102] In an essay on the rights of juries, Adams wrote: "Juries are taken by lot or by suffrage from the mass of the people, and no man can be condemned of life, or limb, or property or reputation, without the concurrence of the voice of the people." He added that "the common people should have as complete a control, as decisive a negative, in every judgment of a court of judicature."[103] Expressing the colonists' struggle against the Crown, Adams condemned the attempts of judges to usurp the power of juries and vindicated jury nullification.[104] This history is difficult to square with the assertion in *Harris* that the Founders approved of judicial fact-finding to decide accusations in criminal cases with devastating consequences to defendants.

If anything was certain, it was that factual determinations are within the province of the jury. John Marshall stated this principle in simple but forceful language at the Virginia ratification convention in 1788:

> What is the object of a jury trial? To inform the court of the facts. I hope that in this country, where impartiality is so much admired, the laws will direct facts to be ascertained by a jury.[105]

Moreover, the Fifth Amendment provides that "[n]o person shall be held to answer for a capital, or otherwise infamous crime, unless

---

[100] *Jones*, 526 U.S. at 246, quoting 4 BLACKSTONE, COMMENTARIES *342–344. "Providing an accused with the right to be tried by a jury of his peers gave him an inestimable safeguard . . . against the compliant, biased, or eccentric judge." Duncan v. Louisiana, 391 U.S. 145, 156 (1968). The jury guarantee reflects "a reluctance to entrust plenary powers over the life and liberty of the citizen to one judge or to a group of judges." *Id. See* United States v. Gaudin, 515 U.S. 506, 510–11 (1995).

[101] 3 BLACKSTONE, COMMENTARIES, *378.

[102] LEGAL PAPERS OF JOHN ADAMS 219 (1965).

[103] *Id.* at 229.

[104] *See id.* at 210–27.

[105] 3 JONATHAN ELLIOT, THE DEBATES IN THE SEVERAL STATE CONVENTIONS ON THE ADOPTION OF THE FEDERAL CONSTITUTION 557–58 (1836).

on a presentment or indictment of a Grand Jury." Justice Story wrote, "The grand jury performs most important public functions; and, is a great security to the citizens against vindictive prosecutions."[106]

The term "crime," a fundamental concept in the Constitution's vocabulary, has an objective meaning and is assuredly not just anything the legislature or a court says it is (or is not).[107] When what is really a "crime" is declared by the legislature or construed by the judiciary to be a sentencing factor, the power of the grand jury to accuse (or not accuse) a person of crime and of the petit jury to try the person is shifted to the judiciary. Yet the jury is just as much a constitutional decision-maker as are the other branches of government, and its power cannot be usurped by wordsmithery.

The Court in *Jones* reiterated the long-established rule that "Where a statute is susceptible of two constructions, by one of which grave and doubtful constitutional questions arise and by the other of which such questions are avoided, our duty is to adopt the latter."[108] In *Harris*, constitutional doubt existed as to whether facts requiring an increased mandatory minimum sentence must be found by the jury, while in *Jones* doubt existed as to whether facts requiring an increased maximum sentence must be found by the jury.[109] The latter issue was resolved in favor of the jury in *Apprendi v. New Jersey* (2000).[110] Some background to that decision is in order.

---

[106] JOSEPH STORY, A FAMILIAR EXPOSITION OF THE CONSTITUTION OF THE UNITED STATES § 390 (1840).

[107] TVA v. Hill, 437 U.S. 153, 173 n.18 (1978):

> This recalls Lewis Carroll's classic advice on the construction of language: "'When I use a word,' Humpty Dumpty said, in rather a scornful tone, 'it means just what I choose it to mean—neither more nor less.'"

[108] *Jones*, 526 U.S. at 239 (citations omitted).

[109] *Jones*, 526 U.S. 243 n.6, explained the principle as follows:

> [U]nder the Due Process Clause of the Fifth Amendment and the notice and jury trial guarantees of the Sixth Amendment, any fact (other than prior conviction) that increases the maximum penalty for a crime must be charged in an indictment, submitted to a jury, and proven beyond a reasonable doubt. Because our prior cases suggest rather than establish this principle, our concern about the Government's reading of the statute rises only to the level of doubt, not certainty.

[110] Apprendi v. New Jersey, 530 U.S. 466 (2000).

To begin with, the Court noted in *In re Winship* (1970) that "the Due Process Clause protects the accused against conviction except upon proof beyond a reasonable doubt of every fact necessary to constitute the crime with which he is charged."[111] This burden cannot be avoided by judicially redefining a crime as a sentencing factor.

Further, *Mullaney v. Wilbur* (1975) invalidated a murder statute providing that malice is presumed on proof of intent to kill resulting in death, except that the crime is manslaughter if the defendant proves provocation in the heat of passion.[112] The rebuttable presumption relieved the state of its due process burden to prove every element of the crime beyond a reasonable doubt. *Mullaney* stated,

> Moreover, if *Winship* were limited to those facts that constitute a crime as defined by state law, a State could undermine many of the interests that decision sought to protect without effecting any substantive change in its law. It would only be necessary to redefine the elements that constitute different crimes, characterizing them as factors that bear solely on the extent of punishment.[113]

But *Patterson v. New York* (1977) upheld a definition of murder as causing death with intent, subject to an affirmative defense of extreme emotional disturbance.[114] There was no presumption of malice, and at common law the prosecution need not disprove beyond a reasonable doubt every fact constituting an affirmative defense.[115] The Court noted,

> This view may seem to permit state legislatures to reallocate burdens of proof by labeling as affirmative defenses at least some elements of the crimes now defined in their statutes. But there are obviously constitutional limits beyond which the States may not go in this regard.[116]

This is open to the broad reading that "the State lacked the discretion to omit 'traditional' elements from the definition of crimes and instead to require the accused to disprove such elements."[117]

---

[111] *In re Winship*, 397 U.S. 358, 364 (1970).

[112] Mullaney v. Wilbur, 421 U.S. 684, 686 & n.3 (1975).

[113] *Id.* at 697.

[114] Patterson v. New York, 432 U.S. 197, 205–06 (1977).

[115] *Id.* at 202, 210–11.

[116] *Id.* at 210.

[117] *Jones*, 526 U.S. at 241–42.

Underlying *Winship*, *Mullaney*, and *Patterson*, regardless of how each case resolved the burden shifting, is the premise that the jury determines all of the pertinent facts. By contrast, transforming an element into a sentencing factor completely removes the fact-finding from the jury.

McMillan v. Pennsylvania (1986) upheld a state statute imposing a minimum 5-year sentence for which the court finds the fact of visible possession of a firearm at sentencing by a preponderance of evidence.[118] The enhancement was lower than the 20- and 10-year maximum sentences authorized for the actual offenses, and thus "the statute gives no impression of having been tailored to permit the visible possession finding to be a tail which wags the dog of the substantive offense."[119] The claim that visible possession is really an offense element "would have at least more superficial appeal if a finding of visible possession exposed them to greater or additional punishment but it does not."[120]

While upholding *McMillan*, the court in *Harris* disregards the "tail which wags the dog" implicit in its interpretation of amended § 924(c). Because it imposes only minimums and authorizes life imprisonment for every offense, § 924(c) breaks out of the *McMillan* paradigm altogether. *McMillan* was decided before the Brave New World in which all crimes of a class, from the lowest level to the most aggravated, have the same maximum of life imprisonment. Under this regime, the *McMillan* framework cannot protect the basic constitutional values at stake.

Almendarez-Torres v. United States (1998) held that recidivism, which is "as typical a sentencing factor as one might imagine," is not an element of the crime of unlawful reentry after deportation under 8 U.S.C. § 1326.[121] By contrast, brandishing is prosecuted as a crime in every state in the United States. Moreover, recidivism is rarely contested and may create unfair prejudice with the jury.[122] But in determining whether a firearm was "used," the jury will invariably determine if it was brandished or discharged, which is

---

[118] McMillan v. Pennsylvania, 477 U.S. 79, 88 (1986).

[119] *Id.* at 88.

[120] *Id.*

[121] Almendarez-Torres v. United States, 523 U.S. 224, 230 (1998).

[122] *Id.* at 235.

frequently contested. Finally, unlike other allegations, "a prior conviction must itself have been established through procedures satisfying the fair notice, reasonable doubt, and jury trial guarantees."[123]

Almendarez-Torres was a 5–4 decision authored by Justice Breyer and joined by the Chief Justice and Justices O'Connor, Kennedy, and Thomas. Justice Scalia wrote a strong dissent joined by Justices Stevens, Souter, and Ginsburg. However, in *Apprendi*, Justice Thomas wrote a concurring opinion in which he confessed error in joining with the majority in *Almendarez-Torres* and argued that the right to jury trial requires that the existence of a prior conviction be considered an element of the offense.[124] It is apparent that only four Justices now agree with the opinion in *Almendarez-Torres*.

Interpretation of aggravated crimes as sentencing factors reduces the jury function, in the words of *Jones*, to "low-level gatekeeping," that is, the jury's fact-finding necessary for the basic offense with the lowest level punishment opens the door to a judicial finding sufficient to impose far higher sentences.[125] The jury's fact-finding for a minimum 5-year sentence in *Harris* opened the door to a judicial finding triggering minimum 7- and 10-year sentences, respectively.

Apprendi v. New Jersey (2000) held that facts that result in an increase in the maximum punishment must be found by the jury.[126] Its underlying premises would also apply to facts that increase mandatory minimum penalties. With the exception of the fact of a prior conviction, *Apprendi* endorsed the following: "It is unconstitutional for a legislature to remove from the jury the assessment of facts that increase the prescribed range of penalties to which a criminal defendant is exposed."[127]

Apprendi found the essence of a "crime" to be as follows: "The law threatens certain pains if you do certain things, intending thereby to

---

[123] *Jones*, 526 U.S. at 249.

[124] *Apprendi*, 530 U.S. 466, 520 (Thomas, J., concurring).

[125] *Id.* at 243–44.

[126] Apprendi v. New Jersey, 530 U.S. 466, 120 S. Ct. 2348 (2000).

[127] 120 S. Ct. at 2363 (quoting *Jones*, 526 U.S. at 252–253 (Stevens, J., concurring)). Justice Stevens added in that concurrence: "A proper understanding of this principle encompasses facts that increase the minimum as well as the maximum permissible sentence. . . ." *Id.* at 253.

give you a new motive for not doing them."[128] "[T]he procedural safeguards designed to protect Apprendi from unwarranted pains should apply equally to the two acts that New Jersey has singled out for punishment."[129]

Where a "crime" is concerned, the Constitution repeatedly addresses the role of the grand jury and the petit jury.[130] *Apprendi* relates about the original intent: "Any possible distinction between an 'element' of a felony offense and a 'sentencing factor' was unknown to the practice of criminal indictment, trial by jury, and judgment by court as it existed during the years surrounding our Nation's founding."[131]

Brandishing includes the specific intent of making the presence of a firearm known to intimidate another, and criminal intent has always been a jury matter. "The defendant's intent in committing a crime is perhaps as close as one might hope to come to a core criminal offense 'element.'"[132] The legislature cannot define and punish a crime, but then remove it from the jury's purview by referring to it as a sentencing factor:

> [A] State cannot through mere characterization change the nature of the conduct actually targeted. It is as clear as day that this hate crime law defines a particular kind of prohibited intent, and a particular intent is more often than not the sine qua non of a violation of a criminal law.[133]

The harsher minimum imprisonment and additional blameworthiness also make clear that brandishing is a crime. *Apprendi* states, "Both in terms of absolute years behind bars, and because of the

---

[128] *Id.* at 2356 (quoting O. HOLMES, THE COMMON LAW 40 (1963)). Justice Thomas wrote in *Apprendi* that "This case turns on the seemingly simple question of what constitutes a 'crime.'" *Id.* at 2367–68 (Thomas, J., concurring) (quoting Fifth and Sixth Amendment guarantees). "[A] 'crime' includes every fact that is by law a basis for imposing or increasing punishment (in contrast with a fact that mitigates punishment.") *Id.* at 2369.

[129] *Id.*

[130] U.S. CONST., art. III, § 2; amdts. 5 & 6.

[131] 120 S. Ct. at 2356.

[132] *Id.* at 2364.

[133] *Id.* at 2364 n.18.

more severe stigma attached, the differential here is unquestionably of constitutional significance."[134]

Thus, the principles set forth in *Apprendi* apply just as much to increases in mandatory minimum sentences as to increases in the maximum sentence. As Justice Thomas, joined by Justice Scalia, wrote in his concurrence,

> The mandatory minimum "entitles the government" to more than it would otherwise be entitled. Those courts, in holding that such a fact was an element, did not bother with any distinction between changes in the maximum and the minimum. What mattered was simply the overall increase in the punishment provided by law.[135]

Happily, the *Harris* Court did not allude to legislative history, but a word on that subject is in order. The Court did affirm the decision of the Fourth Circuit, which held that the legislative history established that brandishing is a sentencing factor.[136] However, "principles of lenity preclude our resolution of the ambiguity against petitioner on the basis of legislative history."[137] Even where there are "contrary indications in the statute's legislative history," a court must "resolve any doubt in favor of the defendant."[138] Nor can legislative history override the doctrine of constitutional doubt.

Statutes with identical structures—the two versions of § 924(c) and the statute in *Jones*—cannot be construed differently regarding elements versus sentencing factors on the basis of a court's rendition of legislative history.[139] Under this discordant linguistic methodology, citizens may not rely on uniformity in the language or structure

---

[134]*Id.* at 2365.

[135]*Id.* at 2379–80 (Thomas, J., concurring) (citation omitted).

[136]*Harris*, 243 F.3d at 810–11.

[137]Hughey v. United States, 495 U.S. 411, 422 (1990).

[138]Ratzlaf v. United States, 510 U.S. 135, 147–48 (1994). *See* United States v. Thompson/Ctr. Arms Co., 504 U.S. 505, 517–18 (1992) (applying rule of lenity); *Id.* at 521 (Scalia, J., concurring, joined by Thomas, J.) ("that last hope of lost interpretive causes, that St. Jude of the hagiology of statutory construction, legislative history" is "particularly inappropriate in determining the meaning of a statute with criminal application").

[139]*See* United States v. R.L.C., 503 U.S. 291, 309 (1992) (Scalia, J., concurring, joined by Kennedy and Thomas, JJ.) (the fiction that one is presumed to know the criminal law "descends to needless farce when the public is charged even with knowledge of Committee Reports").

of criminal laws, but are subject to prosecution on the basis of a court's *post hoc* portrayal of "legislative history." Rather than rely on legislative history, the Supreme Court in *Harris* relied on the more illusive but related concept that brandishing just was not the kind of thing that Congress had a history of making into a crime, and thus it must be a sentencing factor.

That said, factually the legislative history regarding amended § 924(c) verifies that brandishing was considered to be a crime.[140] Not one proponent cited any need to transform the acts condemned in § 924(c) from elements of the offense to sentencing factors, and not one opponent criticized the bills for usurping the right to jury trial.[141]

Had Congress intended the disputed portions of § 924(c) to be mere sentencing factors, it could have declared just that in the statute itself. At the very least, a proponent or opponent of the bill would have mentioned it. Neither was the case. *Harris* is the product of the campaign by the Department of Justice to transform crimes into sentencing factors to ease the path to conviction and imprisonment, particularly in questionable cases in which the jury probably would not convict. It was able to muster five votes on the Supreme Court and thus succeeded in its objective in *Harris*, as it had in *Almendarez-Torres*. However, it failed to do so in *Jones*, *Castillo*, and *Apprendi*.

Whither Harris?

The most immediate effect of *Harris* will be felt elsewhere in § 924(c), and its outcome is by no means clear. As noted earlier, *Harris* relied in part on *Castillo*, which applied some of the same factors to reach the opposite conclusion concerning the types of firearms that are used or carried, graduating from 5 years for a

---

[140] *See* H.R. REP. No. 105-344, at 12 (1997) ("To sustain a *conviction* for brandishing or discharging a firearm"); 144 CONG. REC. H533 (Feb. 24, 1998) (remarks of Rep. McCollum) (bill provided that "a crime be the possession or the brandishing or the discharging of the gun"); *Id.* at H10, 329 (Oct. 9, 1998) (remarks of Rep. McCollum) (House-Senate compromise bill "clarifies Congress' intent as to the type of criminal conduct which should trigger the statute's application,' including "using a gun, possessing in the course of a crime a gun, or certainly brandishing or discharging that gun."); *Id.* (remarks of Rep. Scott) (comparing brandishing and discharge penalties "to the penalties for *other crimes*").

[141] *See* Castillo v. United States, 530 U.S. 120, 130 (2000) ("the 'mandatory sentencing' statements to which the Government points show only that Congress believed that the 'machine gun' and 'firearm' provisions would work similarly").

normal firearm to 30 years for a machine gun. *Castillo* held the firearm types to be offense elements, not sentencing factors.

Castillo arose out of the 1993 tragedy at Waco, Texas. The few Branch Davidians who were not killed in the fire were indicted for conspiracy to murder federal agents, but the jury acquitted them of this charge. Because the prosecution essentially lost its case, it seized upon the conviction of the defendants for carrying firearms under § 924(c), a 5-year offense. Contrary to all previous precedents, the prosecution argued that the type of firearm is a mere sentencing factor, that someone at Waco had machine guns, that whoever was not killed was responsible for whoever used machine guns, and thus the defendants must be sentenced to 30 years for constructively carrying machine guns. The district court obliged, sentencing the defendants to 30 years for accusations that were not in the indictment and/or decided by the jury, and the Fifth Circuit affirmed twice.[142] Then other circuits began to hold the same, creating a circuit conflict.[143]

That saga reveals how what is considered a crime was judicially transformed into a sentencing factor, and how the precedent creating the transformation spread to other circuits. But in this instance, the Supreme Court put its foot down, rendering a 9–0 opinion in *Castillo* that held that firearm types in § 924(c) are elements of the offense. Surprisingly, the opinion was authored by Justice Breyer, who in other cases has been associated with favoring the taking of fact-finding from juries to sentencing judges. This author argued *Castillo* both times in the Fifth Circuit and then in the Supreme Court.

The opinion of the Court in *Harris* relied on *Castillo* for propositions that support the continued interpretation of firearm types as offense elements. Firearm types are traditionally offense elements. *Harris* states, "Tradition and past congressional practice were perhaps the most important guideposts in *Jones*. The fact at issue there—serious bodily injury—is an element in numerous federal statutes; and the *Jones* Court doubted that Congress would have made this fact a sentencing factor in one isolated instance." *Harris* then cites the pages of *Castillo* that made this same point about firearm types.[144]

---

[142] United States v. Branch, 91 F.3d 699 (5th Cir. 1996), *cert. denied sub nom.*, Castillo v. United States, 520 U.S. 1185 (1997), *aff'd. after remand*, 179 F.3d 321 (5th Cir. 1999), *rev'd.*, 530 U.S. 120 (2000), *final remand*, 220 F.3d 648 (5th Cir. 2000).

[143] For a detailed account, see HALBROOK, FIREARMS LAW DESKBOOK: FEDERAL AND STATE CRIMINAL PRACTICE § 2.15.

[144] Harris v. United States, 2002 U.S. LEXIS 4652, at *16 (2002) (citing *Castillo*, 530 U.S. at 126–127).

Harris also quotes *Castillo* for the proposition that "traditional sentencing factors often involve special features of the manner in which a basic crime was carried out,"[145] and *Castillo* rejected the government's argument that firearm types were in that category.

The dramatic increase in penalties in the statutes in *Jones* and *Castillo* also contrasted with the mere two-year difference in the brandishing provision in *Harris* in the calculus for whether something is an element or a sentencing factor. In *Castillo*,[146] mandatory minimum sentences for firearm use jumped from 5 to 30 years if the firearm is a machine gun. The 1998 amendments recodified the provision at § 924(c)(1)(B) to provide for the same leaps in minimum sentences if the firearms are of certain specified types. For a subsequent conviction, subpart (C) requires a 25-year minimum sentence, and life imprisonment if the firearm is of certain types.

Other factors listed as decisive in *Castillo* continue to apply after the 1998 amendments. It bears repeating that *Castillo* was a 9–0 opinion and that *Harris* was 5–4, with part of the opinion being only a plurality opinion. But the issue of whether firearm types continue to be offense elements and not sentencing factors will be hotly contested in the future.

The above is only a preview of what is already taking place regarding numerous federal criminal statutes. *Harris* for the time being resolves the constitutional issue that facts that form the basis for mandatory minimum sentences need not be alleged in the indictment, found by the jury, or proven beyond a reasonable doubt. But the basis of the opinion was agreed to only by a plurality of the Court.

Like other guarantees in the Bill of Rights, the protections under the Fifth and Sixth Amendments for persons accused of crimes are in a state of flux. The current transformation of "crimes" into sentencing factors, while on rare occasions have been explicitly enacted by the Congress or state legislatures, is primarily the work of prosecutorial agendas and judicial activism. It remains to be seen how extensively this linguistic manipulation will serve to erode the right to be informed in an indictment of the accusations, the right of trial by jury, and the right to proof beyond a reasonable doubt.

---

[145] *Id.* at *17 (citing *Castillo*, 530 U.S. at 126).

[146] *Id.* at *18 (citing *Castillo*, 530 U.S. at 131).

Tenants, Students, and Drugs: A Comment on the War on the Rule of Law

Roger Pilon

Introduction: The Expansive War on Drugs

For two decades now the nation has been waging a war on drugs—far longer than we waged war on alcohol, yet with no greater success.[1] Over that period numerous legal disputes arising from the war have reached the Supreme Court. Too often, however, the Court has decided those disputes not as a dispassionate adjudicator securing the rule of law but as a handmaiden to the political branches—one more agency in the war.[2] Rather than apply the law to check the zeal of government agents seemingly steeped in moral certitude, the Court itself, in case after case, has carved out a "drug exception"

---

[1] The current phase of the war is ordinarily taken to have begun with President Reagan in 1982. President's Radio Address to the Nation (October 2, 1982), *in* 18 *Weekly Compilation of Presidential Documents,* at 1249. In 1989 President Bush aggressively escalated the war. ("We need, fully and completely, to marshal the nation's energy and intelligence in a true all-out war against drugs.") *Quoted in Excerpts from News Session by Bush, Watkins and Bennet,* N.Y. TIMES, Jan. 13, 1989, at D16 (Statement by President Bush). But this is the most recent phase in a long line of wars on drugs. U.S. Treasury agents fought the original war in the decade following passage of the Harrison Narcotics Act of 1914, 38 Stat. 785, which brought cocaine and opiates under federal control for the first time. *See* EDWARD EPSTEIN, AGENCY OF FEAR 103 (1977). The Marihuana Tax Act of 1937 led to a second war. Federal Bureau of Narcotics Commissioner Harry Anslinger told Congress it was necessary to stop the "marihuana menace" exemplified by teenage gangs who became violent and murderous after smoking marijuana. *Id.* at 33. President Nixon declared a third drug war. In a message to Congress he labeled drug abuse a "national emergency," branding it "public enemy number one," and called for a "total offensive." *Id.* at 178. *See generally* AFTER PROHIBITION (Timothy Lynch ed., 2000); STEVEN B. DUKE & ALBERT C. GROSS, AMERICA'S LONGEST WAR (1993).

[2] *See* Steven Duke, *The Drug War and the Constitution, in* AFTER PROHIBITION, *supra* note 1, at 41–59. Steven Wisotsky, *A Society of Suspects: The War on Drugs and Civil Liberties,* CATO POL'Y ANALYSIS No. 180, Oct. 2, 1992.

to the Constitution,[3] as if we were engaged in a moral crusade with the law serving not as a check but as a weapon. Looking back in 1981, but as if he were looking ahead to the massive legislation that would soon unfold, then-Justice Rehnquist remarked that "[t]he history of the narcotics legislation in this country reveals the determination of Congress to turn the screw of the criminal machinery—detection, prosecution and punishment—tighter and tighter."[4]

Two decisions handed down during the 2001 term give ample evidence of that approach to drug cases. In *Department of Housing and Urban Development v. Rucker*,[5] Chief Justice Rehnquist, writing for a unanimous Court, begins his opinion in what must seem to him a matter-of-fact tone: "With drug dealers 'increasingly imposing a reign of terror on public and other federally assisted low-income housing tenants,' Congress passed the Anti-Drug Abuse Act of 1988."[6] Never mind that tenants themselves had brought the suit against the act, the Court reversed an en banc panel of the Court of Appeals for the Ninth Circuit,[7] reading the act to allow HUD officials discretion to evict four elderly Oakland, California, tenants from public housing. HUD's grounds? The grandsons of two tenants were caught in the building's parking lot smoking marijuana; the mentally disabled daughter of another was found three blocks from the building with cocaine and a crack cocaine pipe; and the caregiver to a disabled 75-year-old tenant was found in possession of cocaine in the tenant's apartment. So much for the reign of terror.

In the second case, *Board of Education of Independent School District No. 92 of Pottawatomie County v. Earls*,[8] Justice Thomas, writing for Chief Justice Rehnquist and Justices Scalia, Kennedy, and Breyer, upheld a Tecumseh, Oklahoma, school district's policy of requiring all students who participate in competitive extracurricular activities—from athletics to band, choir, Future Homemakers of America,

---

[3] "There is no drug exception to the Constitution." Skinner v. Ry. Labor Executive Ass'n, 489 U.S. 602, 641 (1989) (Marshall, J., dissenting). *See generally*, Erik Luna, *Drug Exceptionalism*, 47 VILL. L. REV. 753 (2002).

[4] Albernaz v. United States, 450 U.S. 333, 343 (1981).

[5] 122 S. Ct. 1230 (2002).

[6] *Id.* at 1232.

[7] Rucker v. Davis, 237 F.3d 1113 (2001).

[8] 122 S. Ct. 2559; 70 U.S.L.W. 4737 (2002). Here, too, the court below was reversed. Earls by Earls v. Bd. of Educ., 242 F.3d 1264 (2001).

and the academic team—to submit to drug testing by urinalysis. The Court's attitude in this case is best revealed, perhaps, by the exchanges at oral argument. Reporting for the *New York Times*, Linda Greenhouse described them as "spirited, intense and sometimes downright nasty":

> The justices appeared unusually snappish. When Justice Souter was invoking the small number of positive drug tests to question the district's need for drug testing, Chief Justice William H. Rehnquist offered a helping hand to [the district's lawyer]. "The existence of the policy might be expected to deter drug use, wouldn't it?" he asked the lawyer.
>
> "Then we'll never know, will we," Justice Souter said with some asperity.
>
> "Let her answer the question," the chief justice said sharply.
>
> But most surprising was Justice Kennedy's implied slur on the plaintiffs in the case. He had posed to [Lindsay Earls's lawyer] the hypothetical question of whether a district could have two schools, one a "druggie school" and one with drug testing. As for the first, Justice Kennedy said, "no parent would send a child to that school, except maybe your client."[9]

Lindsay Earls, a model student who had passed her drug test and was by then in her first year at Dartmouth College, was in the audience that day.

Given the almost religious fervor that has surrounded the war on drugs, even on the Court, it is hardly surprising that reasoned argument and the rule of law itself are among the war's casualties— collateral damage, so to speak. Congress has made the manufacture, distribution, sale, possession, and use of some drugs—marijuana, for example, but not alcohol—a federal crime. Its constitutional authority for doing so has never been squarely addressed by the Court.[10] Yet neither has a Court otherwise rightly concerned about

---

[9] Linda Greenhouse, *Supreme Court Seems Ready To Extend School Drug Tests*, N.Y. Times, Mar. 20, 2002, at A1.

[10] In *United States v. Jin Fuey Moy*, 241 U.S. 394 (1916), the Court expressed serious doubts about the constitutionality of the Harrison Act but avoided the enumerated powers question by construing the act as authorized under the federal government's taxing and revenue power. *United States v. Doremus*, 249 U.S. 86 (1919), presented a direct challenge to the act on enumerated powers grounds. Over a one-paragraph dissent by four justices, the act was upheld. *See* Eric Luna, *Our Vietnam: The Prohibition Apocalypse*, 46 DePaul L. Rev. 483 (1997). It is noteworthy that when we sought to prohibit alcohol, we found the federal power to do so only through a constitutional amendment.

federalism, the limits of congressional power, and the integrity of state government addressed those issues seriously as they arise in the context of growing state efforts—by the voters of the states, no less—to free themselves from the war's federal chains, especially regarding the medical use of marijuana.[11] Rather than address the first principles of the matter, the Court instead has narrowed its focus, finding comfort in precedent, prior mistakes notwithstanding. Thus we have today a federal government with vast resources dedicated to this single crusade—hardly a government with powers "few and defined," as Madison promised in *Federalist* No. 45.

Assume, however, that the Constitution does authorize the federal government to wage a "war on drugs"—either because there is some general federal police power to do so, despite the Court's repeated admonitions that there is no such power,[12] or because the power of Congress to ensure the free flow of commerce among the states entails, as a necessary and proper means to that end, a power to prohibit commerce in drugs. On such dubious assumptions— plus the equally dubious assumption that the general police power of states entails not only the power to secure rights, as John Locke argued,[13] but the power to police "morals" as well, whatever that may mean—it remains to be asked how government may wage that war. One imagines that federal and state governments would do so directly—by arresting and prosecuting those who manufacture, distribute, sell, possess, and use the prohibited drugs—since private enforcement through civil actions is unavailable, there being no individual rights violated by those acts. And that, precisely, is how our governments do wage the war, in the main, by prosecuting,

---

[11] I have discussed those issues more fully in Roger Pilon, *The Illegitimate War on Drugs, in* AFTER PROHIBITION, *supra* note 1, at 23–39.

[12] *See* United States v. Morrison, 529 U.S. 598, 618–19 (2000): "The Constitution . . . withhold[s] from Congress a plenary police power," citing United States v. Lopez, 514 U.S. 549, 566 (1995); *Lopez*, 514 U.S. at 584. ("[W]e *always* have rejected readings of the Commerce Clause and the scope of federal power that would permit Congress to exercise a police power.") (Thomas, J., concurring) (original emphasis); *id.* at 596–97, n.6 (noting that the first Congresses did not enact nationwide punishments for criminal conduct under the Commerce Clause) (Thomas, J., concurring).

[13] JOHN LOCKE, THE SECOND TREATISE OF GOVERNMENT, *in* TWO TREATISES OF GOVERNMENT § 13 (Peter Laslett ed., 1960).

convicting, and incarcerating hundreds of thousands of otherwise law-abiding citizens.[14]

But that is not the only way this war is waged. Conventional prosecution is not enough for zealous drug warriors. In their quest for a "drug-free America" they insinuate themselves and their cause into every area of life. Public housing and education have thus been conscripted in the war on drugs. Public housing tenants are effectively deputized; if they fail in their duties, they lose their housing. Public schools too become arms of law enforcement, prophylactically testing students who, if they fail, lose their eligibility for extracurricular activities. We're all in this together—checking, monitoring, policing, changing behavior. Private housing and education have not yet been enlisted so directly,[15] but given the ubiquity of government lending and spending programs, one imagines it only a matter of time before they too will be required to do their parts. That is what we've come to in this truly insidious war. What ever happened to that "most comprehensive of rights and the right most valued by civilized men"[16]—the right to be let alone?

One would hope to see such issues raised in the Court's drug opinions—the larger constitutional issues, at least. Instead, those opinions too often read like policy statements on social problems. Just to be clear on that, drug abuse is a problem, to be sure, although it would be less a public and more a private problem were it not for the war on drugs—much like alcoholism has been since the end of Prohibition. But the private problems of drug abuse pale compared with the very public problems of crime, corruption, and cost that are brought on by the war on drugs.[17] Yet the typical drug opinion from the Court rarely notices that. Constrained by its post-New Deal deference to the political branches, which undermines the very reason for separating powers, the Court treats the policies of

---

[14] *See* Julie Stewart, *Effects of the Drug War, in* AFTER PROHIBITION, *supra* note 1, at 141–45.

[15] Private institutions are involved indirectly, however. *See* Diane Jean Schemo, *Students Find Drug Law Has Big Price: Student Aid*, N.Y. TIMES. May 3, 2001, at A12 (college student found guilty of smoking marijuana in a car sentenced to $250 fine, suspension of driver's license, 20 hours of community service, a year's probation, and then is denied student financial aid under the federal Higher Education Act).

[16] Olmstead v. United States, 277 U.S. 438, 478 (1928) (Brandeis, J., dissenting).

[17] *See especially,* AMERICA'S LONGEST WAR, *supra* note 1.

those branches uncritically, taking them as given and presumptively legitimate. Such is the Court's deference that when the policies are balanced against objections on the other side, rarely do they lose. We see that in the cases before us here.

Statutory Construction

The statute at issue in *Rucker* required public housing agencies to use leases for their properties providing that "any drug-related criminal activity on or off such premises, engaged in by a public housing tenant, any member of the tenant's household, or any guest or other person under the tenant's control, shall be cause for termination of tenancy."[18] Pursuant to that provision, the four elderly plaintiffs noted earlier signed leases obligating them to "assure that the tenant, any member of the household, a guest, or another person under the tenant's control, shall not engage in . . . [a]ny drug-related activity on or near the premise[s]."[19] To administer the statute, HUD wrote regulations that gave local authorities discretion to evict even in situations in which the tenant "did not know, could not foresee, or could not control behavior by other occupants of the unit."[20]

After the Oakland Housing Authority initiated eviction proceedings based on the facts noted earlier, the tenants challenged HUD's interpretation of the statute under the Administrative Procedures Act,[21] arguing that it does not require lease terms authorizing the eviction of "innocent" tenants and, in the alternative, if it does, the statute violates, among other things, the Due Process Clause of the Fourteenth Amendment.

The Court disagreed, finding that the statute "unambiguously" allows authorities to evict tenants for drug-related activity, "whether or not the tenant knew, or should have known, about the activity." That conclusion "seems evident from the plain language of the statute," Rehnquist continued for the Court. In fact, "Congress' decision not to impose any qualification in the statute, combined with its use of the term 'any' to modify 'drug-related criminal activity,' precludes

---

[18] *Rucker*, 122 S. Ct. at 1232.
[19] *Id.*
[20] *Id.*
[21] 5 U.S.C. § 706(2)(A).

any knowledge requirement.''[22] Let us examine those final two points in reverse order.

The word "any" has an expansive meaning, Rehnquist says. He continues: "Thus, *any* drug-related activity engaged in by the specified persons is grounds for termination, not just drug-related activity that the tenant knew, or should have known, about.''[23] In truth, however, the word "any" adds nothing to the phrase that follows. It serves simply to make it emphatic that "drug-related activity engaged in by the specified persons [as later qualified] is grounds for termination." With or without the addition of "any," that is, the phrase means the same thing. To be sure, the rejected reading that follows *that* phrase—"not just drug-related activity that the tenant knew, or should have known, about"—*narrows* the class denoted by the previous phrase. But those words are no part of the statute. They are invoked, and rejected, by Rehnquist to help indicate *his* understanding of the force of "any." Yet "any" has no such force. It emphasizes; it does not expand the phrase that immediately follows. We are left, then, with the assertion that "drug-related activity engaged in by the specified persons [as later qualified] is grounds for termination." We will return to the actual text in a moment.

The second ground Rehnquist gives for precluding any knowledge requirement is "Congress' decision not to impose any qualification in the statute." He then moves to reinforce that point by citing civil forfeiture provisions from the same act that *do* contain an "innocent owner defense." Thus, presumably, Congress could have provided such a defense in the section of the act dealing with evictions, but it did not. As Rehnquist says:

> It is entirely reasonable to think that the Government, when seeking to transfer private property to itself in a forfeiture proceeding, should be subject to an "innocent owner defense," while it should not be when acting as a landlord in a public housing project. The forfeiture provision shows that Congress knew exactly how to provide an "innocent owner" defense. It did not provide one in [the eviction section of the bill].[24]

---

[22] *Rucker*, 122 S. Ct. at 1233.

[23] *Id.* (original emphasis).

[24] *Id.* at 1234.

That would be a powerful argument if Congress were as thought-ful and orderly as Rehnquist seems to presume, especially when he speaks of Congress's "decision" not to impose any qualification in the statute. One imagines Congress gathered to thoughtfully deliber-ate and then affirmatively decide the matter, when in truth the lawmaking process is anything but thoughtful and deliberative. Thus, it may be "reasonable" to include innocent owner defenses in forfeiture measures—and over the past decade Congress has done so to a considerable extent. But of the more than 100 federal statutes today with forfeiture provisions, many still do not include innocent owner defenses, however reasonable they may be.[25]

More generally, however, the idea that Congress "decided" not to impose any qualification in the eviction language simply strains credulity. As is well known beyond the realm of civics textbooks, few if any members of Congress ever even read the bills on which they vote. Most of Congress's work is done by staff. Bills invariably are written in cryptic language, referring to and amending language in existing statutes (e.g., "In sec. 123, delete 'and' and add 'but.'"). Only those few who are deeply conversant with the issue at hand know what is going on. Yet despite that common knowledge about how Congress actually works, the Court, especially in its post–New Deal deferential mode, continues to elevate "congressional intent" to a stature not remotely warranted by the evidence.

The business of interpretation is rarely easy, to be sure.[26] And one element in it is congressional intent, however illusory. But it is only one element, and should never be given more credit than it warrants. At bottom, interpretation, whether of statutory or of constitutional language, involves a "rational reconstruction" of the material at hand, starting with the text, then moving, if necessary, to other elements, including background principles. There is no set formula for the process, of course, and there is often room for reasonable disagreement, except in fairly rare cases that truly are unambiguous. When the text is ambiguous, one wants the "best" reading, all things considered, even if the criteria for that may themselves be open to debate.

---

[25] *See* DAVID B. SMITH, PROSECUTION AND DEFENSE OF FORFEITURE CASES (2002).

[26] *See generally* KEITH E. WHITTINGTON, CONSTITUTIONAL INTERPRETATION (1999).

We return, then, to the text that Rehnquist believes is "unambiguous." (If the text were truly unambiguous, it is hard to understand how the en banc panel below could have read it so differently.) His parsing of that text is worth quoting in its entirety:

> The en banc Court of Appeals also thought it possible that "under the tenant's control" modifies not just "other person," but also "member of the tenant's household" and "guest." The court ultimately adopted this reading, concluding that the statute prohibits eviction where the tenant "for a lack of knowledge or other reason, could not realistically exercise control over the conduct of a household member or guest." But this interpretation runs counter to basic rules of grammar. The disjunctive "or" means that the qualification applies only to "other person." Indeed, the view that "under the tenant's control" modifies everything coming before it in the sentence would result in the nonsensical reading that the statute applies to "a public housing tenant . . . under the tenant's control." HUD offers a convincing explanation for the grammatical imperative that "under the tenant's control" modifies only "other person": "by 'control,' the statute means control in the sense that the tenant has permitted access to the premises." Implicit in the terms "household member" or "guest" is that access to the premises has been granted by the tenant. Thus, the plain language of [the statute] requires leases that grant public housing authorities the discretion to terminate tenancy without regard to the tenant's knowledge of the drug-related criminal activity.[27]

As both the en banc panel and Rehnquist recognize, the heart of the matter is the meaning and scope of the qualification, "under the tenant's control." The en banc panel thought it modified not just "other person" but also "member of the tenant's household" and "guest." Rehnquist thinks it modifies "other person" only. Why? Because "the disjunctive 'or' means that the qualification applies only to 'other person.'" Yet that is hardly self-evident. Moreover, taking the provision as a whole, it leads not only to an unnatural reading but to a mistaken reading of the text.

The term "or" is systematically ambiguous. Logicians speak of its exclusive and nonexclusive senses.[28] "A or B" can mean either

---

[27] *Rucker*, 122 S. Ct. at 1233–34.

[28] *See, e.g.*, WILLARD VAN ORMAN QUINE, METHODS OF LOGIC 3–12 (1967).

"A or B but not both," the exclusive sense; or "A or B and possibly both," the nonexclusive sense. Which sense is intended can be determined only in context. Considered with reference to truth conditions, however, "A or B" is true when "or" is used in the exclusive sense only if A or B but not both are true. By contrast, "A or B" is true when "or" is used in the nonexclusive sense if A or B or both are true. Thus, unless the context suggests otherwise, one presumes that the nonexclusive use is intended.

At the least, then, "under the tenant's control" must be presumed to modify not simply "other person" but "guest" as well; for the linguistic context, following the last comma, is "or any guest or other person under the tenant's control." In that construction, why would "under the tenant's control" apply any less to "guest" than to "other person"? In the context of a home, the term "guest" has a somewhat different signification than "other person"—a friend versus, say, a plumber called for a repair—although nothing turns on that distinction. But if "under the tenant's control" modifies "guest" as well as "other person," it could also be read to modify "any member of the tenant's household" and even "tenant." For the commas in the statutory language are deceptive: the four categories of people reached by the statute—tenants, household members, guests, and other persons—are actually separated by "or." In fact, the statute can be read that way with perfect fidelity: In brief, "any criminal activity engaged in by a tenant or household member or guest or other person under the tenant's control shall be cause for termination of the tenancy."

When that is done, however, it turns out that the crucial word, for interpretive purposes, is "other." Absent that word, only "person" would be modified by "under the tenant's control." With that word, however, "under the tenant's control" modifies "other person" and "guest" for sure, and probably "household member" and "tenant" as well. For in a very realistic sense, they are *all* presumed to be "under the tenant's control"—even the tenant. (Thus, Rehnquist is mistaken to say that including the tenant as "under the tenant's control" is "nonsensical." It is redundant. They are different.) The force of "other" in the provision is thus explicated as follows: "or any other person *who, like the foregoing,* is presumed to be under the tenant's control." How to treat that presumption is another matter, of course, to be discussed below. What is plain, however, is that

Congress, despite its ambiguous construction, meant at bottom to distinguish those under from those not under the tenant's control.

Thus, once the provision is better, more naturally explicated, it makes far more sense. Under the reading Rehnquist gave it, a tenant could be evicted if a plumber or a cable installer with marijuana in his pocket, unbeknown to the tenant, was "permitted access to the premises." Difficult as it may be to determine what Congress intended, that surely cannot be it. Congress wanted tenants to be responsible, to take responsibility for their premises. How else to explain Congress's use of "under the tenant's control"? Rehnquist's reading, by contrast, makes tenants strictly—indeed, almost absolutely—liable. So too does the HUD explanation—"the statute means control in the sense that the tenant has permitted access to the premises." What is a tenant to do? Check the pockets of itinerant repairmen to ensure that they are not lying if asked whether they are carrying any drugs? Police the parking lot? The neighborhood within three blocks? Three miles? Congress could have written "permitted access to the premises" if it had wanted to. It did not, for that means something different than "under the tenant's control."

Indeed, if Congress had wanted to make tenants strictly liable, why did it add the words "under the tenant's control"? Presumably, Congress did not want to have tenants evicted for actions by persons *not* under the tenant's control, which truly would have amounted to absolute liability. But that still leaves us asking how to treat the presumption that persons in the four categories are under the tenant's control. HUD's administrative regulations give local authorities discretion to evict even in situations in which the tenant "did not know, could not foresee, or *could not control* behavior by other occupants of the unit." To be sure, there is a distinction between *persons* not under the tenant's control and *behavior* not under the tenant's control, but as a practical matter it is a distinction without a difference. Does it really make sense to say that B is under A's control if B's *behavior* is not under A's control? Practically, B is under A's control only to the extent that B's *behavior* is under A's control. Thus, HUD's regulations holding tenants liable for behavior they "could not control" runs contrary to Congress's intent to hold tenants liable only for persons "under their control." Because they are inconsistent with congressional intent, therefore, the regulations must be rejected under the first step of the *Chevron* doctrine.[29]

[29] Chevron U.S.A., Inc. v. Natural Ress. Def. Council, Inc., 467 U.S. 837, 842–43 (1984).

The larger problem remains, however. It is that the statute itself is foolish. On one hand, assuming that government should be in the housing business to begin with, much less has constitutional authority to be, we surely do not want to evict people like these plaintiffs. Herman Walker, after all, was 75 years old and partly paralyzed from a stroke. He was hardly in a position to police the drug-related behavior of the caretakers he was fortunate enough to have. But even if he were in a better position to "control" such behavior, it hardly follows that he could. The president of the United States, after all, and his brother, the governor of Florida, both of whom live in public housing, have had their own troubles lately controlling the behavior of their grown children as it relates to controlled substances.[30] The folly of this statute lies in its effort to hold some people liable for the behavior of others—just one more extension of the war on drugs. Yet not once in the Court's opinion do we find that issue addressed. Only below, when District Judge Charles R. Breyer issued a preliminary injunction against the evictions, did we glimpse a bit of candor: "This policy on its face appears irrational."[31]

Suspicionless Searches

As with public housing, public education is now an arm of law enforcement if the issue is drugs. In *Rucker*, the federal government conscripted public housing tenants to help fight the war on drugs. In *Earls*, it was a local school district that stepped in to do its part, drug-testing students who participated in extracurricular activities, excluding them from such activities if they failed the tests. Given the state of public education today and the problems of simply educating students, one wonders why schools have taken on such responsibilities, distracting as they are from a school's main business. Yet so officious have public schools become that we learn just now of a rural South Dakota school in which the principal ordered two recent "lockdowns" of every classroom from kindergarten through high school. Local police officials and a federal law enforcement

---

[30] Dana Canedy, *Jeb Bush's Daughter Is Arrested On Charge of Faking Prescription*, N.Y. TIMES, Jan. 30, 2002, at A12.

[31] Rucker v. Davis, No. C 98-00781, 1998 U.S. Dist. LEXIS 9345, at *32 (N.D. Cal. June 19, 1998).

officer then arrived with a drug-sniffing German shepherd dog that went up and down the aisles as the students, some as young as six, were ordered to keep their hands on their desks in order not to startle the dog. Students were terrorized, reports said, especially after the dog broke from its handler in one classroom, chasing students around the room.[32] Plainly, this is war. Children as young as six are among its targets.

In *Rucker* the issue was primarily one of statutory interpretation. In *Earls* the issue was constitutional—whether suspicionless searches like the ones before the Court are permitted under the Fourth Amendment. In both cases, however, the decisions below were overturned—and in *Earls* the Court split 5 to 4—suggesting that the outcomes were not foreordained. It is in such cases that one wants to examine the reasoning especially closely. The reasoning in *Earls*, unfortunately, is conclusory at every turn. It is one long circular argument, the conclusion seemingly foreordained from the start. Justice Thomas, writing for the majority, gives it away in his second sentence: "Because this Policy reasonably serves the School District's important interest in detecting and preventing drug use among its students, we hold that it is constitutional."[33] Note the school's "important interest"—detecting and preventing drug use, as if it were a law enforcement agency. Because the school's policy "reasonably serves" that interest, it is constitutional. That is the kind of uncritical, means/end analysis that speaks volumes about deference to the political branches.

The Fourth Amendment guards against "unreasonable" searches and seizures, of course. In that regard, a government search is unreasonable if conducted without good reason; and "good reason" means not simply that the search serves the government's interest—a matter for the government to determine in any event—but that officials have "probable cause" to believe that the person searched has done something to warrant the search, if only harbor information about a crime. Thus, "good reason" looks backward, to the person or property to be searched, not forward to the government's aim: "[No]

---

[32] Tamar Lewin, *Drug Dogs Sniff Even 6-Year-Olds; Parents Sue*, N.Y. TIMES, July 26, 2002, at A17; Helen Rumbelow, *Use of Dog to Search Children For Drugs Prompts ACLU Suit*, WASH. POST, July 28, 2002, at A10.

[33] *Earls*, 70 U.S.L.W. at 4737.

Warrant shall issue, but upon probable cause, supported by Oath or affirmation, and particularly describing the place to be searched, and the persons or things to be seized." In a nutshell, the Fourth Amendment erects a clear presumption in favor of privacy and against government searches; if government does act, it must have a good reason; and that reason must relate to the person (or property) searched, to something that person is suspected of having done.

It is that presumption in favor of privacy and against government intrusions on privacy that is conspicuously absent from the *Earls* opinion, which goes out of its way to give the government the benefit of the doubt. To be sure, a "reasonableness" standard involves judgment, which means that reasonable people may reasonably differ about the standard and its application. For that very reason, however, it is essential that the Court have a sound theory of the matter—quite apart from the case law—a clear understanding of the presumptions and burdens of proof, grounded in first principles. When the opinion reads like a policy argument that could have been written by the government, we know we are far from that—and probably in the realm of drug policy.

Setting aside the case law for the moment, the problem here begins with the idea of an "administrative search"—as distinct from searches conducted in a criminal context. Administrative searches came to the fore with the modern administrative state, of course.[34] As governments began increasingly to regulate in the name of health and safety, as those grounds grew increasingly pretextual, and as unrelated grounds came to justify regulation, the administrative search became more common—to ensure that the law was being obeyed. In an uncertain world, some health and safety regulations are necessary, to be sure, as are the administrative searches that accompany them to ensure not simply that harm is rectified, after the fact, but prevented before it occurs. Among our unenumerated rights, after all, is the right to be free from the excessive risk others might create.

The road to health and safety is paved with peril, however, not least the peril of overregulation and loss of privacy.[35] Indeed, in

---

[34] *See, e.g.*, Timothy Lynch, *Polluting Our Principles: Environmental Prosecutions and the Bill of Rights*, 15 TEMP. L. & TECH. J., 161, 171–77 (1996).

[35] In fact, it turns out that most regulation in this area cannot be justified from a cost-benefit perspective. *See generally*, W. KIP VISCUSI, FATAL TRADEOFFS (1992).

arguing that students who participate in extracurricular activities voluntarily subject themselves to intrusions on their privacy, Thomas likens them to "adults who choose to participate in a closely regulated industry." As a comment on the Court's reasoning, the analogy is instructive. Because government closely regulates an industry, those who enter it are said, as here, to have no complaint because they consented to the regulation. Absent an independent justification for the regulation, however, the argument is patently circular. It is like the mugger who demands your money or your life. Your "choice" is bogus because he has no right to either your money or your life and hence no right to put you to such a "voluntary" choice. Without an independent justification, therefore, the closely-regulated-industry rationale becomes a circular argument for both initial and subsequent regulation.

What one wants to know, then, is whether there is an independent justification for an administrative search—much as there has to be an independent justification for a more conventional search, one related to something the person searched may have done to give rise to a probable-cause rationale for the search. But administrative searches are called "suspicionless" precisely because there is no *individualized* cause for suspicion. How, then, can they be called "reasonable"?

The answer involves both probability and practicality: probability concerning risk arising from actions of certain kinds by many actors; practicality regarding the inefficacy of suspicion-based searches. Unfortunately, as in the individualized context, there are few bright lines here either—doubtless, there are fewer. In general, however, if actions of certain kinds by many actors entail risk to others, and the risk is of sufficient magnitude, then prophylactic regulation, with enforcement through administrative searches, may be justified. The justification is still backward looking, however: just as in the individualized context, it looks to what those searched are doing—putting others at risk—to justify an otherwise impermissible intrusion on their privacy, not to any policies of the government that go beyond its main business of protecting rights. And in such cases suspicion-based searches are often inefficacious as well. Thus, everything from vision exams for drivers to the screening of airline passengers can be justified along those lines, without any individualized suspicion. Plainly, however, not any rationale will do. In fact, it is because such

241

searches are *not* based on individualized suspicion that courts must be especially careful about approving them and especially skeptical of the government's rationale. Indeed, it was precisely the use of blanket searches and general warrants against the colonists that led to the Fourth Amendment in the first place.[36]

Earls *and Extracurricular Activities*

Under that amendment, then, suspicionless searches are "reasonable" only in situations in which suspicion-based searches would be impractical and would not protect others from excessive risk. Thus, it is mainly to the rights of others that we must look to justify such searches. And in *Earls*, that is where Thomas begins: the probable cause standard, he says, "may be unsuited to determining the reasonableness of administrative searches where the 'Government seeks to *prevent* the development of hazardous conditions.'"[37] In elaborating on that rationale, however, he slowly broadens the focus:

> "[I]n certain limited circumstances, the Government's need to . . . [prevent harm] is sufficiently compelling to justify the intrusion on privacy entailed by conducting such searches without any measure of individualized suspicion." Therefore, in the context of safety and administrative regulations, a search unsupported by probable cause may be reasonable "when 'special needs, beyond the normal need for law enforcement, make the warrant and probable-cause requirement impracticable.'"
>
> Significantly, this Court has previously held that "special needs" inhere in the public school context. While schoolchildren do not shed their constitutional rights when they enter the schoolhouse, Fourth Amendment rights . . . are different in public schools than elsewhere; the "reasonableness" inquiry cannot disregard the school's custodial and tutelary responsibility for children." In particular, a finding of individualized suspicion may not be necessary when a school conducts drug testing.[38]

---

[36] NELSON B. LASSON, THE HISTORY AND DEVELOPMENT OF THE FOURTH AMENDMENT TO THE CONSTITUTION OF THE UNITED STATES, ch. 1–3 (1937).

[37] *Earls*, 70 U.S.L.W at 4738, (citing Treasury Employees v. Von Raab, 489 U.S. 656, 667–68 (1989)) (original emphasis).

[38] *Earls*, 70 U.S.L.W. at 4738–39 (internal citations omitted).

Notice the move from "hazardous conditions" and "safety" to "special needs" and finally to a school's "custodial and tutelary responsibilities for children." Citing *Vernonia School District 47J v. Acton*,[39] in which the Court upheld drug testing for school athletes, Thomas concludes that what is required to determine if a suspicionless search is justified is "a fact-specific balancing of the intrusion on the children's Fourth Amendment rights against the promotion of legitimate governmental interests."[40] The outcome of the balance is buried in that final phrase, of course. To get there, however, and to do the balancing, Thomas considers (1) the nature of the privacy interest allegedly compromised by the drug testing, (2) the character of the intrusion imposed by the policy, and (3) the nature and immediacy of the government's concerns and the efficacy of the policy in meeting them.

Regarding the nature of students' privacy interests, Thomas says that in the public school context, the most significant element is that the policy is undertaken in furtherance of the government's responsibilities "as guardian and tutor of children entrusted to its care." Thus, "[W]hen the government acts as guardian and tutor the relevant question is whether the search is one that a reasonable guardian and tutor might undertake."[41] If that in fact is the relevant question, let us ask it: Would parents, surely a child's most important guardians and tutors, conduct suspicionless drug tests on their children? Not likely. Indeed, why would anyone, parent or nonparent guardian alike, conduct a drug test on a child in his charge without some reason to do so—some reason related to something the child had done?

Thomas neither asks nor answers that question. He simply assumes that testing is what a reasonable guardian would do, then goes on to argue that a student's privacy interests are limited in a public school environment because "the State is responsible for maintaining discipline, health, and safety."[42] And he adds that the lowered expectations of privacy that athletes enjoy, which the *Vernonia* Court cited to justify drug-testing that group, apply also to

---

[39] 515 U.S. 646 (1995).

[40] *Earls*, 70 U.S.L.W. at 4739.

[41] *Id.*

[42] *Id.*

students who participate in nonathletic activities. The arguments here are so thin that one is almost relieved to find them irrelevant in the end; for Thomas says that the distinction between the privacy expectations of athletes and those of nonathletes "was not essential to our decision in *Vernonia*, which depended primarily upon the school's custodial responsibility and authority."[43] Better circular than thin arguments, apparently. The school's testing authority rested on its custodial authority, we are told, not on the students' status as athletes. Why then stop at athletes, or at students who participate in nonathletic extracurricular activities? Why not test all students? It is at this point that Thomas points to the voluntary nature of such participation, as mentioned above—trying thereby, apparently, to stop the slide made inevitable by the premise. The effort is futile. The custodial arguments in *Earls* will justify testing all students.

Turning to the second element in the balance, the character of the intrusion, the school's policy requires a faculty monitor to wait outside a closed restroom stall for the student to produce a urine sample and to "listen for the normal sounds of urination in order to guard against tampered specimens and to insure an accurate chain of custody." Thomas calls this process "minimally intrusive."[44] He adds, however, that test results are not turned over to any law enforcement authority. Instead, if a student fails a test, the school calls his parents or guardians for a meeting with school officials; and the student must show proof of receiving drug counseling and submit to a second test in two weeks. If he fails that test he is suspended from all extracurricular activities for 14 days; and he must complete four hours of substance abuse counseling and submit to monthly drug tests. A third failed test results in a one-year suspension from all extracurricular activities. Obviously, the school does not have to turn results over to law enforcement authorities. It is itself a law enforcement agency.

As should be clear from what has already been argued, the final element to be balanced—"the nature and immediacy of the government's concerns and the efficacy of the Policy in meeting them"—will tip the scale beyond retrieval. In fact, Thomas begins his discussion of this factor in a noteworthy way:

[43] *Id.*
[44] *Id.* at 4739–40.

> The drug abuse problem among our Nation's youth has hardly abated since *Vernonia* was decided in 1995. In fact, evidence suggests that it has only grown worse. As in *Vernonia*, "the necessity for the State to act is magnified by the fact that this evil is being visited not just upon individuals at large, but upon children for whom it has undertaken a special responsibility of care and direction." The health and safety risks identified in *Vernonia* apply with equal force to Tecumseh's children. Indeed, the nationwide drug epidemic makes the war against drugs a pressing concern in every school.[45]

No indifference there. No studied neutrality between the competing litigants. Here is a Court firmly committed to the war on drugs, anxious to do its part.

Given that beginning, the rest of the argument follows naturally. To the objection that the school had virtually no drug problem, Thomas responds that teachers had seen students who appeared to be under the influence of drugs and had heard students speaking openly about using drugs. Again, a drug dog had found marijuana cigarettes near the school parking lot, and police officers "once found drugs or drug paraphernalia in a car driven by a Future Farmers of America member." If that were not enough, "the school board president reported that people in the community were calling the board to discuss the 'drug situation.'"[46] In point of fact, over the testing years, to the date of summary judgment in the case, only 3 or 4 students of more than 500 tested showed evidence of drug use.[47] Never mind: just as the distinction between athletes and nonathletes did not matter in the end, neither does the evidence matter here, for "'[a] demonstrated problem of drug abuse . . . [is] not in all cases necessary to the validity of a testing regime.'"[48] And again, "this Court has not required a particularized or pervasive drug problem before allowing the government to conduct suspicionless drug testing. . . . In response to the lack of evidence relating to drug use,

---

[45] *Id.* at 4740 (citing *Vernonia*, 515 U.S. at 662).

[46] *Id.*

[47] Greenhouse, *supra* note 9, at A22.

[48] *Earls*, 70 U.S.L.W. at 4740 (citing Chandler v. Miller, 520 U.S. 305, 319 (1997)).

the Court noted generally that 'drug abuse is one of the most serious problems confronting our society today.'"[49]

The reasoning implicit in that final sentence is striking. It moves from the general to the particular in a way the Fourth Amendment was written, precisely, to block. Indeed, for "drug use" and "drug abuse" substitute "crime," "drunken driving," "Internet porn," what have you. The implication seems to be that if there is some "social problem" in the nation, the individualized suspicion required by the Fourth Amendment can be ignored. Thus, Thomas writes: "As we cannot articulate a threshold level of drug use that would suffice to justify a drug testing program for schoolchildren, we refuse to fashion what in effect would be a constitutional quantum of drug use necessary to show a 'drug problem.'"[50] In other words, no particularized evidence is necessary. A general "drug abuse problem" in society will do. The Fourth Amendment's presumption has effectively shifted. It was *against* government intrusion on privacy, unless there is individualized suspicion. Now, a general "social problem" suffices to establish a presumption *in favor of* government intrusion. And the presumption is effectively unrebuttable.[51]

Only at the end of his opinion does Thomas return, cursorily, to the safety issue, one of the two main rationales for suspicionless searches. Responding to a claim that "the testing of nonathletes does not implicate any safety concerns, and that safety is a 'crucial factor' in applying the special needs framework," Thomas agrees "that safety factors into the special needs analysis, but the safety interest furthered by drug testing is undoubtedly substantial for all children,

---

[49] *Id.* (citing Treasury Employees v. Von Raab, 489 U.S. 656, 673).

[50] *Id.* at 4741.

[51] One wonders what happened to the Thomas who dissented in *City of Indianapolis v. Edmond*, 531 U.S. 32 (2000): "Taken together, our decisions in *Michigan Dept. of State Police v. Sitz*, 496 U.S. 444 (1990), and *United States v. Martinez-Fuerte*, 428 U.S. 543 (1976), stand for the proposition that suspicionless roadblock seizures are constitutionally permissible if conducted according to a plan that limits the discretion of the officers conducting the stops. I am not convinced that Sitz and Martinez-Fuerte were correctly decided. Indeed, I rather doubt that the Framers of the Fourth Amendment would have considered "reasonable" a program of indiscriminate stops of individuals not suspected of wrongdoing." *Id.* at 56 (Because respondent Edmond did not advocate overruling Sitz or Martinez-Fuerte, and thus did not brief or argue doing so, Thomas was reluctant to consider that step. Given those precedents, therefore, he dissented and voted to uphold the searches before the Court.).

athletes and nonathletes alike. We know all too well that drug use carries a variety of health risks for children, including death from overdose."[52]

Here again, Thomas tries to justify suspicionless searches by invoking a general proposition about the dangers of drug use rather than a specific situation in which some are exposing others to excessive risk. In dissent, Justice Ginsburg nails the issue solidly. The risks Thomas cites, she says,

> are present for *all* schoolchildren. *Vernonia* cannot be read to endorse invasive and suspicionless drug testing of all students upon any evidence of drug use, solely because drugs jeopardize the life and health of those who use them. Many children, like many adults, engage in dangerous activities on their own time; that the children are enrolled in schools scarcely allows government to monitor all such activities. . . . Had the *Vernonia* Court agreed that public school attendance, in and of itself, permitted the State to test each student's blood or urine for drugs, the opinion in *Vernonia* could have saved many words.[53]

In *Vernonia*, from which *Earls* purports to flow, Ginsburg wrote a one-paragraph *concurrence* stating her understanding that the Court there reserved the question whether, on those facts, *all* students could be drug tested. In *Earls*, in which she found the facts to be quite different, she *dissented*, saying that the balance should have come out other than it did. She was joined by Justices Stevens, O'Connor, and Souter. Separately, O'Connor also dissented, joined by Souter, saying simply that she continues to believe that *Vernonia* was wrongly decided. She had written the dissent in *Vernonia*, joined by Stevens and Souter. Unfortunately, because Ginsburg's dissent in *Earls* proceeds on the assumption that *Vernonia* was rightly decided—whereas *Earls* goes "too far," as it were—it fails to get to the heart of the matter, even if it does smartly dispatch the majority's opinion. To get to the bottom of things, therefore, we have to look back to O'Connor's dissent in *Vernonia*.

---

[52] *Earls*, 70 U.S.L.W. at 4741
[53] *Id.* at 4743.

Vernonia *and Athletes*

The question in that case, again, was whether student *athletes* could be subjected to random, suspicionless drug tests. Writing for the majority, Justice Scalia noted that the Court had found suspicion-less searches reasonable " 'when special needs, beyond the normal need for law enforcement, made the warrant and probable-cause requirement impracticable.' "[54] The Court had also found that "spe-cial needs" existed in the public school context in which the power of the state was "custodial and tutelary."[55] Scalia then invoked a simple balancing test, pitting the intrusion on the students' privacy against the school's interests. On the students' side he found a reduced expectation of privacy within the school environment and a still lesser expectation among athletes. Moreover, the privacy inter-ests compromised by the tests were "negligible," he concluded. On the other side, by contrast, was the school's interest in deterring drug use, especially among athletes who were said to be leaders in the school's drug culture, had caused disciplinary problems in the school, and were at greater risk of sports injuries because of drug use. Because Scalia believed the balance favored the school, he upheld the suspicionless tests as reasonable under the Fourth Amendment.

In her dissent, O'Connor began by noting that the majority had dispensed with the requirement of individualized suspicion on "con-sidered policy grounds"; yet whether a blanket search was "better" than one based on suspicion was not for judges to decide, she averred.[56] In fact, for most of the Court's history, she continued, "mass, suspicionless searches have been generally considered *per se* unreasonable."[57] Only in recent years have exceptions been allowed, she noted, and only "where it has been clear that a suspicion-based regime would be ineffectual."[58] After reviewing the history of the matter, O'Connor concluded that suspicionless searches have been upheld only in "unusual circumstances," and after first recognizing the Fourth Amendment's "longstanding preference for a suspicion-based search regime":[59]

---

[54] *Vernonia*, 515 U.S. at 653 (citing Griffin v. Wisconsin, 483 U.S. 868, 873 (1987)).

[55] *Id.* at 655.

[56] *Id.* at 667.

[57] *Id.*

[58] *Id.* at 668.

[59] *Id.* at 674.

"In limited circumstances, where the privacy interests implicated by the search are minimal, and where an important
governmental interest furthered by the intrusion *would be
placed in jeopardy by a requirement of individualized suspicion,*
a search may be reasonable despite the absence of such suspicion." The obvious negative implication of this reasoning is
that, if such an individualized suspicion requirement would
not place the government's objectives in jeopardy, the
requirement should not be forsaken.[60]

Now there is a statement about the Fourth Amendment's presumption in favor of privacy and against government intrusion, the kind
of statement one would hope to have seen from Scalia or Thomas.
It makes it clear how limited the exceptions are, which O'Connor
went on to illustrate with examples involving risk for others and
the impracticability, under the circumstances, of a suspicion-based
regime. She then concluded that "the individualized suspicion
requirement has a legal pedigree as old as the Fourth Amendment
itself, and it may not be easily cast aside in the name of policy
concerns."[61]

But the irony, O'Connor continued, is that the public school context that so colors the Court's view, far from requiring suspicionless
searches, is precisely the kind of setting that lends itself to suspicion-
based searches. "In most schools, the entire pool of potential search
targets—students—is under constant supervision by teachers and
administrators and coaches, be it in the classrooms, the hallways,
or locker rooms."[62] In fact, most of the evidence the school had
presented consisted of stories of "particular, identifiable students
acting in ways that plainly give rise to reasonable suspicion" of
drug use, suspicion that would have justified a search. Given that,
O'Connor drew the inference that utterly escaped the majority: "[A]
vigorous regime of suspicion-based testing would have gone a long
way toward solving Vernonia's school drug problem while preserving the Fourth Amendment rights" of the innocent. In such circumstances, she concluded, "a mass, suspicionless search regime is categorically unreasonable."[63]

---

[60] *Id.* (citing Skinner v. Ry. Labor Executive Ass'n 489 U.S. 602, at 624 (emphasis
added by O'Connor, J.)).

[61] *Id.* at 678.

[62] *Id.*

[63] *Id.* at 679–80.

Having nailed down her conclusion, O'Connor addressed what she called "the principal counterargument," plainly central to both *Vernonia* and *Earls*, that the Fourth Amendment is more lenient regarding school searches. That is true, she noted; but while public school children do not enjoy either the warrant or the probable cause guarantees—which they do enjoy in nonschool settings—they should still enjoy "the individualized suspicion requirement, with its accompanying antipathy toward personally intrusive, blanket searches of mostly innocent people."[64] That students today, after *Earls*, do not enjoy even that protection is nothing short of scandalous. Indeed, the Court's opinions in this area, together with compulsory attendance laws, have effectively stripped public school students of their Fourth Amendment rights.

In his concurrence in *Earls*, Justice Breyer writes, "[a] public school system that fails adequately to [protect students from drugs] may well see parents send their children to private or parochial school instead—with help from the State. See *Zelman v. Simmons-Harris*."[65] That may be true. But a school that addresses the problem of drug use with lockdowns and mass, suspicionless searches of mostly innocent students may well see the same thing. Indeed, a cynic would be forgiven for thinking that the Court's jurisprudence in this area is designed precisely to drive parents to send their children to private schools, where a variety of voluntary arrangements is possible to address the problem of drug use. That, of course, would be the ultimate solution to the problem of drugs in schools—and the only one consistent with a free society.

Conclusion

In sum, whether it concerns tenants in public housing, students in public schools, or any other group or context, the war on drugs continues. Our cities have been devastated, our prisons have been filled, our institutions have been corrupted, and our rights have been trampled and lost, along with our lives, all in a futile effort to stop some of us from consuming substances that others of us think should not be consumed, substances that have been consumed by

---

[64] *Id.* at 681.
[65] *Earls*, 70 U.S.L.W. at 4742.

people from time immemorial. The evidence of failure is so palpable that even the Court can no longer ignore it.

Yet the Court continues to play its part in this lost cause, doing untold damage to the rule of law in the process. It neither questions the authority of the federal government to be exercising what is plainly a general police power—the kind of power the Court itself has repeatedly said does not exist—nor protects the rights of individuals to be free from the tyranny that ensues. That is no proper judicial restraint. It is judicial abdication. And the rule of law is its main victim.

October Term 2002

Erik S. Jaffe

Although almost any case before the Supreme Court has the potential to broach vital questions that shape our republic, some invite the Court to address the first principles of the matter. Already, the upcoming October Term 2002 promises to keep our interest piqued and our appetites whetted with a number of cases involving important constitutional issues. Our preview begins with the First Amendment—well represented by disputes involving topics ranging from cross burning to copyright extensions.

Cross Burning

In *Virginia* v. *Black*, No. 01-1107, the Court will consider whether a statute that prohibits cross burning with the intent to intimidate violates the First Amendment. The case is the latest in a line of challenges to popular laws banning unpopular speech, such as the flag-burning and cross-burning statutes reviewed, respectively, in *Texas* v. *Johnson*, 491 U.S. 397 (1989), and *R.A.V.* v. *City of St. Paul*, 505 U.S. 377 (1992). The Supreme Court of Virginia struck down the statute in *Black* because government may not discriminate based on content or viewpoint when regulating speech, even if the same speech could be regulated on other, neutral, grounds. That the Virginia law applied only to burning a cross, and not to other intimidating pyrotechnics, demonstrated to the court that the law discriminated, and intended to discriminate, based on the disfavored content of the symbolic speech. That the statute also presumed an intent to intimidate from the act of cross burning alone simply confirmed the court's view. Court watchers should stay tuned to see whether the justices will toe the constitutional line and strike down a popular state law, or draw a different line in the face of hateful speech that few would relish defending, even if only on principle.

Anti-Abortion Protests

In the consolidated cases of *Scheidler* v. *NOW, Inc.*, and *Operation Rescue* v. *NOW, Inc.*, Nos. 01-1118 and 01-1119, the Supreme Court will be interpreting the Racketeer Influenced and Corrupt Organizations (RICO) Act and the Hobbs Act as applied to anti-abortion protests. (The Hobbs Act makes it a federal offense to commit robbery or extortion in a manner that obstructs interstate commerce.) Given the context and past cases in this area, the First Amendment likely will be a substantial consideration in shaping the Court's interpretations. But aside from First Amendment concerns, there are other interesting questions: Is injunctive relief available under RICO's civil remedy provisions? Can political protest in the form of sit-ins and demonstrations that obstruct access to abortion clinics be characterized as "extortion" of the "property" right to give and receive services at such clinics?

The balance between the ability to speak when, where, and in a way the speech will be most effective, and the ability of citizens to engage in lawful activities without undue harassment or intimidation, involves a difficult clash of two fundamental aspects of freedom. That clash arises whenever there are issues that inspire strong public views. During the civil rights movement, RICO and the Hobbs Act might have been applied to sit-ins and demonstrations at segregated lunch-counters, or to demonstrators protesting federally ordered integration of schools. Today the fight is over abortion; tomorrow it could be animal experiments, AIDS research, or the teaching of the Koran. The freedom to do what you will within the law, and the freedom of others to protest what you do, will remain in constant tension. How the Supreme Court reconciles that tension promises to be controversial.

Copyrights

In *Eldred* v. *Ashcroft*, No. 01-618, the Court will take up the interrelation between the First Amendment and the Copyright Clause. In assessing whether a law extending the terms of existing and future copyrights is "categorically immune" from First Amendment challenge, the Court will have an opportunity to determine whether Article I copyright powers are subject to the same First Amendment limitations as are all other Article I powers. Prior Supreme Court cases have correctly recognized that certain speech-preserving aspects of the existing copyright laws and jurisprudence generally allowed such laws to survive First Amendment scrutiny. Yet those cases have sometimes been interpreted as giving copyright laws a free pass under the First Amendment, regardless of their content. In *Eldred*, the Court will consider an amendment to the copyright laws that makes them significantly more speech restrictive while providing only uncertain incentives for the creation of new writings. The Court will decide how the First Amendment applies to such speech-restrictive exercises of congressional power.

In addition to the First Amendment question, *Eldred* will construe the text of the Copyright Clause itself. Article I, Section 8, clause 8 of the Constitution gives Congress the power "To promote the Progress of Science and useful Arts, by securing for limited Times to Authors and Inventors the exclusive Right to their respective Writings and Discoveries." The U.S. Court of Appeals for the District of Columbia Circuit held, however, that the exercise of Congressional power to extend the terms of existing copyrights need not promote the progress of science. And in any event, said the court, retroactive extensions incidentally encourage preservation of old materials and advance international uniformity in copyright terms. The D.C. Circuit also held that retroactive extensions, even though repeated a number of times, did not violate the "limited Times" requirement of the Copyright Clause. The Supreme Court's interpretation of "promote the Progress" and "limited Times" will test how the Court gives effect to specific enumerations of Congressional power.

Meagan's Laws

Basic principles constraining the government's approach to crime, punishment, and related matters will command considerable attention in two cases that challenge state sex-offender registries adopted through so-called Meagan's laws. One case addresses the nature of "punishment" for purposes of the constitutional prohibition against *ex post facto* laws. The other examines the scope of any due process protections for reputation interests threatened by the dissemination of truthful information by the government.

In *Godfrey* v. *Doe*, No. 01-729, the Court will consider whether Alaska's publication on the internet of the names and addresses of convicted sex offenders, and the ongoing requirement that offenders report to the state, constitute punishment notwithstanding Alaska's express public-safety justification for the law. The Ninth Circuit, in an opinion by Judge Stephen Reinhardt, held that Alaska's law imposed punishment and thus violated the *Ex Post Facto* Clause as to persons whose crimes were committed before enactment of the law. Although jurisprudence on the difficult question of what constitutes "punishment" for various purposes under the Constitution is less than satisfying, *Godfrey* is not likely to provide much insight in that area.

What may be more significant, however, is how the Court will treat a related question: Assuming that the government is concerned with both punishment and public safety, may it release information that is truthful, of great public interest, and closely tied to the government's own operation of the criminal justice system? Some might even suggest that the government is *obliged* to provide such information to the public. Indeed, the greater accessibility of the information via the internet enhances rather than detracts from its value. As long as the information is truthful, can secondary consequences caused by its dissemination ever be a basis for suppressing information so closely tied to the operation of the criminal justice system?

A slightly different approach to sex-offender registries is at issue in *Connecticut Department of Public Safety* v. *Doe*, No. 01-1231. The Supreme Court will consider whether a sex-offender is entitled to an individualized hearing regarding his current dangerousness before being listed in the registry. Rather than treat listing as "punishment," the Second Circuit treated it as deprivation of a liberty interest in the offender's reputation, and thus subject to pre-deprivation due process. The most interesting aspect of this case could be the Supreme Court's analysis of the fundamental concept of liberty, and whether it includes a privacy interest in *minimizing* access to truthful public information—for example, conviction for a sex offense—that carries with it a significant stigma. It will be curious indeed if the Court finds a liberty interest in a favorable reputation that is based on public ignorance, then finds a deprivation of liberty if the dissemination of truthful information undermines that ignorance and hence the favorable reputation.

A further question is whether the government must have a hearing to establish that the inference of dangerousness likely to be drawn by an informed public will be correct. That question raises the troubling prospect of government as suppressor of information out of distrust that the public will draw the right conclusions. Thus, the First Amendment is a secondary theme in both Meagan's law cases: What rules should apply when the government controls public access to, and therefore use of, valuable information intimately related to the operation of the criminal justice system?

Due Process for Aliens

Demore v. *Kim*, No. 01-1491, addresses due process considerations in a context not bound up with public information issues. Aliens who are deportable for having committed certain felonies in the United States have been civilly detained, without bail, pending final determination regarding deportation. Does the Due Process Clause require an individualized hearing regarding applicability of the law, presence of danger, or risk of flight before those persons are detained? The Ninth Circuit invalidated the mandatory detention provision of the Immigration and Nationality Act, 8 U.S.C. § 1226(c), as applied to otherwise lawful permanent resident aliens. Because individualized hearings would be constitutionally required for civil detention in virtually any other context, at stake is the Court's commitment to basic tenets of due process for all "persons" — even those who are deportable. We shall soon see whether recent events, sensitivity to security concerns, and the last decade's growing hostility toward aliens will cause due process values to lose ground in favor of congressional authority over immigration.

Double Jeopardy

The Double Jeopardy Clause is at issue in *Sattazahn* v. *Pennsylvania*, No. 01-7574, which involves a defendant who obtains a retrial after his conviction is overturned on appeal. The Court will decide whether the failure of a jury to impose the death penalty, and the resulting imposition of a mandatory life sentence as required by statute, bars a subsequent attempt to impose the death penalty. The larger principle is whether government should have the authority to threaten defendants with greater punishment than it was able to obtain in a first trial as a means of deterring appeals that could lead to retrial. Possibly, the Supreme Court will treat the death penalty as different from other types of sentencing. As a result, the Court could limit any potential one-way ratchet of punishment to death-penalty cases while allowing greater sentences on retrial in other cases.

Excessive Punishment

In recent years, the Eighth Amendment restriction against cruel and unusual punishment has received considerable attention in the death-penalty context. But in the coming term, two consolidated cases involve the Eighth Amendment as applied to non-capital sentencing. *Lockyer* v. *Andrade*, No. 01-1127, from the Ninth Circuit, and *Ewing* v. *California*, No. 01-6978, from the California Court of Appeals, challenge California's "three strikes" law mandating 25-year-to-life sentences for third and subsequent felony convictions. The Supreme Court will consider whether such sentences are grossly disproportional to third offenses that would otherwise be misdemeanors. The case may well highlight the inevitable tension between judicial deference to the political branches on substantive matters, and restraint on government authority imposed by the Eighth Amendment. The method by which the Court gives content to the substantive requirement of proportionality will speak as much to the fundamental relationship among courts, legislatures, and the Constitution as to the concept of cruel and unusual punishment.

The issue of proportionality also arises next term in the civil context. In *State Farm Mutual Automobile Insurance Co.* v. *Campbell*, No. 01-1289, the Supreme Court will consider whether punitive damages 145 times the amount of compensatory damages, based on conduct outside the jurisdiction and unrelated to the plaintiff, violate the Due Process Clause of the Fourteenth Amendment. While the case seems unlikely to alter fundamentally the due process balancing test applied to punitive damages, it does implicate interesting and basic issues of punishment versus compensation. Moreover, the case may illuminate constitutional treatment of deterrence as an objective of both civil and criminal law. There is some irony in contrasting the *State Farm* case, which treats intentionally "punitive" damages as civil phenomena, with the Meagan's law cases, which inquire whether the government's release of truthful information about sex-offenders to the public for the express purpose of public safety constitutes criminal punishment.

State Sovereign Immunity

Another group of cases to be heard by the Court concerns a variety of other limitations on government authority and the allocation of authority between different elements of government.

In *Nevada Department of Human Resources* v. *Hibbs*, No. 01-1368, the Court once again will address the interplay of state sovereign immunity and congressional authority under Section 5 of the Fourteenth Amendment. The broad principle of state sovereign immunity as a limit on federal authority has been addressed frequently by the Supreme Court over the last several terms. Although this case is the first in the sovereign immunity series that tests gender-based legislation, it probably will not break new ground on that score. Instead, the case could offer an interesting treatment of Fourteenth Amendment equal protection principles and the degree to which Congress can, under Section 5, legislate against conduct that would not itself rise to the level of an equal protection violation.

The federal government's claim, accepted by the court below, was that the Family and Medical Leave Act was remedial legislation seeking to prevent gender discrimination by ensuring leave on a gender-neutral basis. But the Act goes far beyond requiring gender-neutral leave policies, and includes prohibitions against state conduct that would not remotely violate the Fourteenth Amendment. Thus, the decision below seems to test the limit on claims of prophylactic legislation under Section 5. Because the appellate decision comes from a Ninth Circuit panel that included Judge Reinhardt, odds-makers are likely to favor the petitioner.

"Dormant" Commerce Clause

The application of the "dormant" Commerce Clause to a state program that indirectly exacts a price rebate from out-of-state prescription drug manufacturers is at issue in *Pharmaceutical Research & Manufacturers of America* v. *Concannon*, No. 01-188. The program effectively creates a means for individuals to purchase prescription drugs collectively, with the state then negotiating a rebate that is funneled back to each individual purchaser. As a direct bargaining agent, the state does more than authorize and oversee a private buyer's cooperative. That raises interesting economic questions, which probably have more to do with the peculiarities of antitrust policy than with the dormant Commerce Clause. If the Court wanted to tackle first principles in this case, it might revisit the very existence of its dormant Commerce Clause jurisprudence and consider leaving this whole area to Congress under the "active" Commerce Clause. But such reconsideration is unlikely. More likely, the Court will undertake an economic analysis of the state's involvement in negotiating indirect rebates on behalf of private purchasers. How does that involvement impact competition and free markets? Would a federal court be treading on state sovereignty if it rejected a program based on economic considerations not tied to a specific constitutional or congressional command?

Takings

Washington Legal Foundation v. *Legal Foundation of Washington*, No. 01-1325, is the latest phase of a Takings Clause challenge to a state "IOLTA" statute—Interest on Lawyers' Trust Accounts. State IOLTA programs channel client funds—small sums and large sums held for short periods of time—into designated interest-bearing trust accounts. The interest is then funneled through a judicially created legal foundation to various "public interest" legal firms. Fundamental property right principles ought to make this a straightforward case, since the state has asserted control over the equitable interest of client property without consent or just compensation. But the Supreme Court's takings jurisprudence has often followed a more complicated *ad hoc* approach. Because the property taken is money, rather than land, the Court may treat the case as one involving a regulatory rather than a physical taking. If so, the outcome is unpredictable.

Congressional Elections

A last case that raises an interesting, if not quite fundamental, issue is *Branch* v. *Smith*, No. 01-1437 (to be heard together with *Smith* v. *Branch*, No. 01-1596). The Supreme Court will consider the interpretation of Article I, Section 4, of the Constitution, which provides that the times, places, and manners of congressional elections "shall be prescribed in each State by the Legislature thereof." The immediate question for the Court is whether a congressional redistricting plan imposed by a state court under authority of its general jurisdiction, rather than pursuant to an express legislative delegation of authority, violates the constitutional requirement that the state "Legislature" prescribe such matters. That somewhat quirky constitutional issue seems less a matter of overarching principle than of adherence to constitutional details. Still, it should elicit greater attention due to the role of a related constitutional provision (Article II, Section 1) in the *Bush* v. *Gore* dust-up of two terms ago.

Future Cases

Finally, three cases not yet on the docket have reasonable chances of being accepted for the coming term. Each raises a significant constitutional issue: affirmative action, commercial speech, and campaign finance, respectively.

The pending petition in *Grutter* v. *Bollinger*, No. 02-241, will give the Court the opportunity, avoided several times previously, to revisit the question of affirmative action and the role that race can play in state law school admissions. With the contentiousness and emotions surrounding that issue, it may be too much to expect a completely principled resolution, but some incremental progress and greater clarity would surely be welcomed.

In the expected petition for review of *Kasky* v. *Nike, Inc.*, 45 P.3d 243 (Cal. 2002), the Court may get the chance to clarify whether commercial speech should be regarded differently under the First Amendment from all other protected speech. While it would be welcome if the Court retreated from its questionable denigration of commercial speech, it may not have to go very far in that direction to resolve this peculiar case: The speech subject to restriction under state law was Nike's public defense of its business practices against public criticism. Many legal scholars scoff at the categorization of such speech as commercial speech in the first place.

Last, but not least, the 500-pound gorilla sitting in the lower courts is the collection of sweeping challenges to the Bipartisan Campaign Reform Act (BCRA) of 2002. Although the group of challenges will be subject, by statute, to direct appeals to the Supreme Court, argument before a three-judge panel of the District Court is not scheduled until December. Thus, the appeal may not make it onto the coming term's docket. Whether heard during the coming term or the next, the BCRA challenges will involve fundamental principles of free speech and democratic government. One can only trust that the Supreme Court will be more sensitive to the First Amendment than was Congress.

Contributors

Clint Bolick serves as vice president and national director of state chapters at the Institute for Justice, which he cofounded in 1991 to engage in constitutional litigation protecting individual liberty and challenging the regulatory welfare state. Bolick is a leading legal pioneer in several areas. For the past 12 years he has led the nationwide effort to defend school choice programs, with victories in the Wisconsin, Ohio, and Arizona Supreme Courts, culminating in *Zelman v. Simmons-Harris* in the U.S. Supreme Court. In the 1980s and 1990s, he helped lead the effort to increase judicial scrutiny of racial classifications in such areas as public employment and interracial adoptions. He designed a legal strategy to restore judicial protection of economic liberty that has produced several landmark rulings invalidating regulatory barriers to enterprise. In 2001, Bolick moved to Arizona to launch the Institute's first state chapter. From the Phoenix office, he will train and organize other state chapters around the nation. Bolick is one of the subjects profiled in *Gang of Five: Leaders at the Center of the Conservative Crusade* by Nina Easton, who writes that Bolick "confounds his liberal critics because he is something that is not supposed to exist on the right: an idealist." His latest book is *Voucher Wars: Lessons From the Legal Battle Over School Choice*, which will be published in spring 2003 by the Cato Institute. Bolick received his law degree from the University of California at Davis in 1982 and his undergraduate degree from Drew University in 1979.

Robert Corn-Revere is a partner in the Washington, D.C., office of Hogan & Hartson L.L.P., specializing in First Amendment, internet, and communications law. He successfully argued *United States v. Playboy Entertainment Group, Inc.*, 529 U.S. 803 (2000), in which the United States Supreme Court struck down Section 505 of the Telecommunications Act of 1996 as a violation of the First Amendment. Corn-Revere was listed on a 30th Anniversary Roll of Honor by the

American Library Association Office of Intellectual Freedom and Freedom to Read Foundation for his role as lead counsel in *Mainstream Loudoun v. Board of Trustees of the Loudoun County Library*. Before joining Hogan & Hartson in 1994, Corn-Revere served as chief counsel to Interim Chairman James H. Quello of the Federal Communications Commission. He is a coauthor of a three-volume treatise entitled *Modern Communications Law*, published by West Group, and is editor and coauthor of the book, *Rationales and Rationalizations*, published in 1997. He is a member of the Editorial Advisory Board of Pike & Fischer's *Internet Law & Regulation*. From 1987 to 2001 Corn-Revere taught at the Communications Law Institute of the Columbus School of Law, Catholic University of America. He is an adjunct scholar at the Cato Institute and is chairman of the Media Institute's First Amendment Advisory Council.

Richard A. Epstein is the James Parker Hall Distinguished Service Professor of Law at the University of Chicago Law School. He received a B.A. in philosophy *summa cum laude* from Columbia in 1964. He received a B.A. in law with first class honors from Oxford University in 1966, and an LL.B. *cum laude* from the Yale Law School in 1968. Upon his graduation he joined the faculty at the University of Southern California where he taught until 1972. In 1972, he visited the University of Chicago, and became a regular member of the faculty the next year. He was named James Parker Hall Professor in 1982 and Distinguished Service Professor in 1988. He served as Interim Dean of the Law School from February to June of 2001. Epstein has written extensively in many legal areas. His books include *Principles for a Free Society: Reconciling Individual Liberty with the Common Good* (1998); *Mortal Peril: Our Inalienable Right to Health Care?* (1997); *Simple Rules for a Complex World* (1995); *Bargaining with the State* (1993); *Forbidden Grounds: The Case Against Employment Discrimination Laws* (1992); and *Takings: Private Property and the Power of Eminent Domain* (1985). Epstein is also the editor of *Cases and Materials in the Law of Torts* (7th ed.) and has written a one-volume treatise, *Torts* (1999). He has also written many scholarly articles on a broad range of common law, constitutional, economic, historical, and philosophical subjects. Among the subjects that he has taught are contracts, property, torts, and criminal law in the first-year curriculum, and conflicts of law, health law, workers' compensation, real estate development and finance, and political theory in the upper years. Epstein spent the 1977–78 year as a Fellow at the Center for Advanced Studies in the Behavioral Sciences at Stanford. From 1981 to 1991 he was editor of the *Journal of Legal Studies*. Since 1991, he has been an editor of the *Journal of Law & Economics*. Epstein was elected a Fellow of the American Academy of Arts and Sciences in 1985.

Stephen P. Halbrook argued and prevailed in *Castillo v. United States*, 530 U.S. 120 (2000), a decision upholding the right to jury trial arising out of the Waco tragedy; *Printz v. United States*, 521 U.S. 98 (1997), which struck down federal mandates under the Tenth Amendment; and *United States v. Thompson/Center Arms Co.*, 504 U.S. 505 (1992), which applied the rule of lenity in a civil tax case. He is the author of an amici curiae brief in the *Harris* case, discussed in this volume, on behalf of the Cato Institute and the National Association of Criminal Defense Lawyers. From his offices in Fairfax, Virginia, he devotes his litigation practice to federal and state appellate work. He is a Research Fellow with the Independent Institute. Halbrook holds a Ph.D. in philosophy from Florida State University and a J.D. from Georgetown University Law Center. His books include *Firearms Law Deskbook: Federal and State Criminal Practice* (West Group, 2002); *That Every Man Be Armed: The Evolution of a Constitutional Right* (University of New Mexico Press, 1984; Independent Institute, reprint 2000); *A Right to Bear Arms: State and Federal Bills of Rights and Constitutional Guarantees* (Greenwood Press, 1989); and *Freedmen, the Fourteenth Amendment, and the Right to Bear Arms, 1866–1876* (Praeger Publishers, 1998). Halbrook's book *Target Switzerland: Swiss Armed Neutrality in World War II* (Sarpedon Publishers, 1998) has been published in German and French editions, and won the Max Geilinger Foundation award in 2000 for works contributing to Swiss and Anglo-American culture.

Erik S. Jaffe is a solo appellate attorney in Washington, D.C., whose practice emphasizes First Amendment and other constitutional issues. He is a 1986 graduate of Dartmouth College and a 1990 graduate of Columbia Law School. Following law school he clerked for Judge Douglas H. Ginsburg on the U.S. Court of Appeals for the District of Columbia Circuit, practiced for five years at Williams

& Connolly in Washington, D.C., clerked for Justice Clarence Thomas on the U.S. Supreme Court during October Term 1996, and then began his solo appellate practice in 1997. Since 1999 he has been involved in over a dozen cases at the merits stage before the U.S. Supreme Court. He represented one of the successful respondents in the First Amendment case of *Bartnicki* v. *Vopper*, 532 U.S. 514 (2001), and authored amicus briefs for such organizations as the Cato Institute and the Center for Individual Freedom, in constitutional cases such as *Republican Party of Minnesota* v. *Kelly*, 122 S. Ct. 2528 (2002) (judicial speech), *Zelman* v. *Simmons-Harris*, 122 S. Ct. 2460 (2002) (vouchers), *Watchtower Bible and Tract Society* v. *Village of Stratton*, 122 S. Ct. 2080 (2002) (anonymous speech), *United States* v. *United Foods, Inc.*, 533 U.S. 405 (2001) (compelled advertising), *Boy Scouts of America* v. *Dale*, 530 U.S. 640 (2000) (freedom of expressive association); and *United States* v. *Morrison*, 529 U.S. 598 (2000) (Commerce Clause).

Robert A. Levy joined the Cato Institute in 1997 after 25 years in business. He is an adjunct professor at the Georgetown University Law Center, a director of the Institute for Justice, and a trustee of The Objectivist Center. Levy received his Ph.D. in business from American University in 1966. During 1966 he founded CDA Investment Technologies, Inc., a major provider of financial information and software. Levy was chief executive officer of CDA until 1991. He then earned his J.D. in 1994 from George Mason University, where he was chief articles editor of the law review. For the next two years Levy clerked for Judge Royce C. Lamberth on the U.S. District Court in Washington, D.C., and for Judge Douglas H. Ginsburg on the U.S. Court of Appeals for the District of Columbia Circuit. Among Levy's publications are a book, dozens of articles on investments, and, more recently, numerous papers on law and public policy. His work has been published in the *New York Times, Wall Street Journal, USA Today, Washington Post, National Review, Weekly Standard, Journal of the American Medical Association,* and numerous other media. He also has discussed public policy on many national radio and TV programs, including CNN's "Crossfire," ABC's "Nightline," "Geraldo," "Hardball," and NBC's "Today Show."

Timothy Lynch is director of the Cato Institute's Project on Criminal Justice and associate director of Cato's Center for Constitutional Studies. Lynch is an outspoken critic of police misconduct, the drug war, gun control, and the militarization of police tactics. Since September 11, Lynch has decried several antiterrorism initiatives for their impact on civil liberties. Lynch has published articles in the *New York Times, Washington Post, Wall Street Journal, Los Angeles Times, ABA Journal,* and *National Law Journal.* He has appeared on such television programs as the "Lehrer Newshour," "NBC Nightly News," "ABC World News Tonight," Fox News Channel's "The O'Reilly Factor," and C-SPAN's "Washington Journal." Lynch has also filed several amicus briefs in the U.S. Supreme Court in pending cases involving constitutional rights. He is the editor of the book *After Prohibition: An Adult Approach to Drug Policies in the 21st Century.* Lynch is a 1990 graduate of the Marquette University School of Law and is a member of the Wisconsin and District of Columbia bars.

Roger Pilon is vice president for legal affairs at the Cato Institute. He holds Cato's B. Kenneth Simon Chair in Constitutional Studies and is the founder and director of Cato's Center for Constitutional Studies. Established in 1989 to encourage limited constitutional government at home and abroad, the Center has become an important force in the national debate over constitutional interpretation and judicial philosophy. Pilon's work has appeared in the *New York Times, Washington Post, Wall Street Journal, Los Angeles Times, Legal Times, National Law Journal, Harvard Journal of Law & Public Policy, Notre Dame Law Review, Stanford Law & Policy Review, Texas Review of Law & Politics,* and elsewhere. He has appeared, among other places, on ABC's "Nightline," CBS's "60 Minutes II," National Public Radio, Fox News Channel, CNN, MSNBC, and CNBC. He lectures and debates at universities and law schools across the country and testifies often before Congress. Before joining Cato, Pilon held five senior posts in the Reagan administration, including at State and Justice. He has taught philosophy and law and was a national fellow at Stanford's Hoover Institution. Pilon holds a B.A. from Columbia University, an M.A. and a Ph.D. from the University of Chicago, and a J.D. from the George Washington University School of Law. In 1989 the Bicentennial Commission presented him with the Benjamin Franklin Award for excellence in writing on the U.S. Constitution.

In 2001 Columbia University's School of General Studies awarded him its Alumni Medal of Distinction.

James L. Swanson is a senior fellow in constitutional studies at the Cato Institute and editor in chief of the *Cato Supreme Court Review*. A graduate of the University of Chicago and the UCLA School of Law, he was a member of the law review and recipient of a moot court distinguished advocate award. Swanson served as a legal advisor to Chairman Susan Liebeler at the U.S. International Trade Commission, clerked for Judge Douglas H. Ginsburg on the U.S. Court of Appeals for the District of Columbia Circuit, and was a special assistant in the Office of Legal Counsel at the Department of Justice. Swanson is the founding and current editor of the *First Amendment Law Handbook* (West Group), an annual volume on recent developments in constitutional law and freedom of speech. He has written articles on intellectual property, the First Amendment, and other topics, and his work has appeared in the *Chicago Tribune, Los Angeles Times, American Heritage*, and other publications. A member of the National Book Critics Circle, he covers books on law, politics, the presidency, war, and African American history. Swanson's latest book, *Lincoln's Assassins: Their Trial and Execution*, was reviewed widely, including in the *New York Times*, the *Sunday Times* of London, *Wilson Quarterly*, and elsewhere. As an adjunct professor at the John Marshall Law School in 2000 and 2001, he taught First Amendment law.

Jonathan Turley is the J.B. & Maurice C. Shapiro Professor of Public Interest Law at The George Washington University Law School. He is a nationally recognized legal scholar who has written broadly in the areas of constitutional law, legal theory, and legal history. Turley has more than three dozen academic publications. In addition to his academic work, Turley has served as counsel in various well-known constitutional, criminal, and national security cases. These include espionage cases like the Nicholson and King spy cases as well as his representation of four former U.S. Attorneys General opposing the so-called Secret Service privilege during the Clinton impeachment litigation. In addition, Turley is a frequent witness before the House and Senate on constitutional and statutory issues and is a nationally known legal commentator. In a recent study by Judge

Richard Posner, Jonathan Turley was ranked 38 in the top 100 most-cited "public intellectuals," the second most-cited law professor in the country. Turley writes regularly for national newspapers and has published more than 300 articles on legal and policy issues. He has also worked for NBC/MSNBC News and CBS News as an on-air legal expert during the impeachment and election controversies. Turley joined the George Washington University faculty in 1990 and previously taught at Tulane Law School. He clerked on the U.S. Court of Appeals for the Fifth Circuit and served as the executive articles editor of the *Northwestern University Law Review*.

ABOUT THE CATO INSTITUTE

The Cato Institute is a public policy research foundation dedicated to the principles of limited government, individual liberty, free markets, and private property. It takes its name from *Cato's Letters*, popular libertarian pamphlets that helped to lay the philosophical foundation for the American Revolution.

Despite the Founders' libertarian values, today virtually no aspect of life is free from government encroachment. A pervasive intolerance for individual rights is shown by government's arbitrary intrusions into private economic transactions and its disregard for civil liberties.

To counter that trend, the Cato Institute undertakes an extensive publications program that addresses the complete spectrum of policy issues. It holds major conferences throughout the year, from which papers are published thrice yearly in the *Cato Journal*, and also publishes the quarterly magazine *Regulation*.

The Cato Institute accepts no government funding. It relies instead on contributions from foundations, corporations, and individuals and revenue generated from the sale of publications. The Institute is a nonprofit, tax-exempt educational foundation under Section 501(c)(3) of the Internal Revenue Code.

ABOUT THE CENTER FOR CONSTITUTIONAL STUDIES

Cato's Center for Constitutional Studies and its scholars take their inspiration from the struggle of America's founding generation to secure liberty through limited government and the rule of law. Under the direction of Roger Pilon, the center was established in 1989 to help revive the idea that the Constitution authorizes a government of delegated, enumerated, and thus limited powers, the exercise of which must be further restrained by our rights, both enumerated and unenumerated. Through books, monographs, conferences, forums, op-eds, speeches, congressional testimony, and TV and radio appearances, the center's scholars address a wide range of constitutional and legal issues—from judicial review to federalism, economic liberty, property rights, civil rights, criminal law and procedure, asset forfeiture, tort law, and term limits, to name just a few. The center is especially concerned to encourage the judiciary to be "the bulwark of our liberties," as James Madison put it, neither making nor ignoring the law but interpreting and applying it through the natural rights tradition we inherited from the founding generation.

CATO INSTITUTE
1000 Massachusetts Ave., N.W.
Washington, D.C. 20001